ROUTLEDGE LIBRARY EDITIONS:
19TH CENTURY RELIGION

Volume 10

THE UNITARIAN CONTROVERSY, 1819–1823

THE UNITARIAN CONTROVERSY, 1819–1823

Volume One

Edited by
BRUCE KUKLICK

LONDON AND NEW YORK

First published in 1987 by Garland Publishing, Inc.

This edition first published in 2018
by Routledge
2 Park Square, Milton Park, Abingdon, Oxon OX14 4RN

and by Routledge
711 Third Avenue, New York, NY 10017

Routledge is an imprint of the Taylor & Francis Group, an informa business

© 1987 Bruce Kuklick, Introduction

All rights reserved. No part of this book may be reprinted or reproduced or utilised in any form or by any electronic, mechanical, or other means, now known or hereafter invented, including photocopying and recording, or in any information storage or retrieval system, without permission in writing from the publishers.

Trademark notice: Product or corporate names may be trademarks or registered trademarks, and are used only for identification and explanation without intent to infringe.

British Library Cataloguing in Publication Data
A catalogue record for this book is available from the British Library

ISBN: 978-1-138-06800-1 (Set)
ISBN: 978-1-315-10089-0 (Set) (ebk)
ISBN: 978-1-138-10344-3 (Volume 10) (hbk)
ISBN: 978-1-138-10345-0 (Volume 10) (pbk)
ISBN: 978-1-315-10271-9 (Volume 10) (ebk)

Publisher's Note
The publisher has gone to great lengths to ensure the quality of this reprint but points out that some imperfections in the original copies may be apparent.

Disclaimer
The publisher has made every effort to trace copyright holders and would welcome correspondence from those they have been unable to trace.

The Unitarian Controversy 1819–1823

Edited with an Introduction by
Bruce Kuklick

In Two Volumes
VOLUME ONE

Garland Publishing, Inc.
New York & London
1987

For a complete list of the titles in this series, see the final pages of volume two.

Introduction copyright © 1987 by Bruce Kuklick

The facsimile of *Unitarian Christianity* has been made from a copy in the New York Public Library; the remaining facsimiles are from copies in the Yale University Library.

Library of Congress Cataloging-in-Publication Data

The Unitarian controversy, 1819–1823.

(American religious thought of the 18th and 19th centuries)
  Reprint of works published 1820–1841.
   1. Unitarianism—Collected works. 2. Calvinism—Collected works. 3. Unitarian Universalist churches—New England—Doctrines—Collected works.
4. Congregational churches—New England—Doctrines—Collected works. 5. Reformed Church—New England—Doctrines—Collected works. 6. Theology—Collected works—19th century. I. Kuklick, Bruce, 1941– II. Series.
BX9841.A1U523 1987   288'.74   87-12837
ISBN 0-8240-6958-7 (alk. paper)

The volumes in this series are printed on acid-free, 250-year-life paper.

Printed in the United States of America

CONTENTS

Introduction
    by Bruce Kuklick

Unitarian Christianity
    by William Ellery Channing

Letters to Unitarians Occasioned by the Sermon of the Reverend William E. Channing at the Ordination of the Rev. J. Sparks
    by Leonard Woods

Letters Addressed to Trinitarians and Calvinists Occasioned by Dr. Woods' Letters to Unitarians
    by Henry Ware

A Reply to Dr. Ware's Letters to Trinitarians and Calvinists
    by Leonard Woods

Answer to Dr. Woods' Reply, in a Second Series of Letters Addressed to Trinitarians and Calvinists
    by Henry Ware

Remarks on Dr. Ware's Answer
    by Leonard Woods

A Postscript to the Second Series of Letters Addressed to Trinitarians and Calvinists
    by Henry Ware

INTRODUCTION

A liberal impulse grew up in New England Calvinism after the Great Awakening, the series of revivals that swept religious centers in the late 1730s and early 1740s. For a long time moderate churchmen were able to contain these impulses within traditional channels. In and around Boston, however, the religious leadership persistently strayed from what orthodox men thought was appropriate. Stimulated by a hopeful view of the human condition, liberals by 1800 had well-nigh repudiated their Calvinism. By 1820 Boston and its locale were "Unitarian" rather than Calvinist in religious philosophy. The new ideas prompted an acrimonious debate as well as, it turned out, a fierce institutional rivalry.

The primary dispute between Unitarians and Calvinists nominally concerned the unity or trinity of the godhead, but, of greater moment for almost every discussion, the Unitarians had a moral and social perspective different from Trinitarians. Reared in a more sophisticated environment, Unitarians could not sustain a creed based on mystery and faith. They demanded that Christianity be made more rationally credible, that its tenets conform to what a literate urban middle class considered believable.

The Unitarians at least initially were not interested in systematic theology, preferring to avoid abstruse theological controversy. Their spiritual leader was William Ellery Channing (1780–1842), a prominent Boston minister and a man renowned for his Christian character and practical piety. Largely because of his fear of the dangers of overintellectualization to religion, it was not until 1819 that a major codification of the Unitarian position was undertaken.

Channing's eloquent essay of that year, "Unitarian Christianity," is reprinted in this volume and gives a succinct elaboration of American Unitarian beliefs. Channing, however, was unwilling to engage in learned argument over matters of the soul and left the field after his initial foray. Nonetheless, at Harvard a separate school of divinity had emerged in the second decade of the century that was a bastion of Unitarian ideas. At Andover, in 1808, strict Calvinists had established their own clerical training school in prudent anticipation of Harvard's final apostasy. What became known as the Unitarian controversy was the debate between the rival theologians of these two institutions.

Leonard Woods (1774–1854) spoke for Andover and wrote initially so that Channing would not go unanswered. But the sustained responses to Woods came from Henry Ware (1764–1845) who defended Unitarianism from a position at Harvard.

The famous "Wood 'n' Ware" dispute went on for four years and is reprinted here in its entirety. Although the combatants were concerned over whether God's nature was one or three, other issues were more important for them. The Unitarians asserted the spontaneous freedom of the will and denied the innate depravity of man. Woods was forced to come to grips with many conundrums of Edwardsean Calvinism in his defense of human depravity and a deterministic will. Critics at the time thought Ware got the better of the debate; of greater significance, however, is the manner in which the great issues of Reformed Protestantism became codified in America for theological professionals.

Bruce Kuklick

UNITARIAN CHRISTIANITY.

1 Thessalonians v. 21.

"Prove all things; hold fast that which is good."

The peculiar circumstances of this occasion not only justify, but seem to demand, a departure from the course generally followed by preachers at the introduction of a brother into the sacred office. It is usual to speak of the nature, design, duties, and advantages of the Christian ministry; and on these topics I should now be happy to insist, did I not remember that a minister is to be given this day to a religious society, whose peculiarities of opinion have drawn upon them much remark, and, may I not add, much reproach. Many good minds, many sincere Christians, I am aware, are apprehensive that the solemnities of this day are to give a degree of influence to principles which they deem false and injurious. The fears and anxieties of such men I respect; and, believing that they are grounded in part on mistake, I have thought it my duty to lay before you. as clearly as I can, some of the distinguishing opinions of that class of Christians in our country who are known to sympathize with this religious society. I must ask your patience, for such a subject is not to be despatched in a narrow compass. I must also ask you to remember, that it is impossible to exhibit, in a single discourse, our views of every doctrine of revelation, much less the differences of opinion which are known to subsist among ourselves. I shall confine myself to topics on which our sentiments have been misrepresented, or which distinguish us most widely from others. May I not hope to be heard with candor? God deliver us all from prejudice and unkindness, and fill us with the love of truth and virtue.

There are two natural divisions under which my thoughts will be arranged. I shall endeavour to unfold, 1st, The principles which we adopt in interpreting the Scriptures. And, 2dly, Some of the doctrines which the Scriptures, so interpreted, seem to us clearly to express.

I. We regard the Scriptures as the records of God's successive revelations to mankind, and particularly of the last and most perfect revelation of his will by Jesus Christ. Whatever doctrines seem to us to be clearly taught in the Scriptures, we receive without reserve or exception. We do not, however, attach equal importance to all the books in this collection. Our religion, we believe, lies chiefly in the New Testament. The dispensation of Moses, compared with that of Jesus, we consider as adapted to the childhood of the human race, a preparation for a nobler system, and chiefly useful now as serving to confirm and illustrate the Christian Scriptures. Jesus Christ is the only master of Christians, and whatever he taught, either during his personal ministry, or by his inspired apostles, we regard as of Divine authority, and profess to make the rule of our lives.

This authority which we give to the Scriptures is a reason, we conceive, for studying them with peculiar care, and for inquiring anxiously into the principles of interpretation by which their true meaning may be ascertained. The principles adopted by the class of Christians in whose name I speak need to be explained, because they are often misunderstood. We are particularly accused of making an unwarrantable use of reason in the interpretation of Scripture. We are said to exalt reason above revelation, to prefer our own wisdom to God's. Loose and undefined charges of this kind are circulated so freely, that we think it due to ourselves, and to the cause of truth, to express our views with some particularity.

Our leading principle in interpreting Scripture is this, that the Bible is a book written for men, in the language of men, and that its meaning is to be sought in the same manner as that of other books. We believe that God, when he speaks to the human race, conforms, if we may so say, to the established rules of speaking and writing. How else would the Scriptures avail us more than if communicated in an unknown tongue?

Now all books, and all conversation, require in the reader or hearer the constant exercise of reason; or their true import is only to be obtained by continual comparison and inference. Human language, you well know, admits various interpretations; and every word and every sentence must be modified and explained according to the subject which is discussed, according to the purposes, feelings, circumstances, and principles of the writer, and according to the genius and idioms of the language which he uses. These are acknowledged principles in the interpretation of human writings, and a man, whose words we should explain without reference to these principles, would reproach us justly with a criminal want of candor, and an intention of obscuring or distorting his meaning.

Were the Bible written in a language and style of its own, did it consist of words which admit but a single sense, and of sentences wholly detached from each other, there would be no place for the principles now laid down. We could not reason about it, as about other writings. But such a book would be of little worth; and perhaps, of all books, the Scriptures correspond least to this description. The word of God bears the stamp of the same hand which we see in his works. It has infinite connections and dependences. Every proposition is linked with others, and is to be compared with others, that its full and precise import may be understood. Nothing stands alone. The New Testament is built on the Old. The Christian dispensation is a continuation of the Jewish, the completion of a vast scheme of Providence, requiring great extent of view in the reader. Still more, the Bible treats of subjects on which we receive ideas from other sources besides itself; such subjects as the nature, passions, relations, and duties of man; and it expects us to restrain and modify its language by the known truths which observation and experience furnish on these topics.

We profess not to know a book which demands a more frequent exercise of reason than the Bible. In addition to the remarks now made on its infinite connections, we may observe, that its style nowhere affects the precision of science, or the accuracy of definition. Its language is singularly glowing, bold, and figurative, demanding more frequent departures from the literal sense than that of our own age and country, and consequently demanding more continual exercise of judgment. We find, too, that the different portions of this book, instead of being confined to general truths, refer perpetually to the times when they were written, to states of society, to modes of thinking, to controversies in the Church, to feelings and usages, which have passed away, and without the knowledge of which we are constantly in danger of extending to all times and places what was of temporary and local application. We find, too, that some of these books are strongly marked by the genius and character of their respective writers, that the Holy Spirit did not so guide the Apostles as to suspend the peculiarities of their minds, and that a knowledge of their feelings, and of the influences under which they were placed, is one of the preparations for understanding their writings. With these views of the Bible, we feel it our bounden duty to exercise our reason upon it perpetually; to compare, to infer, to look beyond the letter to the spirit, to seek in the nature of the subject, and the aim of the writer, his true meaning; and, in general, to make use of what is known for explaining what is difficult, and for discovering new truths.

Need I descend to particulars to prove that the Scriptures demand the exercise of reason? Take, for example, the style in which they generally speak of God, and observe how habitually they apply to him human passions and organs. Recollect the declarations of Christ, that he came, not to send peace, but a sword; that unless we eat his flesh, and drink his blood, we have no life in us; that we must hate father and mother, and pluck out the right eye; and a vast number of passages equally bold and unlimited. Recollect the unqualified manner in which it is said of Christians, that they possess all things, know all things, and can do all things. Recollect the verbal contradiction between Paul and James, and the apparent clashing of some parts of Paul's writings with the general doctrines and end of Christianity. I might extend the enumeration indefinitely; and who does not see that we must limit all these passages by the known attributes of God, of Jesus Christ, and of human nature, and by the circumstances under which they were written, so as to give the language a quite different import from what it would require had it been applied to different beings, or used in different connections?

Enough has been said to show in what sense we make use of reason in interpreting Scripture. From a variety of possible interpretations, we select that which accords with the nature of the subject and the state of the writer, with the connection of the passage, with the general strain of Scripture, with the known character and will of God, and with the obvious and acknowledged laws of nature. In other words, we believe that God never contradicts, in one part of Scripture, what he teaches in another; and never contradicts, in revelation, what he teaches in his works and providence. And we, therefore, distrust every interpretation which, after deliberate attention, seems repugnant to any established truth. We reason about the Bible precisely as civilians do about the constitution under which we live; who, you know, are accustomed to limit one provision of that venerable instrument by others, and to fix the precise import of its parts by inquiring into its general spirit, into the intentions of its authors, and into the prevalent feelings, impressions, and circumstances of the time when it was framed. Without these principles of interpretation, we frankly acknowledge that we cannot defend the Divine authority of the Scriptures. Deny us this latitude, and we must abandon this book to its enemies.

We do not announce these principles as original or peculiar to ourselves. All Christians occasionally adopt them, not excepting those who most vehemently decry them when they happen to menace some favorite article of their creed. All Christians are compelled to use them in their controversies with infidels. All sects employ them in their warfare with one another. All willingly avail themselves of reason, when it can be pressed into the service of their own party, and only complain of it when its weapons wound themselves. None reason more frequently than those from whom we differ. It is astonishing what a fabric they rear from a few slight hints about the fall of our first parents; and how ingeniously they extract, from detached passages, mysterious doctrines about the Divine nature. We do not blame them for reasoning so abundantly, but for violating the fundamental rules of reasoning, for sacrificing the plain to the obscure, and the general strain of Scripture to a scanty number of insulated texts.

We object strongly to the contemptuous manner in which human reason is often spoken of by our adversaries, because it leads, we believe, to universal skepticism. If reason be so dreadfully darkened by the fall, that its most decisive judgments on religion are unworthy of trust, then Christianity, and even natural theology, must be abandoned; for the existence and veracity of God, and the Divine original of Christianity, are conclusions of reason, and must stand or fall with it. If revelation be at war with this faculty, it subverts itself, for the great question of its truth is left by God to be decided at the bar of reason. It is worthy of remark, how nearly the bigot and the skeptic approach. Both would annihilate our confidence in our faculties, and both throw doubt and confusion over truth We honor revelation too highly to make it the antagonist of reason, or to believe that it calls us to renounce our highest powers.

We indeed grant, that the use of reason in religion is accompanied with danger. But we ask any honest man to look on the history of the Church, and say, whether the renunciation of it be not still more dangerous. Besides, it is a plain fact, that men reason as erroneously on all subjects as on religion. Who does not know the wild and groundless theories which have been framed in physical and political science? But who ever supposed that we must cease to exercise reason on nature and society, because men have erred for ages in explaining them? We grant, that the passions continually, and sometimes fatally, disturb the rational faculty in its inquiries into revelation. The ambitious contrive to find doctrines in the Bible which favor their love of dominion. The timid and dejected discover there a gloomy system, and the mystical and fanatical, a visionary theology. The vicious can find examples or assertions on which to build the hope of a late repentance, or of acceptance on easy terms. The falsely refined contrive to light on doctrines which have not been soiled by vulgar handling. But the passions do not distract the reason in religious, any more than in any other inquiries, which excite strong and general interest; and this faculty of consequence, is not to be renounced in religion, unless we are prepared to discard it universally. The true inference from the almost endless errors which have darkened theology is, not that we are to neglect and disparage our powers, but to exert them more patiently, circumspectly, uprightly. The worst errors, after all, have sprung up in that church which proscribes reason, and demands from its members implicit faith. The most pernicious doctrines have been the growth of the darkest times, when the general credulity encouraged bad men and enthusiasts to broach their dreams and inventions, and to stifle the faint remonstrances of reason by the menaces of everlasting perdition. Say what we may, God has given us a rational nature, and will call us to account for it. We may let it sleep, but we do so at our peril. Revelation is addressed to us as rational beings. We may wish, in our sloth, that God had given us a system, demanding no labor of comparing, limiting, and inferring. But such a system would be at variance with the whole character of our present existence; and it is the part of wisdom to take revelation as it is given to us, and to interpret it by the help of the faculties which it everywhere supposes, and on which it is founded.

To the views now given, an objection is commonly urged from the character of God. We are told, that, God being infinitely wiser than men, his discoveries will surpass human reason. In a revelation from such a teacher, we ought to expect propositions which we cannot reconcile with one another, and which may seem to contradict established truths; and it becomes us not to question or explain them away, but to believe and adore, and to submit our weak and carnal reason to the Divine word. To this objection, we have two short answers. We say, first, that it is impossible that a teacher of infinite wisdom should expose those whom he would teach to infinite error. But if once we admit that propositions, which in their literal sense appear plainly repugnant to one another, or to any known truth, are still to be literally understood and received, what possible limit can we set to the belief of contradictions? What shelter have we from the wildest fanaticism, which can always quote passages that, in their literal and obvious sense, give support to its extravagances? How can the Protestant escape from transubstantiation, a doctrine most clearly taught us, if the submission of reason now contended for be a duty? How can we even hold fast the truths of revelation? for if one apparent contradiction may be true, so may another, and the proposition, that Christianity is false, though involving inconsistency, may still be a verity.

We answer, again, that, if God be infinitely wise, he cannot sport with the understandings of his creatures. A wise teacher discovers his wisdom in adapting himself to the capacities of his pupils, not in perplexing them with what is unintelligible, not in distressing them with apparent contradictions, not in filling them with a skeptical distrust of their own powers. An infinitely wise teacher, who knows the precise extent of our minds, and the best method of enlightening them, will surpass all other instructers in bringing down truth to our apprehension, and in showing its loveliness and harmony. We ought, indeed, to expect occasional obscurity in such a book as the Bible, which was written for past and future ages, as well as for the present. But God's wisdom is a pledge, that whatever is necessary for us, and necessary for salvation, is revealed too plainly to be mistaken, and too consistently to be questioned, by a sound and upright mind. It is not the mark of wisdom to use an unintelligible phraseology, to communicate what is above our capacities, to confuse and unsettle the intellect by appearances of contradiction. We honor our heavenly teacher too much to ascribe to him such a revelation. A revelation is a gift of light. It cannot thicken our darkness, and multiply our perplexities.

II. Having thus stated the principles according to which we interpret Scripture, I now proceed to the second great head of this discourse, which is, to state some of the views which we derive from that sacred book, particularly those which distinguish us from other Christians.

1. In the first place, we believe in the doctrine of GOD's UNITY, or that there is one God, and one only. To this truth we give infinite importance, and we feel ourselves bound to take heed, lest any man spoil us of it by vain philosophy. The proposition, that there is one God, seems to us exceedingly plain. We understand by it, that there is one being, one mind, one person, one intelligent agent, and one only, to whom underived and infinite perfection and dominion belong. We conceive, that these words could have conveyed no other meaning to the simple and uncultivated people who were set apart to be the depositaries of this great truth, and who were utterly incapable of understanding those hairbreadth distinctions between being and person which the sagacity of latter ages has discovered. We find no intimation, that this language was to be taken in an unusual sense, or that God's unity was a quite different thing from the oneness of other intelligent beings.

We object to the doctrine of the Trinity, that, whilst acknowledging in words, it subverts in effect, the unity of God. According to this doctrine, there are three infinite and equal persons possessing supreme divinity, called the Father, Son, and Holy Ghost. Each of these persons, as described by theologians, has his own particular consciousness, will, and perceptions. They love each other, converse with each other, and delight in each other's society. They perform different parts in man's redemption, each having his appropriate office, and neither doing the work of the other. The Son is mediator, and not the Father. The Father sends the Son, and is not himself sent; nor is he conscious, like the Son, of taking flesh. Here, then, we have three intelligent agents, possessed of different consciousnesses, different wills, and different perceptions, performing different acts, and sustaining different relations; and if these things do not imply and constitute three minds or beings, we are utterly at a loss to know how three minds or beings are to be formed. It is difference of properties, and acts, and consciousness, which leads us to the belief of different intelligent beings, and if this mark fails us, our whole knowledge falls; we have no proof, that all the agents and persons in the universe are not one and the same mind. When we attempt to conceive of three Gods, we can do nothing more than represent to ourselves three agents, distinguished from each other by similar marks and peculiarities to those which separate the persons of the Trinity; and when common Christians hear these persons spoken of as conversing with each other, loving each other, and performing different acts, how can they help regarding them as different beings, different minds?

We do, then, with all earnestness, though without reproaching our brethren, protest against the irrational and unscriptural doctrine of the Trinity. "To us," as to the Apostle and the primitive Christians, "there is one God, even the Father." With Jesus, we worship the Father, as the only living and true God. We are astonished, that any man can read the New Testament, and avoid the conviction, that the Father alone is God. We hear our Saviour continually appropriating this character to the Father. We find the Father continually distinguished from Jesus by this title. "God sent his Son." "God anointed Jesus." Now, how singular and inexplicable is this phraseology, which fills the New Testament, if this title belong equally to Jesus, and if a principal object of this book is to reveal him as God, as partaking equally with the Father in supreme divinity! We challenge our opponents to adduce one passage in the New Testament where the word God means three persons, where it is not limited to one person, and where, unless turned from its usual sense by the connection it does not mean the Father. Can stronger proof be given that the doctrine of three persons in the Godhead is not a fundamental doctrine of Christianity?

This doctrine, were it true, must, from its difficulty, singularity, and importance, have been laid down with great clearness, guarded with great care, and stated with all possible precision. But where does this statement appear? From the many passages which treat of God, we ask for one, one only, in which we are told that he is a threefold being, or that he is three persons, or that he is Father, Son, and Holy Ghost. On the contrary, in the New Testament, where, at least, we might expect many express assertions of this nature, God is declared to be one, without the least attempt to prevent the acceptation of the words in their common sense; and he is always spoken of and addressed in the singular number, that is, in language which was universally understood to intend a single person, and to which no other idea could have been attached, without an express admonition. So entirely do the Scriptures abstain from stating the Trinity, that, when our opponents would insert it into their creeds and doxologies, they are compelled to leave the Bible, and to invent forms of words altogether unsanctioned by Scriptural phraseology. That a doctrine so strange, so liable to misapprehension, so fundamental as this is said to be, and requiring such careful exposition, should be left so undefined and unprotected, to be made out by inference, and to be hunted through distant and detached parts of Scripture, — this is a difficulty which, we think, no ingenuity can explain.

We have another difficulty. Christianity, it must be remembered, was planted and grew up amidst sharp-sighted enemies, who overlooked no objectionable part of the system, and who must have fastened with great earnestness on a doctrine involving such apparent contradictions as the Trinity. We cannot conceive an opinion, against which the Jews, who prided themselves on an adherence to God's unity, would have raised an equal clamor. Now, how happens it that in the Apostolic writings, which relate so much to objections against Christianity, and to the controversies which grew out of this religion, not one word is said implying that objections were brought against the Gospel from the doctrine of the Trinity, not one word is uttered in its defence and explanation, not a word to rescue it from reproach and mistake? This argument has almost the force of demonstration. We are persuaded, that, had three divine persons been announced by the first preachers of Christianity, all equal and all infinite, one of whom was the very Jesus who had lately died on a cross, this peculiarity of Christianity would have almost absorbed every other, and the great labor of the Apostles would have been to repel th continual assaults which it would have awakened. But the fact is, that not a whisper of objection to Christianity, on that account, reaches our ears from the Apostolic age. In the Epistles we see not a trace of controversy called forth by the Trinity

We have further objections to this doctrine, drawn from its practical influence. We regard it as unfavorable to devotion, by dividing and distracting the mind in its communion with God. It is a great excellence of the doctrine of God's unity, that it offers to us ONE OBJECT of supreme homage, adoration, and love, one Infinite Father, one Being of beings, one original and fountain, to whom we may refer all good, in whom all our powers and affections may be concentrated, and whose lovely and venerable nature may pervade all our thoughts. True piety, when directed to an undivided Deity, has a chasteness, a singleness, most favorable to religious awe and love. Now the Trinity sets before us three distinct objects of supreme adoration; three infinite persons, having equal claims on our hearts; three divine agents, performing different offices, and to be acknowledged and worshipped in different relations. And is it possible we ask, that the weak and limited mind of man can attach itself to these with the same power and joy as to one Infinite Father, the only First Cause, in whom all the bless ings of nature and redemption meet as their centre and source? Must not devotion be distracted by the equal and rival claims of three equal persons, and must not the worship of the conscientious, consistent Christian be disturbed by an apprehension, lest he withhold from one or another of these his due proportion of homage?

We also think, that the doctrine of the Trinity injures devotion, not only by joining to the Father other objects of worship, but by taking from the Father the supreme affection which is his due, and transferring it to the Son. This is a most important view. That Jesus Christ, if exalted into the infinite Divinity, should be more interesting than the Father, is precisely what might be expected from history, and from the principles of human nature. Men want an object of worship like themselves, and the great secret of idolatry lies in this propensity. A God, clothed in our form, and feeling our wants and sorrows, speaks to our weak nature more strongly than a Father in heaven, a pure spirit, invisible, and unapproachable, save by the reflecting and purified mind. — We think, too, that the peculiar offices ascribed to Jesus by the popular theology make him the most attractive person in the Godhead. The Father is the depositary of the justice, the vindicator of the rights, the avenger of the laws, of the Divinity. On the other hand, the Son, the brightness of the Divine mercy, stands between the incensed Deity and guilty humanity, exposes his meek head to the storms, and his compassionate breast to the sword of the Divine justice, bears our whole load of punishment, and purchases with his blood every blessing which descends from heaven. Need we state the effect of these representations, especially on common minds for whom

Christianity was chiefly designed, and whom it seeks to bring to the Father as the loveliest being? We do believe, that the worship of a bleeding, suffering God tends strongly to absorb the mind, and to draw it from other objects, just as the human tenderness of the Virgin Mary has given her so conspicuous a place in the devotions of the Church of Rome. We believe, too, that this worship, though attractive is not most fitted to spiritualize the mind, that it awakens human transport rather than that deep veneration of the moral perfections of God which is the essence of piety.

2. Having thus given our views of the unity of God, I proceed in the second place to observe, that we believe in the unity of Jesus Christ. We believe that Jesus is one mind, one soul, one being, as truly one as we are, and equally distinct from the one God. We complain of the doctrine of the Trinity, that, not satisfied with making God three beings, it makes Jesus Christ two beings, and thus introduces infinite confusion into our conceptions of his character. This corruption of Christianity, alike repugnant to common sense and to the general strain of Scripture, is a remarkable proof of the power of a false philosophy in disfiguring the simple truth of Jesus.

According to this doctrine, Jesus Christ, instead of being one mind, one conscious intelligent principle, whom we can understand, consists of two souls, two minds; the one divine, the other human; the one weak, the other almighty; the one ignorant, the other omniscient. Now we maintain, that this is to make Christ two beings. To denominate him one person, one being, and yet to suppose him made up of two minds, infinitely different from each other, is to abuse and confound language, and to throw darkness over all our conceptions of intelligent natures. According to the common doctrine, each of these two minds in Christ has its own consciousness, its own will, its own perceptions. They have in fact no common properties. The divine mind feels none of the wants and sorrows of the human, and the human is infinitely removed from the perfection and happiness of the divine. Can you conceive of two beings in the universe more distinct? We have always thought that one person was constituted and distinguished by one consciousness. The doctrine, that one and the same person should have two consciousnesses, two wills, two souls, infinitely different from each other, — this we think an enormous tax on human credulity.

We say, that if a doctrine so strange, so difficult, so remote from all the previous conceptions of men, be indeed a part and an essential part of revelation, it must be taught with great distinctness, and we ask our brethren to point to some plain, direct passage, where Christ is said to be composed of two minds infinitely different, yet constituting one person. We find none. Other Christians, indeed, tell us, that this doctrine is necessary to the harmony of the Scriptures; that some texts ascribe to Jesus Christ human, and others divine properties, and that to reconcile these we must suppose two minds to which these properties may be referred. In other words, for the purpose of reconciling certain difficult passages, which a just criticism can in a great degree, if not wholly, explain, we must invent an hypothesis vastly more difficult, and involving gross absurdity. We are to find our way out of a labyrinth by a clue which conducts us into mazes infinitely more inextricable.

Surely, if Jesus Christ felt that he consisted of two minds, and that this was a leading feature of his religion, his phraseology respecting himself would have been colored by this peculiarity. The universal language of men is framed upon the idea, that one person is one person, is one mind, and one soul; and when the multitude heard this language from the lips of Jesus, they must have taken it in its usual sense, and must have referred to a single soul all which he spoke, unless expressly instructed to interpret it differently. But where do we find this instruction? Where do you meet, in the New Testament, the phraseology which abounds in Trinitarian books, and which necessarily grows from the doctrine of two natures in Jesus? Where does this divine teacher say, "This I speak as God, and this as man; this is true only of my human mind, this only of my divine"? Where do we find in the Epistles a trace of this strange phraseology? Nowhere. It was not needed in that day. It was demanded by the errors of a later age.

We believe, then, that Christ is one mind, one being, and, I add, a being distinct from the one God. That Christ is not the one God, not the same being with the Father, is a necessary inference from our former head, in which we saw that the doctrine of three persons in God is a fiction. But on so important a subject I would add a few remarks. We wish that those from whom we differ would weigh one striking fact. Jesus, in his preaching, continually spoke of God. The word was always in his mouth. We ask, does he, by this word, ever mean himself? We say, never. On the contrary, he most plainly distinguishes between God and himself, and so do his disciples. How this is to be reconciled with the idea, that the manifestation of Christ, as

God, was a primary object of Christianity, our adversaries must determine.

If we examine the passages in which Jesus is distinguished from God, we shall see that they not only speak of him as another being, but seem to labor to express his inferiority. He is continually spoken of as the Son of God, sent of God, receiving all his powers from God, working miracles because God was with him, judging justly because God taught him, having claims on our belief because he was anointed and sealed by God, and as able of himself to do nothing. The New Testament is filled with this language. Now we ask what impression this language was fitted and intended to make. Could any who heard it have imagined, that Jesus was the very God to whom he was so industriously declared to be inferior, — the very being by whom he was sent, and from whom he professed to have received his message and power? Let it here be remembered, that the human birth, and bodily form, and humble circumstances, and mortal sufferings of Jesus must all have prepared men to interpret, in the most unqualified manner, the language in which his inferiority to God was declared. Why, then, was this language used so continually, and without limitation, if Jesus were the Supreme Deity, and if this truth were an essential part of his religion? I repeat it, the human condition and sufferings of Christ tended strongly to exclude from men's minds the idea of his proper Godhead; and, of course, we should expect to find in the New Testament perpetual care and effort to counteract this tendency, to hold him forth as the same being with his Father, if this doctrine were, as is pretended, the soul and centre of his religion. We should expect to find the phraseology of

Scripture cast into the mould of this doctrine, to hear familiarly of God the Son, of our Lord God Jesus, and to be told, that to us there is one God, even Jesus. But instead of this, the inferiority of Christ pervades the New Testament. It is not only implied in the general phraseology, be repeatedly and decidedly expressed, and unaccompanied with any admonition to prevent its application to his whole nature. Could it, then, have been the great design of the sacred writers to exhibit Jesus as the Supreme God?

I am aware that these remarks will be met by two or three texts in which Christ is called God, and by a class of passages, not very numerous, in which divine properties are said to be ascribed to him. To these we offer one plain answer. We say that it is one of the most established and obvious principles of criticism, that language is to be explained according to the known properties of the subject to which it is applied. Every man knows that the same words convey very different ideas, when used in relation to different beings. Thus Solomon *built* the temple in a different manner from the architect whom he employed; and God *repents* differently from man. Now we maintain, that the known properties and circumstances of Christ, his birth, sufferings, and death, his constant habit of speaking of God as a distinct being from himself, his praying to God, his ascribing to God all his power and offices,—these acknowledged properties of Christ, we say, oblige us to interpret the comparatively few passages which are thought to make him the Supreme God in a manner consistent with his distinct and inferior nature. It is our duty to explain such texts by the rule which we apply to other texts, in which human beings are called gods, and are said to be partakers of the Divine nature, to know and possess all things, and to be filled with all God's fulness. These latter passages we do not hesitate to modify, and restrain, and turn from the most obvious sense, because this sense is opposed to the known properties of the beings to whom they relate; and we maintain, that we adhere to the same principle, and use no greater latitude, in explaining as we do the passages which are thought to support the Godhead of Christ.

Trinitarians profess to derive some important advantages from their mode of viewing Christ. It furnishes them, they tell us, with an infinite atonement, for it shows them an infinite being suffering for their sins. The confidence with which this fallacy is repeated astonishes us. When pressed with the question, whether they really believe that the infinite and unchangeable God suffered and died on the cross, they acknowledge that this is not true, but that Christ's human mind alone retained the pains of death. How have we, then, an infinite sufferer? This language seems to us an imposition on common minds, and very derogatory to God's justice, as if this attribute could be satisfied by a sophism and a fiction.

We are also told, that Christ is a more interesting object, that his love and mercy are more felt, when he is viewed as the Supreme God, who left his glory to take humanity and to suffer for men. That Trinitarians are strongly moved by this representation, we do not mean to deny; but we think their emotions altogether founded on a misapprehension of their own doctrines. They talk of the second person of the Trinity's leaving his glory and his Father's bosom, to visit and save the world. But this second person being the unchangeable and infinite God, was evidently incapable of parting with the least degree of his perfection and felicity. At the moment of his taking flesh, he was as intimately present with his Father as before, and equally with his Father filled heaven, and earth, and immensity. This Trinitarians acknowledge; and still they profess to be touched and overwhelmed by the amazing humiliation of this immutable being! But not only does their doctrine when fully explained, reduce Christ's humiliation to a fiction, it almost wholly destroys the impressions with which his cross ought to be viewed. According to their doctrine, Christ was, comparatively, no sufferer at all. It is true, his human mind suffered; but this, they tell us, was an infinitely small part of Jesus, bearing no more proportion to his whole nature, than a single hair of our heads to the whole body, or than a drop to the ocean. The divine mind of Christ, and which was most properly himself, was infinitely happy, as the very moment of the suffering of his humanity. Whilst hanging on the cross, he was the happiest being in the universe, — as happy as the infinite Father; so that his pains, compared with his felicity, were nothing. This Trinitarians do and must acknowledge. It follows necessarily from the immutableness of the divine nature which they ascribe to Christ; so that their system, justly viewed, robs his death of interest, weakens our sympathy with his sufferings, and is, of all others, most unfavorable to a love of Christ, founded on a sense of his sacrifices for mankind. We esteem our own views to be vastly more affecting. It is our belief, that Christ's ilumiliation was real and entire, that the whole Saviour, and not a part of him, suffered; that his crucifixion was a scene of deep and unmixed agony. As we stand round his cross, our minds are not distracted, nor our sensibility weakened, by contemplating him as composed of incongruous and infinitely differing minds, and as having a balance of infinite felicity. We recognize in the dying Jesus but one mind. This, we think, renders his sufferings, and his patience and love in bearing them, incomparably more impressive and affecting, than the system we oppose.

3. Having thus given our belief on two great points, namely, that there is one God, and that Jesus Christ is a being distinct from and inferior to God, I now proceed to another point on which we lay still greater stress. We believe in the *moral perfection of God*. We consider no part of theology so important as that which treats of God's moral character; and we value our views of Christianity chiefly as they assert his amiable and venerable attributes.

It may be said, that, in regard to this subject, all Christians agree; that all ascribe to the Supreme Being infinite justice, goodness, and holiness. We reply, that it is very possible to speak of God magnificently, and to think of him meanly; to apply to his person high-sounding epithets, and to his government principles which make him odious. The heathens called Jupiter the greatest and the best; but his history was black with cruelty and lust. We cannot judge of men's real ideas of God by their general language, for in all ages they have hoped to soothe the Deity by adulation. We must inquire into their particular views of his purposes, of the principles of his administration, and of his disposition towards his creatures.

We conceive that Christians have generally leaned towards a very injurious view of the Supreme Being. They have too often felt as if he were raised, by his greatness and sovereignty, above the principles of morality, above those eternal laws of equity and rectitude to which all other beings are subjected. We believe, that in no being is the sense of right so strong, so omnipotent, as in God. We believe that his almighty power is entirely submitted to his perceptions of rectitude; and this is the ground of our piety. It is not because he is our Creator merely, but because he created us for good and holy purposes; it is not because his will is irresistible, but because his will is the perfection of virtue, that we pay him allegiance. We cannot bow before a being, however great and powerful, who governs tyrannically. We respect nothing but excellence, whether on earth or in heaven. We venerate, not the loftiness of God's throne, but the equity and goodness in which it is established.

We believe that God is infinitely good, kind, benevolent, in the proper sense of these words; good in disposition, as well as in act; good, not to a few, but to all; good to every individual, as well as to the general system.

We believe, too, that God is just; but we never forget that his justice is the justice of a good being, dwelling in the same mind, and acting in harmony with perfect benevolence. By this attribute, we understand God's infinite regard to virtue or moral worth, expressed in a moral government; that is, in giving excellent and equitable laws, and in conferring such rewards, and inflicting such punishments, as are best fitted to secure their observance. God's justice has for its end the highest virtue of the creation, and it punishes for this end alone, and thus it coincides wish be nevolence; for virtue and happiness, though not the same, are inseparably conjoined.

God's justice, thus viewed, appears to us to be in perfect harmony with his mercy. According to the prevalent systems of theology, these attributes are so discordant and jarring, that to reconcile them is the hardest task, and the most wonderful achievement, of infinite wisdom. To us they seem to be intimate friends, always at peace, breathing the same spirit, and seeking the same end. By God's mercy, we understand not a blind, instinctive compassion, which forgives without reflection, and without regard to the interests of virtue. This, we acknowledge, would be incompatible with justice, and also with enlightened benevolence. God's mercy, as we understand it, desires strongly the happiness of the guilty, but only through their penitence. It has a regard to character as truly as his justice. It defers punishment, and suffers long, that the sinner may return to his duty, but leaves the impenitent and unyielding to the fearful retribution threatened in God's word.

To give our views of God in one word, we believe in his Parental character. We ascribe to him, not only the name, but the dispositions and principles of a father. We believe that he has a father's concern for his creatures, a father's desire for their improvement, a father's equity in proportioning his commands to their powers, a father's joy in their progress, a father's readiness to receive the penitent, and a father's justice for the incorrigible. We look upon this world as a place of education, in which he is training men by prosperity and adversity, by aids and obstructions, by conflicts of reason and passion, by motives to duty and temptations to sin, by a various discipline suited to free and moral beings, for union with himself, and for a sublime and ever growing virtue in heaven.

Now we object to the systems of religion which prevail among us, that they are adverse, in a greater or less degree, to these purifying, comforting, and honorable views of God, that they take from us our father in heaven, and substitute for him a being, whom we cannot love if we would, and whom we ought not to love if we could. We object particularly, on this ground, to that system which arrogates to itself the name of Orthodoxy, and which is now industriously propagated through our country. This system, indeed, takes various shapes, but in all it casts dishonor on the Creator. According to its old and genuine form, it teaches that God brings us into life wholly depraved, so that under the innocent features of our childhood is hidden a nature averse to all good, and propense to all evil, a nature which exposes us to God's displeasure and wrath, even before we have acquired power to understand our duties, or to reflect upon our actions. According to a more modern exposition, it teaches that we came from the hands of our Maker with such a constitution, and are placed under such influences and circumstances, as to render certain and infallible the total depravity of every human being, from the first moment of his moral agency; and it also teaches, that the offence of the child, who brings into life this ceaseless tendency to unmingled crime, exposes him to the sentence of everlasting damnation. Now, according to the plainest principles of morality, we maintain, that a natural constitution of the mind, unfailingly disposing it to evil and to evil alone, would absolve it from guilt; that to give existence under this condition would argue unspeakable cruelty, and that to punish the sin of this unhappily constituted child with endless ruin would be a wrong unparalleled by the most merciless despotism.

This system also teaches, that God selects from this corrupt mass a number to be saved, and plucks them, by a special influence, from the common ruin; that the rest of mankind, though left without that special grace which their conversion requires, are commanded to repent under penalty of aggravated woe; and that forgiveness is promised them on terms which their very constitution infallibly disposes them to reject, and in rejecting which they awfully enhance the punishments of hell. These proffers of forgiveness and exhortations of amendment, to beings born under a blighting curse, fill our minds with a horror which we want words to express.

That this religious system does not produce all the effects on character which might be anticipated, we most joyfully admit. It is often, very often, counteracted by nature, conscience, common sense, by the general strain of Scripture, by the mild example and precepts of Christ, and by the many positive declarations of God's universal kindness and perfect equity. But still we think that we see its unhappy influence. It tends to discourage the timid, to give excuses to the bad, to feed the vanity of the fanatical, and to offer shelter to the bad feelings of the malignant. By shocking, as it does, the fundamental principles of morality, and by exhibiting a sev e and partial Deity, it tends strongly to pervert the moral faculty, to form a gloomy, forbidding, and servile religion, and to lead men to substitute censoriousness, bitterness, and persecution for a tender and impartial charity. We think, too, that this system, which begins with degrading human nature, may be expected to end in pride; for pride grows out of a consciousness of high distinctions, however obtained, and no distinction is so great as that which is made between the elected and abandoned of God.

The false and dishonorable views of God which have now been stated, we feel ourselves bound to resist unceasingly. Other errors we can pass over with comparative indifference. But we ask our opponents to leave to us a GOD worthy of our love and trust, in whom our moral sentiments may delight, in whom our weaknesses and sorrows may find refuge. We cling to the Divine perfections. We meet them everywhere in creation, we read them in the Scriptures, we see a lovely image of them in Jesus Christ; and gratitude, love, and veneration call on us to assert them. Reproached, as we often are, by men, it is our consolation and happiness, that one of our chief offences is the zeal with which we vindicate the dishonored goodness and rectitude of God.

4. Having thus spoken of the unity of God; of the unity of Jesus, and his inferiority to God; and of the perfections of the Divine character; I now proceed to give our views of the mediation of Christ and of the purposes of his mission. With regard to the great object which Jesus came to accomplish, there seems to be no possibility of mistake. We believe that he was sent by the Father to effect a moral or spiritual deliverance of mankind; that is, to rescue men from sin and its consequences, and to bring them to a state of everlasting purity and happiness. We believe, too, that he accomplishes this sublime purpose by

a variety of methods; by his instructions respecting God's unity, parental character, and moral government, which are admirably fitted to reclaim the world from idolatry and impiety to the knowledge, love, and obedience of the Creator, by his promises of pardon to the penitent, and of Divine assistance to those who labor for progress in moral excellence; by the light which he has thrown on the path of duty; by his own spotless example, in which the loveliness and sublimity of virtue shine forth to warm and quicken, as well as guide us to perfection; by his threatenings against incorrigible guilt; by his glorious discoveries of immortality; by his sufferings and death; by that signal event, the resurrection, which powerfully bore witness to his Divine mission, and brought down to men's senses a future life; by his continual intercession, which obtains for us spiritual aid and blessings; and by the power with which he is invested, of raising the dead, judging the world, and conferring the everlasting rewards promised to the faithful.

We have no desire to conceal the fact, that a difference of opinion exists among us in regard to an interesting part of Christ's mediation; I mean, in regard to the precise influence of his death on our forgiveness. Many suppose that this event contributes to our pardon, as it was a principal means of confirming his religion, and of giving it a power over the mind; in other words, that it procures forgiveness by leading to that repentance and virtue which is the great and only condition on which forgiveness is bestowed. Many of us are dissatisfied with this explanation, and think that the Scriptures ascribe the remission of sins to Christ's death with an emphasis so peculiar, that we ought to consider this event as having a special influence in removing punishment, though the Scriptures may not reveal the way in which it contributes to this end.

Whilst, however, we differ in explaining the connection between Christ's death and human forgiveness,—a connection which we all gratefully acknowledge,—we agree in rejecting many sentiments which prevail in regard to his mediation. The idea which is conveyed to common minds by the popular system, that Christ's death has an influence in making God placable or merciful, in awakening his kindness towards men, we reject with strong disapprobation. We are happy to find, that this very dishonorable notion is disowned by intelligent Christians of that class from which we differ. We recollect, however, that not long ago it was common to hear of Christ as having died to appease God's wrath, and to pay the debt of sinners to his inflexible justice; and we have a strong persuasion, that the language of popular religious books, and the common mode of stating the doctrine of Christ's mediation, still communicate very degrading views of God's character. They give to multitudes the impression, that the death of Jesus produces a change in the mind of God towards man, and that in this its efficacy chiefly consists. No error seems to us more pernicious. We can endure no shade over the pure goodness of God. We earnestly maintain, that Jesus, instead of calling forth, in any way or degree the mercy of the Father, was sent by that mercy, to be our Saviour; that he is nothing to the human race but what he is by God's appointment; that he communicates nothing but what God empowers him to bestow; that our Father in heaven is originally, essentially, and eternally placable, and disposed to forgive; and that his unborrowed, underived, and unchangeable love is the only fountain of what flows to us through his Son. We conceive that Jesus is dishonored, not glorified, by ascribing to him an influence which clouds the splendor of Divine benevolence.

We farther agree in rejecting, as unscriptural and absurd, the explanation given by the popular system of the manner in which Christ's death procures forgiveness for men. This system used to teach, as its fundamental principle, that man, having sinned against an infinite being, has contracted infinite guilt, and is consequently exposed to an infinite penalty. We believe, however, that this reasoning, if reasoning it may be called, which overlooks the obvious maxim, that the guilt of a being must be proportioned to his nature and powers, has fallen into disuse. Still the system teaches that sin, of whatever degree, exposes to endless punishment, and that the whole human race, being infallibly involved by their nature in sin, owe this awful penalty to the justice of their Creator. It teaches, that this penalty cannot be remitted, in consistency with the honor of the Divine law, unless a substitute be found to endure it or to suffer an equivalent. It also teaches that, from the nature of the case, no substitute is adequate to this work, save the infinite God himself; and accordingly, God, in his second person, took on him human nature, that he might pay to his own justice the debt of punishment incurred by men, and might thus reconcile forgiveness with the claims and threatenings of his law. Such is the prevalent system. Now, to us, this doctrine seems to carry on its front strong marks of absurdity, and we maintain that Christianity ought not to be encumbered with it, unless it be laid down in the New Testament fully and expressly. We ask our adversaries, then, to point to some plain passages where it is taught We ask for one text in which we are told that God took human nature, that he might make an infinite satisfaction to his own justice; for one text which tells us that human guilt requires an infinite substitute, that Christ's sufferings owe their efficacy to their being borne by an infinite being, or that his divine nature gives infinite value to the sufferings of the human. Not *one word* of this description can we find in the Scriptures; not a text, which even hints at these strange doctrines. They are altogether, we believe, the fictions of theologians. Christianity is in no degree responsible for them. We are astonished at their prevalence. What can be plainer, than that God cannot, in any sense, be a sufferer, or bear a penalty in the room of his creatures? How dishonorable to him is the supposition, that his justice is now so severe as to exact infinite punishment for the sins of frail and feeble men, and now so easy and yielding as to accept the limited pains of Christ's human soul as a full equivalent for the endless woes due from the world! How plain is it, also, according to this doctrine, that God, instead of being plenteous in forgiveness, never forgives! for it seems absurd to speak of men as forgiven, when their whole punishment, or an equivalent to it, is borne by a substitute. A scheme more fitted to obscure the brightness of Christianity and the mercy of God, or less suited to give comfort to a guilty and troubled mind, could not, we think, be easily framed.

We believe, too, that this system is unfavorable to the character. It naturally leads men to think that Christ came to change God's mind, rather than their own that the highest object of his mission was to avert punishment, rather than to communicate holiness; and that a large part of religion consists in disparaging good works and human virtue, for the purpose of magnifying the value of Christ's vicarious sufferings. In this way a sense of the infinite importance and indispensable necessity of personal improvement is weakened, and high-sounding praises of Christ's cross seem often to be substituted for obedience to his precepts. For ourselves, we have not so learned Jesus. Whilst we gratefully acknowledge that he came to rescue us from punishment, we believe that he was sent on a still nobler errand, namely, to deliver us from sin itself, and to form us to a sublime and heavenly virtue. We regard him as a Saviour, chiefly as he is the light, physician, and guide of the dark, diseased, and wandering mind. No influence in the universe seems to us so glorious as that over the character; and no redemption so worthy of thankfulness, as the restoration of the soul to purity. Without this, pardon, were it possible would be of little value. Why pluck the sinner from hell if a hell be left to burn in his own breast? Why raise him to heaven, if he remain a stranger to its sanctity and love? With these impressions, we are accustomed to value the Gospel chiefly as it abounds in effectual aids, motives, excitements, to a generous and divine virtue. In this virtue, as in a common centre, we see all its doctrines, precepts, promises, meet; and we believe that faith in this religion is of no worth, and contributes nothing to salvation, any farther than as it uses these doctrines, precepts, promises, and the whole life, character, sufferings, and triumphs of Jesus, as the means of purify ing the mind, of changing it into the likeness of his celestial excellence.

5. Having thus stated our views of the highest object of Christ's mission, that it is the recovery of men to virtue, or holiness, I shall now, in the last place, give our views of the nature of Christian virtue, or true holiness. We believe that all virtue has its foundation in the moral nature of man, that is, in conscience, or his sense of duty, and in the power of forming his temper and life according to conscience. We believe that these moral faculties are the grounds of responsibility, and the highest distinctions of human nature, and that no act is praiseworthy any farther than it springs from their exertion. We believe that no dispositions infused into us without our own moral activity are of the nature of virtue, and therefore we reject the doctrine of irresistible Divine influence on the human mind, moulding it into goodness, as marble is hewn into a statue. Such goodness, if this word may be used, would not be the object of moral approbation, any more than the instinctive affections of inferior animals, or the constitutional amiableness of human beings.

By these remarks, we do not mean to deny the importance of God's aid or Spirit; but by his Spirit we mean a moral, illuminating, and persuasive influence, not physical, not compulsory, not involving a necessity of virtue. We object strongly to the idea of many Christians respecting man's impotence and God's irresistible agency on the heart, believing that they subvert our responsibility and the laws of our moral nature, that they make men machines, that they cast on God the blame of all evil

deeds, that they discourage good minds, and inflate the
fanatical with wild conceits of immediate and sensible
inspiration.

Among the virtues, we give the first place to the love of
God. We believe, that this principle is the true end and
happiness of our being, that we were made for union with
our Creator, that his infinite perfection is the only sufficient object and true resting-place for the insatiable desires
and unlimited capacities of the human mind, and that without him our noblest sentiments — admiration, veneration,
hope, and love — would wither and decay. We believe, too,
that the love of God is not only essential to happiness, but
to the strength and perfection of all the virtues; that conscience, without the sanction of God's authority and retributive justice, would be a weak director; that benevolence,
unless nourished by communion with his goodness, and
encouraged by his smile, could not thrive amidst the selfishness and thanklessness of the world; and that self-government, without a sense of the Divine inspection, would
hardly extend beyond an outward and partial purity. God,
as he is essentially goodness, holiness, justice, and vir
tue, so he is the life, motive, and sustainer of virtue in the
human soul.

But whilst we earnestly inculcate the love of God, we
believe that great care is necessary to distinguish it from
counterfeits. We think that much, which is called piety,
is worthless. Many have fallen into the error, that there
can be no excess in feelings which have God for their
object; and, distrusting as coldness that self-possession
without which virtue and devotion lose all their dignity,
they have abandoned themselves to extravagances, which

have brought contempt on piety. Most certainly, if the love of God be that which often bears its name, the less we have of it, the better. If religion be the shipwreck of understanding, we cannot keep too far from it. On this subject, we always speak plainly. We cannot sacrifice our reason to the reputation of zeal. We owe it to truth and religion to maintain, that fanaticism, partial insanity, sudden impressions, and ungovernable transports are any thing rather than piety.

We conceive, that the true love of God is a moral sentiment, founded on a clear perception, and consisting in a high esteem and veneration, of his moral perfections. Thus it perfectly coincides, and is in fact the same thing, with the love of virtue, rectitude, and goodness. You will easily judge, then, what we esteem the surest and only decisive signs of piety. We lay no stress on strong excitements. We esteem him, and him only, a pious man, who practically conforms to God's moral perfections and government; who shows his delight in God's benevolence, by loving and serving his neighbour; his delight in God's justice, by being resolutely upright; his sense of God's purity, by regulating his thoughts, imagination, and desires; and whose conversation, business, and domestic life are swayed by a regard to God's presence and authority. In all things else, men may deceive themselves. Disordered nerves may give them strange sights, and sounds, and impressions. Texts of Scripture may come to them as from heaven. Their whole souls may be moved, and their confidence in God's favor be undoubting. But in all this there is n religion. The question is, do they love God's commands, in which his character is fully expressed, and

give up to these their habits and passions? Without this,
ecstasy is a mockery. One surrender of desire to God's
will is worth a thousand transports. We do not judge
of the bent of men's minds by their raptures, any more
than we judge of the natural direction of a tree during a
storm. We rather suspect loud profession, for we have
observed that deep feeling is generally noiseless, and least
seeks display.

We would not, by these remarks, be understood as wishing to exclude from religion warmth, and even transport.
We honor and highly value true religious sensibility. We
believe that Christianity is intended to act powerfully on
our whole nature,—on the heart, as well as the understanding and the conscience. We conceive of heaven as
a state where the love of God will be exalted into an unbounded fervor and joy; and we desire, in our pilgrimage
here, to drink into the spirit of that better world. But we
think that religious warmth is only to be valued, when it
springs naturally from an improved character, when it
comes unforced, when it is the recompense of obedience,
when it is the warmth of a mind which understands God
by being like him, and when, instead of disordering, it
exalts the understanding, invigorates conscience, gives a
pleasure to common duties, and is seen to exist in connection with cheerfulness, judiciousness, and a reasonable
frame of mind. When we observe a fervor, called religious, in men whose general character expresses little re
finement and elevation, and whose piety seems at war with
reason, we pay it little respect. We honor religion too
much to give its sacred name to a feverish, forced fluctuating zeal, which has little power over the life

Another important branch of virtue we believe to be love to Christ. The greatness of the work of Jesus, the spirit with which he executed it, and the sufferings which he bore for our salvation, we feel to be strong claims on our gratitude and veneration. We see in nature no beauty to be compared with the loveliness of his character, nor do we find on earth a benefactor to whom we owe an equal debt. We read his history with delight, and learn from it he perfection of our nature. We are particularly touched o/ his death, which was endured for our redemption, and oy that strength of charity which triumphed over his pains. His resurrection is the foundation of our hope of immortality. His intercession gives us boldness to draw nigh to the throne of grace, and we look up to heaven with new desire, when we think that, if we follow him here, we shall there see his benignant countenance and enjoy his friendship for ever.

I need not express to you our views on the subject of the benevolent virtues. We attach such importance to these, that we are sometimes reproached with exalting them above piety. We regard the spirit of love, charity, meekness, forgiveness, liberality, and beneficence, as the badge and distinction of Christians, as the brightest image we can bear of God, as the best proof of piety. On this subject, I need not and cannot enlarge; but there is one branch of benevolence which I ought not to pass over in silence, because we think that we conceive of it more highly and justly than many of our brethren. I refer to the duty of candor, charitable judgment, especially towards those who differ in religious opinion. We think hat in nothing have Christians so widely departed from their religion, as in this particular. We read with astonishment and horror the history of the Church; and sometimes, when we look back on the fires of persecution, and on the zeal of Christians in building up walls of separation and in giving up one another to perdition, we feel as if we were reading the records of an infernal, rather than a heavenly kingdom. An enemy to every religion, if asked to describe a Christian, would, with some show of reason, depict him as an idolater of his own distinguishing opinions, covered with badges of party, shutting his eyes on the virtues and his ears on the arguments of his opponents, arrogating all excellence to his own sect and all saving power to his own creed, sheltering under the name of pious zeal the love of domination, the conceit of infallibility, and the spirit of intolerance, and trampling on men's rights under the pretence of saving their souls.

We can hardly conceive of a plainer obligation on beings of our frail and fallible nature, who are instructed in the duty of candid judgment, than to abstain from condemning men of apparent conscientiousness and sincerity, who are chargeable with no crime but that of differing from us in the interpretation of the Scriptures, and differing, too, on topics of great and acknowledged obscurity. We are astonished at the hardihood of those, who, with Christ's warnings sounding in their ears, take on them the responsibility of making creeds for his Church, and cast out professors of virtuous lives for imagined errors, for the guilt of thinking for themselves. We know that zeal for truth is the cover for this usurpation of Christ's prerogative; but we think that zeal for truth, as it is called, is very suspicious, except in men whose capacities and advantages, whose patient deliberation, and whose improvements in humility, mildness, and candor, give them a right to hope that their views are more just than those of their neighbours. Much of what passes for a zeal for truth we look upon with little respect, for it often appears to thrive most luxuriantly where other virtues shoot up thinly and feebly; and we have no gratitude for those reformers, who would force upon us a doctrine which has not sweetened their own tempers, or made them better men than their neighbours.

We are accustomed to think much of the difficulties attending religious inquiries; difficulties springing from the slow development of our minds, from the power of early impressions, from the state of society, from human authority, from the general neglect of the reasoning powers, from the want of just principles of criticism and of important helps in interpreting Scripture, and from various other causes. We find, that on no subject have men, and even good men, ingrafted so many strange conceits, wild theories, and fictions of fancy, as on religion; and remembering, as we do, that we ourselves are sharers of the common frailty, we dare not assume infallibility in the treatment of our fellow-Christians, or encourage in common Christians, who have little time for investigation, the habit of denouncing and contemning other denominations, perhaps more enlightened and virtuous than their own. Charity, forbearance, a delight in the virtues of different sects, a backwardness to censure and condemn, — these are virtues, which, however poorly practised by us, we admire and recommend, and we would rather join ourselves to the church in which they abound, than to any other communion, however elated with the belief of its own orthodoxy, however strict in guarding its creed, however burning with zeal against imagined error.

I have thus given the distinguishing views of those Christians in whose names I have spoken. We have embraced this system, not hastily or lightly, but after much deliberation, and we hold it fast, not merely because we believe it to be true, but because we regard it as purifying truth, as a doctrine according to godliness, as able to "work mightily" and to "bring forth fruit" in them who believe. That we wish to spread it, we have no desire to conceal; but we think that we wish its diffusion, because we regard it as more friendly to practical piety and pure morals than the opposite doctrines, because it gives clearer and nobler views of duty, and stronger motives to its performance, because it recommends religion at once to the understanding and the heart, because it asserts the lovely and venerable attributes of God, because it tends to restore the benevolent spirit of Jesus to his divided and afflicted Church, and because it cuts off every hope of God's favor, except that which springs from practical conformity to the life and precepts of Christ. We see nothing in our views to give offence, save their purity, and it is their purity which makes us seek and hope their extension through the world.

My friend and brother: — You are this day to take upon you important duties; to be clothed with an office which the Son of God did not disdain; to devote yourself to that religion which the most hallowed lips have preached, and the most precious blood sealed. We trust that you will bring to this work a willing mind, a firm purpose, a martyr's spirit, a readiness to toil and suffer for the truth, a devotion of your best powers to the interests of piety and virtue. I have spoken of the doctrines which you will probably preach; but I do not mean that you are to give yourself to controversy. You will remember that good practice is the end of preaching, and will labor to make your people holy livers, rather than skilful disputants. Be careful, lest the desire of defending what you deem truth, and of repelling reproach and misrepresentation, turn you aside from your great business, which is to fix in men's minds a living conviction of the obligation, sublimity, and happiness of Christian virtue. The best way to vindicate your sentiments is to show, in your preaching and life their intimate connection with Christian morals, with a high and delicate sense of duty, with candor towards your opposers, with inflexible integrity, and with an habitual reverence for God. If any light can pierce and scatter the clouds of prejudice, it is that of a pure example. My brother, may your life preach more loudly than your lips Be to this people a pattern of all good works, and may your instructions derive authority from a well-grounded belief in your hearers, that you speak from the heart, tha you preach from experience, that the truth which you dispense has wrought powerfully in your own heart, that God, and Jesus, and heaven are not merely words on your lips but most affecting realities to your mind, and springs of hope, and consolation, and strength in all your trials. Thus laboring, may you reap abundantly, and have a testimony of your faithfulness, not only in your own conscience, but in the esteem, love, virtues, and improvements of your people

To all who hear me, I would say, with the Apostle,— 'Prove all things, hold fast that which is good." Do not, brethren, shrink from the duty of searching God's word for yourselves, through fear of human censure and denunciation. Do not think that you may innocently follow the opinions which prevail around you, without investigation on the ground, that Christianity is now so purified from errors as to need no laborious research. There is much reason to believe that Christianity is at this moment dishonored by gross and cherished corruptions. If you remember the darkness which hung over the Gospel for ages; if you consider the impure union which still subsists in almost every Christian country between the church and the state, and which enlists men's selfishness and ambition on the side of established error; if you recollect in what degree the spirit of intolerance has checked free inquiry, not only before, but since, the Reformation; you will see that Christianity cannot have freed itself from all the human inventions which disfigured it under the Papal tyranny. No. Much stubble is yet to be burnt; much rubbish to be removed; many gaudy decorations, which a false taste has hung around Christianity, must be swept away; and the earth-born fogs which have long shrouded it must be scattered, before this divine fabric will rise before us in its native and awful majesty, in its harmonious proportions, in its mild and celestial splendors. This glorious reformation in the Church, we hope, under God's blessing, from the progress of the human intellect, from the moral progress of society, from the consequent decline of prejudice and bigotry, and, though last not least, from the subversion of human authority in matters of religion, from the fall of those hierarchies, and other human institutions, by which the minds of individuals are oppressed under the weight of numbers, and a Papal dominion is perpetuated in the Protestant Church. Our earnest prayer to God is, that he will overturn, and overturn, and overturn, the strongholds of spiritual usurpation, until HE shall come whose right it is to rule the minds of men; that the conspiracy of ages against the liberty of Christians may be brought to an end; that the servile assent so long yielded to human creeds may give place to honest and devout inquiry into the Scriptures; and that Christianity, thus purified from error, may put forth its almighty energy, and prove itself, by its ennobling influence on the mind, to be indeed "the power of God unto salvation."

LETTERS

TO

UNITARIANS

OCCASIONED BY THE SERMON

OF THE REVEREND WILLIAM E. CHANNING

AT THE ORDINATION OF THE

REV. J. SPARKS.

BY LEONARD WOODS, D.D.
ABBOT PROFESSOR OF CHRISTIAN THEOLOGY IN THE THEOL.
SEMINARY, ANDOVER.

———

ANDOVER:
PUBLISHED BY FLAGG AND GOULD.
1820.

DISTRICT OF MASSACHUSETTS, TO WIT:

District Clerk's Office.

BE it remembered, that on the twenty eighth day of March, A.D. 1820, and in the forty fourth year of the independence of the United States of America, FLAGG & GOULD of the said district, have deposited in this office the title of a book, the right whereof they claim as proprietors, in the words following, viz.—"Letters to Unitarians occasioned by the Sermon of the Rev. William E. Channing at the ordination of the Rev. J. Sparks. By Leonard Woods, D.D. Abbot Professor of Christian Theology in the Theol. Sem. Andover.—In conformity to the act of the congress of the United States of America, entitled "An Act for the encouragement of learning, by securing the copies of maps, charts and books, to the authors and proprietors of such copies during the times therein mentioned:" and also to an Act entitled, "An act supplementary to an Act, entitled, An Act for the encouragement of learning, by securing the copies of maps, charts and books, to the authors and proprietors of such copies during the times therein mentioned; and extending the benefits thereof to the arts of designing, engraving and etching historical, and other prints."

JNO. W. DAVIS, *Clerk of the District of Massachusetts.*

CONTENTS.

LETTER I.

Introductory remarks . . . . 3—7

LETTER II.

The propriety of a creed.—The right of declaring our own opinions.—This right infringed.—Opinions represented as peculiar to Unitarians, which belong to the Orthodox;—particularly as to God's unity, and moral perfection . . . . 8—17

LETTER III.

Views of the Orthodox respecting the character and government of God.—His paternal character illustrated 18—24

LETTER IV.

The proof that the Orthodox deny the moral perfection of God, considered.—Native character of man.—Proper mode of reasoning on this subject . . . 24—30

LETTER V.

The doctrine of man's depravity stated, and proved.—Argument from the Old Testament;—confirmed by Paul's reasoning, Rom. iii.—The principle involved in the reasoning . . . . 31—41

LETTER VI.

Another argument from the Old Testament, Jer. xvi. 9, in proof of man's depravity.—Arguments from the New

Testament, John iii. 1—7. Rom. v. 12.—Imputation considered, Ephes. ii. 3.—Argument from the call to repent.—Moral character of God and human depravity not inconsistent . . . . 41—52

LETTER VII.

The doctrine of Election.—Preliminary remarks.—Proof of the doctrine, from John xvii, Ephes. i. 3—11, Rom. ix. 11—24, &c. . . . . . . 52—62

LETTER VIII.

Misrepresentations of the doctrine of Election, and the common objections against it, considered . . 63—83

LETTER IX.

Atonement.—Misrepresentations.—Metaphorical language employed by the Orthodox, and by the Scriptures.—Cautions to be observed respecting the use of metaphorical language.—Two classes of texts respecting forgiveness.—The nature and design of the atonement.—Objection as to the value of Christ's sufferings, considered . . . . . 83—106

LETTER X.

The doctrine of divine influence illustrated, and guarded against misstatements and objections . . 106—120

LETTER XI.

Additional remarks on representations in the Sermon.—Object of Christ's mission.—Nature of holiness.—Principle of moral government . . . . 120—132

LETTER XII.

Practical influence of the two systems, generally, and particularly.—Love to God.—Gratitude to God.—

Love to Christ.—Faith in Christ.—Dread of sin, and care to obey the divine precepts.—Reverence for the Bible.—Benevolent action, particularly the spread of the Gospel.—Closing remarks   132—160

ERRATA.

Page 12, line 2 from bottom, read *conduct*.
    15,   1,   *Mathers*.
    25,   13,   *could*, for would.
    36,   15,   *whatsoever*.
  106, read, Letter *X*.   P. 120, Letter *XI*.
  132,   Letter *XII*.

LETTER I.

My respected friends,

It has been the general sentiment of those, who are denominated *Unitarians* in this country, that *religious controversy* is undesirable, and of dangerous tendency; and that it is the duty of Christians of different parties to look with candor on each other's opinions, and not to magnify, beyond necessity, the points of difference. To this sentiment of yours respecting the danger of controversy, and the importance of candor and forbearance, I cordially agree. I regard it, as one of the great ends, which remains to be achieved by the influence of the christian religion, that all bitterness and strife should be banished from the world, and the spirit of love and peace universally prevail. With a view to this momentous end, I have made it my care, to guard, as far as possible, against introducing any thing disputatious into the pulpit,—especially on an occasion of so much interest, and so much tender emotion, as that of ordaining a Christian Minister. By these views I have actually governed myself for many years. I admit, indeed, the lawfulness, and, in some cases, the expedience and necessity of religious controversy; and I have endeavored to form some definite views of the principles, on which it ought to be conducted. But I will frankly express my apprehension, that it may require more caution, meekness, and self control, than I possess, to secure an exact observance of those rules of controversy, which I should prescribe for others. At the present time, and in my present undertaking, I cannot be insensible of special danger, as the controversy between the two parties has, for several years, been carried on in various forms, and with no inconsiderable warmth, and there are, I am sorry to say, on both sides, and even among the more moderate, too many symptoms of strong excitement. But whatever may be the circumstances of the present time, or the nature of the business I have undertaken, I wish here to declare my utter abhorrence of the practice, which has been too common, of applying reproachful epithets to an opponent, and of misrepresenting his real opinions, or endeavoring, by painting them in the most glaring colors, to expose them to contempt;—especially, of any disposition to sully his reputation, to inflict a wound on his feelings, or to triumph at the discovery of his imperfections. Such things are totally repugnant to the legitimate ends of controversy, and ought to be reprobated by all Christians, just as we reprobate the ferocities and cruelties of savage war.

The sermon, which occasions these Letters to you, is entitled to particular attention, on account of the talents and public character of the author, and, most of all, because he feels himself authorised to speak in *your name*. The sermon comes forth, as the voice of your denomination, and is extensively circulated, as an instrument of promoting your cause. On such an occasion, it is unquestionably proper, that our attention should be turned afresh to the question, whether the cause, which this sermon advocates, is indeed *the cause of God*.

To men, who are friends to unfettered inquiry, I shall think it unnecessary to offer any apology for the freedom of my remarks on the various subjects, which will be brought into view in these Letters. And I hope you will not deem it improper, that my remarks should be addressed to *you*,—inasmuch as the subjects of the discussion, on which I am entering, have been introduced by one, who appears before the public, as *your representative ;*—especially, as the manner, in which he treats these subjects is, in most respects, not unlike the manner, in which they have generally been treated by those, who have embraced the Arian or Socinian faith. This sermon is a fair specimen of the mode, in which we have been accustomed to see our religious opinions opposed in the writings of Unitarians. Now it must be allowed to be a sufficient justification of this attempt of mine, if I am fully convinced, that my opinions, and those of the Orthodox generally, are misunderstood, and essentially misrepresented by *Unitarians*, and particularly by the author of this sermon. I am convinced of this. And I think too, that the mistaken views, exhibited in the sermon, are exhibited in a manner, which, after cool and sober examination, neither the writer, nor his readers, will be much disposed to justify.

It seems there has, for some time, been a general expectation in this vicinity of some publication from me relative to the sermon which has occasioned these Letters; and inquiries have not unfrequently been made, as to the reasons of such a delay. Those reasons I will now frankly suggest. First. The regular duties of my office are sufficient to occupy my whole time; and I found it would require some effort in me, to be able to devote only a few hours in a week to such an employment as this. Another reason was, that I wished not to interrupt the attention, which the public were inclined to give to what had already been written, on one of the principal subjects of discussion between the two parties. Besides; I hoped that by taking a longer time, I should keep myself at a greater distance from the agitation and heat of controversy, and more perfectly avoid every appearance of wishing to make a personal attack upon any man; and that I should be better able to fix your attention, as well as my own, upon the subjects themselves, which were to be investigated, without regard to any considerations whatever, not conducive to a fair and thorough investigation.

The favor which I now ask of you is, not that you would treat my opinions and arguments with lenity and forbearance, but that you would give me a patient and candid hearing, while I attempt, on several important points, to explain and defend the religious sentiments of the Orthodox in New-England; and while I attempt to show, in what respects the writings of Unitarians essentially misrepresent our faith, and go into a manner of reasoning which is liable to just exceptions. I wish, particularly, to state the objections I feel, to several representations and modes of argumentation, contained in this Sermon, and to suggest some reasons, why the Author himself, and those who have implicitly relied upon the correctness of his positions, should allow themselves time for a serious review of the ground of this controversy. I wish, in short, as far as the limits which I must prescribe for myself will allow, to embrace the present opportunity, to do justice to myself and my brethren, and to satisfy those, who differ from us, as to the character and the evidence of that system of religion, which we believe.

The subjects, which have been discussed by my beloved Colleague, the Rev. Moses Stuart, will here be omitted. I regret, with many others, that his health and professional labors did not permit him to employ his talents and erudition on all the remaining topics of the Sermon. It is at his suggestion, and by his request, that I have turned aside from my common labors, and, let me say too, from my prevailing determination, so much as to take a part publicly in the controversy, which unhappily divides this region of our country. But, though I am urged to this undertaking by the request of those, in whom I am accustomed to repose entire confidence, and though I am fully persuaded that the opinions of the Orthodox have been treated unjustly; I am almost ready to withdraw my hand from this work, from a painful apprehension, that my efforts may serve but to increase or perpetuate the spirit of prejudice and animosity, which has shown itself among us in so many forms, and which, so far as it prevails, does really cut off all prospect of attaining the ends of free investigation. But I indulge the hope, that a different spirit is gaining ground. And I could wish, that the Reverend Author, who has undertaken to speak in your behalf, might have enjoyed the happiness of a more unruffled mind, and the honor of doing something more for that cause, which he is so well able to promote,—*the cause of love, candor, and gentleness.* I think that he, and many others will acknowledge the benefit they have, in this respect, derived from the example of my worthy Colleague. It is from the hope, that I may be guided by the same motive with him, and that, whatever else I may fail of accomplishing, I may help, in some measure, to diffuse a spirit of unprejudiced inquiry and christian kindness, that I am encouraged to proceed.

LETTER II.

My respected friends,

The Author, who speaks in your name, has at length, it seems, obtained satisfaction, as to the propriety of having a *creed,* or *confession of faith.* In his sermon, he has expressly given to the public the opinions which Unitarians embrace, in distinction from the opinions, commonly called Orthodox. The design is just and honorable. I am utterly unable to conceive, what valid objection there can be against the attempt of any denomination of Christians, to make the public acquainted with their views on religious subjects; or, in other words, to exhibit the *articles of their faith.* The thing is evidently proper in itself, and often necessary, though liable to abuse. With so respectable an example before you, I trust you will be free from any further difficulties on this subject, and will proceed, as occasion may require, to correct any mistaken apprehensions which the public may entertain, as to your opinions, and to give them a just view of what you believe to be the Christian religion. You owe this to the community. You owe it to yourselves. And it is obvious, that justice, in this respect, can be rendered to you by none, but yourselves. Other men, especially those who differ from you, cannot be competent to make known your faith, any farther than they are instructed and authorized by you. Doubtless you have felt that you have had reason to complain of the incorrectness of some Orthodox writers, who have undertaken to make a statement of your views. It is with manifest propriety, that you have now claimed the right, and through him, who acts as your organ of communication, have exercised the right, of declaring your own opinions. If you are just to yourselves, you will not stop here. Whenever others impute to you opinions, which you do not entertain, or deny to you those, which you do entertain; and whenever they are doubtful as to your faith, or in any way misrepresent it; you will feel that, of right, it belongs to you to interpose, and to do yourselves justice. And you would think it a gross violation of the rules of christian candor, for any man to declare your opinions to be different from your own serious declaration.—Grant me, and those with whom I have the happiness to be united in opinion, the same right, which you so justly claim for yourselves,—*the right of forming and declaring our own opinions, and of being believed, when we declare them.* We have a just claim to the last, as well as to the first, unless there are substantial reasons to question our veracity.

By the diligent application of our rational powers to the study of the Scriptures, with the best helps which have been afforded us, we have arrived at some sober, settled views on the subjects of religion. These views we wish, for various reasons, to declare. And if we would declare them justly, we must declare them in *our own language,* and do what is in our power to make that language intelligible to all. Where the meaning of the terms employed is doubtful, or obscure; it belongs to us to give the necessary explanations. Where the terms are liable to be understood with greater latitude, than comports with our views; it belongs to us to give the necessary limitations. And where our positions, in any respect whatever, need modifying; it belongs to us to modify them.—Further. It is certainly reasonable to expect, when dealing with men of candid, liberal minds, that the language which, in any case, we use to express our faith, will be understood, not in the sense which, taken by itself, it would possibly bear, nor in the sense which others might be inclined, for party purposes, to put upon it,—but *precisely according to our explanations.* These explanations, you will understand, do as really make a part of the proper enunciation of our faith, as the words which form the general proposition. Nothing can be more obviously just than all this, especially in relation to a subject, which is of a complex nature, or of difficult illustration.

With respect to this point of equity and honor, I have a few remarks to make on the Sermon now under consideration. The Author informs the public, what opinions he, and those who agree with him, embrace, and what they reject. This he has a right to do. Considering the circumstances of the case, he ought to do it. Nor can any one doubt that he is qualified to do it in the best manner. But he goes farther. He undertakes to give an account of *my* creed, and the creed of others with whom I agree. This is a more delicate task. In this he is evidently liable to mistake; and after all he may say on the subject, we may find it necessary to speak for ourselves. If the account he gives of our faith is not given in our language, and with our explanations and modifications,—certainly if not given in a manner which corresponds with our real opinions; we must notice the incorrectness. Most of all shall we have reason for some animadversion upon him, if he adopts, in any measure, that mode of representation, which men usually adopt, who wish to make the opinions of their opponents appear as exceptionable and absurd as possible.

So far as this sermon shall come under review, my remarks will relate chiefly to two points. *The first is, its affirming that certain opinions belong peculiarly and ex-*

clusively to Unitarians, when in fact they are held by the Orthodox. The second is, the misrepresentations it makes of the opinions which the Orthodox entertain, and of the reasoning commonly used to support them. These two points cannot be kept perfectly distinct in every part of the discussion; but it will be sufficiently evident to which my observations relate. For the present I shall beg your attention to the first.

Heretofore, it has been common for Unitarians in this country, and, if I mistake not, for this Author himself, to assert that, in respect of religious opinions, there is *no essential difference* between them and the Orthodox. For the sake of preventing disunion and strife, they have seemed to think it desirable, that the difference should be made to appear as small as possible. But from the tenor of this discourse, one would be apt to suppose that this Author's judgment or feelings had changed, and that he thought some important end was to be answered, by making the difference between the two parties as wide as possible. If this is a matter of fact, it is easy to see how it may have occasioned some of the mistakes, into which he has been led.

In the Sermon, p. 3, he declares what regard he and his particular friends feel for the Bible, and the principles of interpretation, by which they govern themselves in determining what doctrines it contains.—" We regard the Scriptures," he says, " as the record of God's successive revelation to mankind, and particularly of the last and most perfect revelation of his will by Jesus Christ. Whatever doctrines seem to us to be clearly taught in the Scriptures we receive without reserve or exception."
—It is implied in what he says, that this sentiment of reverence for the Scriptures is *peculiar to Unitarians.* For he first expresses his design to lay before his hear-

ers, "some of the *distinguishing* opinions of that class of Christians," in whose name he speaks, and then at the close says, *that he has given their "distinguishing views;"* that is, their views in *distinction* from those of the Orthodox.—I ask then, is it so? Is this high veneration for the Scriptures peculiar to *Unitarians?*—Do not the Orthodox uniformly declare their reverence for the Bible, and their readiness to submit to all its instructions? Do they not embrace that system of doctrines, which is peculiar to them, purely because they are convinced it is contained in the word of God, and because with this conviction, they cannot reject it, without disrespect to that word?—Read their confessions of faith, their systems of Divinity, their Commentaries, Sermons, catechisms, and books of devotion, and then say, whether they do not manifest as high a regard for the sacred volume, as this Author expresses?—Why then should it be signified, that this veneration for the Bible is among those things, which *distinguish* Unitarians from the Orthodox?—Such a representation must certainly appear somewhat unaccountable to one, who knows what opinions have generally been avowed and defended by these two parties, respecting the regard which is due to the Holy Scriptures.

As to these principles of interpretation, there is no need of adding any thing to what has been written by my Reverend Colleague. You perceive that these principles are not peculiar to Unitarians. They are substantially the principles of the Orthodox; so that, if you adopt them, the question between us is not, as would appear from the Sermon, whether the principles are to be *admitted;* but to what *conclusions* will they coduct us, when fairly applied to the interpretation of Scripture.

In relation to this point, the Author does indeed seem to make a concession in favor of others.—" We do not announce these principles," he says, " as original or peculiar to ourselves."—But immediately he takes occasion to follow his opponents with a train of reproachful insinuations, signifying, that although they occasionally adopt these principles, they vehemently decry them, when their cause requires; that they willingly avail themselves of reason, when it can be pressed into the service of their own party, and only complain of it, when its weapons wound themselves; that they violate the fundamental rules of reasoning, sacrifice the plain to the obscure, &c.

Under the same head I might place the following remarks of this Author.—" God's wisdom is a pledge, that whatever is necessary for *us*, and necessary for salvation, is revealed too plainly to be mistaken, and too consistently to be questioned by a sound and upright mind. It is not a mark of wisdom, to use an unintelligible phraseology, and to confuse and unsettle the intellect by appearances of contradiction."—Here also he evidently means to express sentiments, which belong *peculiarly* to his own party.—I cannot but think it strange, that it did not occur to his recollection, that *the plainness and intelligibleness of the Scriptures on all essential points* is a principle, for which the Orthodox in New England have uniformly contended with great zeal, even in their controversy with Unitarians.

Under the second head of his discourse, the Author undertakes " to state some of the views which Unitarians derive from the sacred book, particularly those which distinguish them from other Christians."—It will be to my purpose just to notice the first doctrine he states, though it has been remarked upon so satisfactorily in the publication above named. This is the *unity* of *God ;* which the Author represents as a doctrine *peculiar* to his party. After reading his remarks, and the remarks of other Unitarians on this subject, who would expect to find, that all respectable writers on the side of Orthodoxy have strenuously asserted the *unity* of *God,* as a fundamental doctrine of revelation, and have declared, times without number, that they could admit no views of the divine character inconsistent with this ? Who would expect to find that, in all Confessions of faith written by Trinitarians, the *unity* of God is one of the first doctrines which is asserted, and in all their systems of Divinity, one of the first, which is distinctly and largely defended ?—Truly, my respected friends, this doctrine is as important in our view, as it can be in yours. And we could not in reality have more reason to charge Unitarian Authors with injustice, should they represent us as denying the *existence* of God, than we have, when they represent us as denying his *unity.*

But we proceed to another point, on which this Author lays still greater stress.—" We believe," he says, " in *the moral perfection of God.*—We value our views of Christianity chiefly, as they assert his amiable and venerable attributes."—From the professed object of the discourse, and the language here employed, it appears, that the Author makes it the grand characteristic of Unitarianism in distinction from Orthodoxy, that it asserts the *moral perfection of God.*—But is this representation, as to the grand distinction between the parties, according to truth? Is it a representation, which he is authorized to make ?—When the most eminent Divines and most enlightened Christians, who have at any time embraced the common doctrines of Orthodoxy,—Luther, Calvin, Boyle, Hale, Baxter, Doddridge, Watts; the Edwardses, the Matthers, the Coopers, and multitudes, not to be numbered, of the same general faith, unite in declaring expressly, and constantly, that they *believe in the moral perfection of God*, that they ascribe to him infinite justice, goodness, and holiness, and continually adore his amiable and venerable attributes;—who is it that thinks himself entitled to look down upon this host of worthies, and reply,—" it is very possible to speak of God magnificently, and to think of him meanly; to apply to his person high sounding epithets, and to his government, principles which make him odious. The heathens called Jupiter the greatest and the best; but his history was black with cruelty and lust."—I make use of no high coloring. This is the reply, which the Author of the sermon makes, actually, and in so many words, to the most serious professions of the Orthodox, whoever they may be, as to their belief in the *moral perfection of God*. If he does not mean to apply what I have quoted, to the *Orthodox*, he has lost sight of the object of his discourse, and his subsequent reasoning, as you will see in a moment, is wholly impertinent.

In another form, he afterwards repeats insinuations of the same sort. " *We* believe," he says,—" *We*," emphatically, and by way of distinction from the Orthodox, —" *We* believe that in no being is the sense of right so strong, so omnipotent, as in God. We believe that his almighty power is entirely submitted to his perception of rectitude.—It is not because he is our Creator merely, but because he created us for good and holy purposes; it is not because his will is irresistible, but because his will is the perfection of virtue, that we pay him allegiance. We cannot bow before a being, however great and powerful, who governs tyrannically. We respect nothing but excellence, whether on earth or in heaven."

—Now the whole body of enlightened Christians, who embrace the common orthodox faith, give their united testimony to the same truths, and declare their veneration and love for a God of the same amiable character. In their creeds, systems, sermons, psalmody, and prayers, they abundantly assert these views respecting the *moral perfection of God.* They have asserted them continually, and publicly. They have taught them to their children. They have repeated them in a thousand forms.—And yet this author, speaking in your name too, feels himself entitled to say to them all in reply;— " It is very possible to speak of God magnificently, and to think of him meanly.—Your system takes from us our Father in heaven, and substitutes for him a being, whom we cannot love if we would, and whom we ought not to love if we could."—*Candor* and *liberality of mind* are virtues which Unitarians have considered peculiarly honorable, and which they have appeared ambitious to advance to the highest degree of influence. I would just inquire, whether these virtues are likely to be improved, or to acquire greater influence, either among Unitarians, or the Orthodox, by such language as this Author uses respecting his opponents,—language apparently expressive of real conviction, and characterized by strength and elegance, but unfortunately wanting in justice and truth.— We claim the right of thinking for ourselves, and of declaring what we think. But according to the principle which seems to govern this writer's pen, there would be no possibility of our ever making a declaration of our opinions, which would be entitled to credit. For suppose we should profess our full assent to the strongest propositions of this author respecting the moral perfection of God; suppose we should say the very things which he says, in the same forms, and in different forms, and should enlarge upon them, and carry them into their practical uses, and should show by our conduct, that such are our sober views of the divine character; he could still meet all this with the reply;—"It is possible to apply to God's person high sounding epithets, and to his government, principles which make him odious. The heathens called Jupiter the greatest and the best; but his history was black with cruelty and lust."—If the picture, which this Author has drawn of our opinions on this subject were chargeable with only a little misrepresentation;—or if it were ever so great a misrepresentation on a subject of no considerable importance; it would be worthy of little notice. But it is, if I mistake not, a great and total misrepresentation, on a subject of vital consequence to religion, both theoretic and practical. And every man, and every child, who has received his impression from this sermon, as to the views of the Orthodox on the subject now under consideration, has been led into a palpable and total mistake as to a matter of fact,—a matter of fact, concerning which the Orthodox must be considered the best, and the only competent judges. To them therefore I appeal. And I am sure they will be sensible of the truth of what I say, and will be compelled, from a sense of justice to themselves, to declare, that, however free from blame the *motives* of this Author may have been, the representation he has here made of their views, is totally incorrect,—that it is false throughout, and in the highest degree.

LETTER III.

My respected friends,

I wish you not to infer from any thing contained in the foregoing letter, nor from the general aspect of it, that I am desirous of avoiding that kind of investigation, which the Author of the sermon has represented, as necessary in this case.—" We cannot," he remarks, "judge of men's real ideas of God from their general language.—We must inquire into their particular views of his purposes, of the principles of his administration, and of his disposition towards his creatures."—To this mode of proceeding I cheerfully accede. Accordingly, I will not ask you to rest ultimately on my bare assertion, that Unitarians give an incorrect account of our opinions, nor upon my *general* declaration, that we believe in the *moral perfection of God*.—That you may be under the best advantages to judge, whether we do in fact, believe in the moral perfection of God, it appears indispensable that I should state, summarily, what *particular* views we entertain of God's character,—" of the principles of his administration, and of his disposition towards his creatures."—For the *correctness* of the statement I shall now make, I must refer you to the writings of those Orthodox Divines, who are the most judicious, and the most generally approved.

Views of the Orthodox respecting the moral character and government of God.

The sentiment, which forms the basis of our system, is, that God is love. This declaration of Scripture we understand in its plain and obvious sense, and believe it happily expresses the whole moral character of God.—

He is a Being of infinite and perfect benevolence;—benevolence without mixture, and without variation. This is the disposition of God toward his creatures; the disposition which prompted him to create, and which prompts him to govern. The object of benevolence, or goodness, is, to do good, to promote real happiness. The object of *infinite* benevolence must be to promote the *highest degree* of happiness.—As to the ways, in which God will secure the greatest amount of happiness to his intelligent creation, we can know nothing, except what God is pleased to reveal. So far as our duty or comfort is concerned, he has given us instruction. According to the Scriptures, the grand means, by which God will promote the happiness of his kingdom, is the administration of a *moral government.* Such a government implies a law, enforced by proper sanctions; that is, by the promise of good to the obedient, and the threat of evil to the disobedient. These promises and threats, being necessary parts of a benevolent moral government, are expressions of the divine goodness. So is the execution of them. Thus the proper punishment of the disobedient, as it is essential to the administration of a perfect moral government, is, in reality, an act of goodness,—an expression of God's benevolent regard to his kingdom. When there is occasion for it, a *good father* will *punish.* He may punish not only *consistently* with his being good, but *because* he is good. God is a father to his kingdom; and will, therefore, show his displeasure against that which tends to injure that kingdom.—As to the degree and duration of the punishment, which will be inflicted on transgressors, we are, of ourselves, wholly incompetent to judge; for the obvious reason, that we are not capable of knowing what the present and future interests of a kingdom, so extensive, will require. We believe that, according to the Scriptures, God will inflict on the wicked a great and everlasting punishment. But, so far as reasoning is concerned, we believe this, as a consequence of believing, that God will feel and manifest displeasure against sin in proportion to the strength of the love, which he feels for his kingdom. In other words, we believe he will inflict on the disobedient that very punishment, which they deserve, and which, *He being judge*, the welfare of his kingdom renders necessary. We consider the demerit of sin to be great, in proportion to the moral excellence of God, against whom it is committed, and to the value of those interests, which it aims to destroy. Here you see why we view *punitive justice*, as a branch of *benevolence*, an exercise of *goodness*. As God is a moral Governor, and the Guardian of the interests of the creation, the want of justice in punishing offences would betray the want of goodness. Thus we believe, as this Author informs us Unitarians believe,—that the justice of God " is the justice of a good being, dwelling in the same mind, and acting in harmony with perfect benevolence." He represents the belief, " that justice and mercy are intimate friends, breathing the same spirit, and seeking the same end," as peculiar to Unitarians; though it is in truth the general belief of the Orthodox.—But in case of transgression, justice and mercy must seek the same end in different ways. In the exercise of *justice*, God seeks the happiness of his kingdom by *punishing* an offence ;—in the exercise of *mercy*, or *grace*, by *forgiving* an offence. This Author says, " God's mercy, as we understand it, desires strongly the happiness of the guilty." We believe the same. But he adds a condition. " God's mercy desires strongly the happiness of the guilty, *but only through their penitence.*" —We go farther. We believe, indeed, that repentance is essential to the happiness of the guilty; but we believe also, because we are so taught in the Scriptures, that repentance itself, without the death of a Mediator, could be of no avail. To forgive sin in any other way, than through *the shedding of blood*, would not consist with a due regard to " the interests of virtue," and so, to use this Author's language, " would be incompatible with justice, and also with enlightened benevolence." On the other hand, we think it equally clear, that the happiness of the *impenitent* would be not only inconsistent with the divine perfections, but in the nature of things impossible.

We believe, as sincerely as Unitarians do, in the *paternal character* of God. You " ascribe to him," as this Author informs us, " not only the name, but the dispositions, and principles of a father." With the qualifications which the divine perfection renders necessary, we do the same.—The language refers to the dispositions of a *human* father. These dispositions belong to God, *so far as is consistent with his infinite perfection.* It is plain, that the dispositions of God, and the conduct flowing from them cannot, in *all* respects, resemble the dispositions and conduct of a human father. The nature of a human father, and the relation he sustains to his children, have but an imperfect analogy to the nature of God, and the relation he sustains to his creatures. From this we conclude, that his treatment of his creatures cannot be fully represented by the treatment, which a human father gives his children. Permit me to illustrate this by a few examples.—What human father, possessing even a common degree of paternal kindness and compassion, would ever treat his children, as God treated his rational offspring, when he destroyed the world by a deluge, or Sodom by fire, or when he caused the earth to open and swallow up the company of Korah? Would a compassionate father drown his children, or consume them by fire, or bury them alive in the earth?—God suffers his rational creatures, even harmless children, to die of hunger, or of sickness, or to be destroyed by some act of cruelty. Could a human father stand and see his children die thus, when it was in the power of his hand to afford relief?—I mention these among a thousand instances, as proof, that the analogy between God and a human father, though a very striking and delightful one, is not perfect, and may be carried too far. Most certainly it is carried too far by those, who undertake to prove what God will do or will not do, as to the punishment of the wicked in the future world, by the consideration, that he is metaphorically called *a father*. The analogy implied in this metaphor must be guarded, and kept within due limits, as carefully as the analogy implied in the metaphors, by which God is called a fire, a man of war, &c. It is not necessary here particularly to exhibit the principles, which we apply in the interpretation of metaphorical language. I will only say, in short, that we can be in no danger of mistake, when we fix upon the analogy, which is suggested by the metaphor itself, and by the manifest design of the writer, and limit the analogy, as we do in common cases, by the knowledge we have obtained of the subject from other sources.——On these principles, the soundness of which will not be called in question, we look to God as a father; we love him as a father; we trust in him as a father. We believe he has a paternal affection for his rational offspring, and takes delight, as a father does, in promoting their welfare. Nay more; we believe that the love of God is not only sincere and durable, like that of a father, but is free from all human imperfection, and distinguished by a purity, elevation, and activity, infinitely superior to what belongs to the love of the best father on earth.

I cannot do justice to Orthodox ministers without adding, that their belief in the moral excellence of God is not a matter of mere speculation. It is in the highest degree practical. They make the infinite and immutable goodness of God the grand motive to religious worship. They inculcate it, as the spring of all pious affections. They present it to the view of Christians to produce higher love, gratitude, and joy. They present it to the view of sinners, to show them the inexcusable guilt and baseness of their disaffection to their Maker, and to induce them to return to him by repentance. They dwell upon the unchangeable love of God, which has a length, and breadth, and depth, and height, passing all understanding, as the source of joy in prosperity, of comfort in affliction, and triumph in death. And they lead Christians to expect, that their highest enjoyments in heaven will arise from the more glorious display, which God will there make, of his infinite benignity and grace.

It would be great injustice to Orthodox ministers and Christians, both in Europe and America, to pass over the influence, which their belief in the divine goodness has, to excite *benevolent exertion*. It is because they believe that *God is love*, and that he is ready to pardon and save all who repent, that they are engaged in such plans of benevolence, and are striving, in various ways, to enlighten and convert the world. In all these benevolent efforts, they are aiming at a humble imitation of Him, who is the supreme object of their veneration and love.

Now when I consider what stress the Orthodox lay upon the moral perfection of God, the variety of ways, in which they acknowledge and affirm it, and the paramount influence which it has upon their conduct; I am not a little surprised that any man should charge them with denying it. It is, in reality, the *very last* thing they would deny. I appeal to millions of witnesses, who will tell you, that they are as far from denying the *moral perfection* of God, as they are from denying that he *exists:* and that his existence would not only cease to afford them satisfaction, but would fill them with anxiety and dread, had they not a certain belief, that he is possessed of perfect rectitude, of unbounded and unchangeable goodness. And after the statement I have now made, and similar statements made by others, of the sentiments of the Orthodox on this subject; I leave it to you candidly to judge, what occasion the Author of this sermon could have for saying what he does, in the following pathetic passage;—"We ask our opponents to leave us a God, worthy of our love and trust, in whom our moral sentiments may delight, in whom our weaknesses and sorrows may find refuge."

LETTER IV.

My respected friends,

I would now ask your attention more particularly to the *manner,* in which the Author of this sermon attempts to make it appear, that we deny the moral perfection of God. If I understand him right, as I think I do, he infers our denial of God's moral perfection from our " particular views of his purposes, of the principles of his administration, and of his disposition towards his creatures."

Now if we admit, for the present, the most that any one could desire,—that our views on these subjects are, in reality, inconsistent with the moral perfection of God; still the allegation here brought against us, is not well supported.—I may *really believe* a certain important doctrine, though I believe other things inconsistent with it. The *consistency* of my belief is one thing; the *reality* of it, another. I may entertain various opinions, which, if examined thoroughly, would appear inconsistent with my belief of some primary truth;—yet the inconsistency may not be apparent to me; and I may as really believe that primary truth, and act as much under its influence, as though I did not entertain those other opinions. In such a case, though an opponent might attack me on the ground of my *consistency*, he would not, with any justice, represent me as *denying* that primary truth. Accordingly, the most which this Author could properly say, even on the admission above supposed, would be that we do not believe the moral perfection of God *consistently*, though we may believe it *really*.

But can the Orthodox be justly charged with entertaining opinions, which are, in fact, inconsistent with their belief in the moral perfection of God? this is the question now to be argued. The Author of the sermon seems to rest the charge chiefly on two points; first, the doctrine we hold as to the *natural character of man;* second, the doctrine we hold, as to *the manner in which God designates the heirs of salvation.*—I shall begin with the first.

Here allow me to remark, with freedom, on the *mode of reasoning* which in my apprehension, ought to be pursued on such a subject as this.—I am happy to find the following principle suggested by the Author of the sermon.—" Whatever doctrines seem to us to be clearly taught in the Scriptures, we receive without reserve or exception." Right. But in relation to this subject, has he adhered to his own principle? With respect to the common doctrine of man's depravity, the grand inquiry which ought to have engaged his attention, was this;—*Do the scriptures, understood according to just rules of interpretation, teach the doctrine? And does the doctrine agree with facts, made known by experience and observation?*—All reasoning *a priori*, in this case especially, is to be rejected. And so is every hypothesis, unless it is evidently founded on Scripture and observation. Independently of revelation, and well known facts, *we are actually incapable of judging, what the goodness of God will require, as to the condition of man; or what man's character and state must be, under the government of a being infinitely wise and benevolent.* Our inability to judge on the subject might be made evident, from the utter impossibility of our having any adequate knowledge respecting either the infinite perfection of God, or the vast and endless scheme of his operations. But without any labored argument to prove, what must be so plain to every intelligent man, it will be sufficient for my present purpose, merely to refer to a few other facts, which are admitted on all hands, but which are quite as different from what we should have previously thought agreeable to the infinite perfections of God, as the moral depravity of man.—Who would have supposed that a God of tender compassion and unbounded goodness would send plagues, hurricanes, and earthquakes, and involve multitudes of affectionate parents, and multitudes of lovely, helpless children in a sudden and dreadful destruction? —Who would have thought that the Lord of the universe, who has an absolute control over all creatures and all events, would suffer the cruelties and horrors of the *Slave-trade* to exist for so long a time?—These are great difficulties. But there is one still greater; namely; *that the God of love, who delights in mercy, and would have all men to be saved, and who has given his Son to die for the redemption of the world, should, after all, suffer the greater part of the world to live and die without any knowledge of the Savior.*—These facts, which are known to all, are as far from being agreeable to what we should naturally imagine the infinite goodness of God would dictate, as the fact, that men are subjects of moral depravity. But our being unable, by the mere exercise of reason, to discover the consistency between these facts and the infinite goodness of God, is no proof that the facts do not exist, and no proof that they are in reality inconsistent with divine goodness.—With regard to all subjects like these, the only mode of reasoning, which can be relied upon to lead us to right conclusions, is that which is pursued in the science of Physics. Regulating ourselves by the maxims of Bacon and Newton, we inquire, not what we should expect the properties and laws of the physical world would be, nor whether this or that thing can be reconciled with the infinite wisdom and goodness of God,—but simply, *what is fact? What do we find from observation and experience, that the properties and laws of nature really are?* This inquiry, to be philosophical, must be perfectly unembarrassed by any other inquiry? The moment we undertake to shape the conclusions we adopt, or the facts we discover, so as to make them conform to any preconceived opinion; we depart from the legitimate rule of philosophical research, and expose ourselves to endless perplexity and error. I might, if necessary, fill a volume with examples of the vagaries of human reason, flowing from the neglect of this grand principle of philosophical research. The importance of this principle, and the hurtful consequences of disregarding it, are now admitted by all enlightened philosophers. And it is to the strict observance of it, that we owe our present advancement in the science of *Physics*.

Now this principle is as applicable to the science of *Theology*, as to the science of *Physics*. Indeed, it will be found that in Theology it is still more necessary, and that any departure from it, is attended with still greater danger, than in Physics. *Theology*, as well as *Philosophy*, is founded on facts. The first thing to be done in either case, is to determine, by the proper method of inquiry, what are the facts, on which the science is founded. In Philosophy, we learn facts merely by observation and experience. In Theology, we have additional aid. Revelation, as well as observation and experience, makes known facts, which form the basis of Theological reasoning. But in both cases, the chief object of inquiry, and the rule of reasoning are the same. We first inquire for the knowledge of facts; and by reasoning from facts, we arrive at general truths. If in either case we neglect this grand principle of reasoning, we are involved in uncertainty, confusion, and error. Suppose a man attempts to prove, from what he thinks divine wisdom or benevolence must dictate, or from what he knows of some other subject, that all parts of the earth must enjoy equal illumination and warmth from the influence of the sun, and must afford equal advantages and comforts to the inhabitants. But what becomes of his arguments, when he looks abroad, and compares the rocks, and ice, and gloomy nights of Greenland, or the sands of Arabia, with the pleasantness and fertility of some other parts of the earth? Or suppose, in any case, he assumes what must be the nature of some particular thing, but afterwards finds, that the phenomena, which that thing exhibits, do not correspond with his assumption. Shall he deny or disregard those phenomena? Or shall he not rather dismiss his assumption?—Now it is not a whit less unphilosophical, to admit any presumptive or hypothetical reasoning in *Ethics*, or *Theology*, than in the science of *Physics*.—Suppose we think it inconsistent with the infinite goodness of God, that he should create an order of rational beings, and place them in such circumstances of temptation, as he certainly knew would be followed by their transgression and ruin; or that a God of infinite power, who has all hearts and all events in his hand, should suffer mankind, through a hundred generations, to be in a state of ignorance, rebellion, and wretchedness, when it is so easy for him to prevent it. But suppose on further inquiry, we find in both cases the existence of facts, which we denied. Shall we deny them still?—It is true we may not be able to reconcile them with the perfections of God. What then? Are we omniscient? Is our understanding above the possibility of mistake?

These remarks are intended to simplify the object of inquiry, with regard to the native character of man. They are intended to show that, according to the just principles of reasoning in such a case, we have nothing to do with the inquiry, whether the common doctrine of depravity can consist with the moral perfection of God, or with any difficulty whatever in the attempt to reconcile them. If I say, *this doctrine cannot be true*, because I cannot reconcile it with the goodness of God; it is the same as saying, *I am an infallible judge*, and my opinion must stand, though opposed by the declarations of Scripture, and the evidence of facts. To take such a position of mind would be an effectual bar to conviction, and render all reasoning absolutely useless. If we would regulate our investigations on this subject by correct principles; we must reject totally every prepossession against the doctrine of depravity, arising from a consideration of the divine perfections, or from any thing else, and must restrict ourselves to this single inquiry, *what is true in fact?* If the subject is one, on which the Scripture undertakes to decide; the question is, *what saith the Scripture?* If experience and observation cast any light on the subject; the question is, what do *they* teach? If when we pursue our inquiry, we find, that the Scripture, interpreted without the influence of any prepossession, and according to just rules, teaches, that man is by nature unholy; this must, unhesitatingly, be admitted as a certain truth. That God declares it, is proof enough. His testimony is an infinitely better foundation for our faith, than all our reasonings. If observation and experience teach the same truth; we are to admit it as doubly confirmed. As to the *goodness of God*, we know it from other evidence. The truth under consideration must, then, according to the supposition, be admitted to be in reality consistent with the goodness of God, however hard it may be for those, who are of yesterday and know nothing, to elucidate that consistency.

The subject under consideration is one, on which we are peculiarly liable to judge erroneously, for the obvious reason, that we have a deep personal concern in it. We are among those, whom the commonly received doctrine arraigns, as polluted and guilty. The doctrine touches our character, and our honor. It aims a blow at our selfesteem. It disturbs our quiet. The consideration of this circumstance should excite us to guard most vigilantly against that prejudice, discoloring of evidence, and partial judgment, to which we know every man, in such a case, is exposed.

LETTER V.

My respected friends,

The doctrine, which the Orthodox in New England hold on the subject, introduced in the last Letter, is briefly this; *that men are by nature destitute of holiness;* or that they are subjects of an *innate moral depravity;* or, in other words, that they are from the first inclined to evil, and that, while unrenewed, their moral affections and actions are wholly wrong. The doctrine, you perceive, is merely the assertion of a general fact. I shall at present consider this fact by itself, entirely unencumbered with any question about the occasion or the mode of it.

It is far from my design to exhibit, in detail, the arguments, by which this doctrine is proved. I shall attain my principal object, if I succeed in attempting to expose a wrong method of reasoning, and contribute any thing towards producing in those, who may honor me with their attention, a steady desire to know the truth, and a disposition to investigate the subject of man's natural character, on right principles, and without being shackled by unreasonable prepossessions. But the case seems to require, that I should lay before you, if not all the particular proofs, at least the general topics of argument, on which I ground my humbling conclusion.— Here then, I contend, and hold myself ready to demonstrate, that there is no principle in the science of Physics, which is established by evidence more uniform, and more conclusive, than the moral depravity of man. I speak now of the evidence which is furnished merely by experience and observation, without looking to the Bible. The appearances of human nature, from infancy to old age, and from the fall of Adam to the present time, prove a deeprooted and universal disease. The existence of this moral disease is practically acknowledged by all, who have any concern in the education of children and youth, or who endeavor, in any form, to bring the actions of men to conform to the rule of duty. The strength of this disease is made evident by all the restraints, which parents are obliged to put upon their children, rulers upon their subjects, and all men, who aim at being virtuous, upon themselves. This disorder of our nature is indicated by as clear, as various, and as uniform symptoms, as ever indicated the existence of a fever, or a consumption, in an individual.—The evidence of human depravity from this source alone, is so great, that, should I reject it as insufficient, I should manifest a strength of prejudice, which, I soberly think, no increase of evidence could overcome. And I would propose it as a serious question, whether, if any of us should stand by, as impartial spectators, and see, in another order of beings, the same indications of character, which we see in the human species, we should hesitate a moment to pronounce them, *depraved.*

But as our views of this subject must depend chiefly on revelation, I shall proceed to exhibit, though in a very summary way, the *principal scripture arguments*, on which the doctrine of man's universal depravity rests. I shall first illustrate the argument, or rather *the principle of reasoning*, from the *Old Testament*. For this purpose I shall take a single passage, which may stand for a multitude of the same nature. Gen. vi. 5. " *And God saw that the wickedness of man was great in the earth, and that every imagination of the thoughts of his heart was only evil continually.*"

It is objected to the argument commonly drawn from this text, that it related to mankind in a season of uncommon corruption, and not to mankind at large, and that it is altogether improper to infer the character of the whole human race from the shocking barbarity and wickedness, which have been perpetrated in any particular age or country. The same objection is thought to lie against our reasoning from any of the numerous passages in the Old Testament, in which human wickedness is declared; namely, that they relate exclusively to those who lived at particular times, when iniquity prevailed to an uncommon degree, and cannot be applied to mankind generally.

We are now to inquire, whether this objection is valid.

The text quoted from Gen. vi. 5, did indeed relate to the corruption of men, who lived before the general deluge. But we find substantially the same testimony given of the human character, soon after the deluge. Gen. viii. 21, " The imagination of man's heart is evil from his youth." There are two reasons for considering this as relating to *mankind universally*, or to *human nature*. The first is, that the language is *general*. " The imagination of *man's* heart is evil;" not Noah's heart, nor the heart of either of his sons *particularly ;* but *man's* heart,—the heart of the *human kind*. Thus we are led to consider it, as the testimony of God respecting the character of our apostate race. The second reason for this construction is, that the *curse* spoken of in the same verse related to mankind in all future ages. " I will not again curse the ground any more for *man's sake ;*" that is, I will not at *any future time*. Immediately after the testimony above quoted, God said, " neither will I again smite any more every living thing, as I have done." It was said in relation to all future time. The description given of man's character must be understood as equally extensive; "*for*," or as it ought, according to the best authorities, and according to the obvious sense of the passage, to be rendered, "*though* the imagination of man's heart is evil from his youth." The meaning of the whole taken together is plainly this; that God would not destroy the world again by a deluge, as he had done, though the character of mankind generally would be, as it had been.—History shows that it has been so in fact.

Further to illustrate the force of the argument, from the Old Testament, and the weakness of the objection against it, I refer my readers to a well known principle of science, namely, *that all, who belong to the same species, have the same nature.* We always consider the actions of any part, certainly of any considerable part of a species, as indicating the character or nature of the whole. And why should we doubt the truth of this principle in relation to man's moral character, any more than in relation to his physical properties, or to the properties of any other order of creatures? In all our treatment of mankind, and in all our maxims of practical wisdom, we admit the principle, that *human nature*, as to its grand moral features, is at all times, and in all circumstances, the same. This is implied also in the fact, that the same precepts, motives, and restraints,—in a word, the same moral discipline has been found suitable and necessary in all ages.

But I do not stop here, but proceed to inquire, whether the *New Testament*, besides furnishing a new argument itself, does not give testimony to the soundness of the argument from the *Old*. The Psalmist, in Psalm xiv. liii. v. cxl. x. xxxvi. and Isaiah, ch. lix. describe the wickedness which prevailed in their day.—" They are corrupt; they have done abominable works; there is none that doeth good. They are all gone aside, they are together become filthy; there is none that doeth good, no, not one. Their throat is an open sepulchre. Their feet run to evil. Their thoughts are thoughts of iniquity; The way of peace they know not;"&c. The objector says, these passages described the corruption of the Jews in times of great degeneracy, and cannot be considered as a just description of mankind generally. But how does the Apostle Paul treat the subject? He takes these same passages, a thousand years afterwards, and applies them, as descriptive of the character of Jews and Gentiles. Rom. iii. 9, he says, referring to ch. i. and ii., "We have before proved both *Jews* and *Gentiles*, that *they are all* under sin; *as it is written*,"—immediately introducing from the Old Testament the texts above quoted, as a true account of the character of mankind without exception; then stating the end he had aimed at in making such a disclosure of the human character; namely, " that *every mouth* may be stopped, and *all the world* become guilty before God;" and then directly bringing us to his final conclusion, that " by the deeds of the law shall *no flesh* be justified in his sight." It is a connected discourse,—an unbroken chain of reasoning. And unless the texts, which the Apostle here cites from the Old Testament, are justly applicable to the whole race of man, " both Jews and Gentiles," and, in connexion with the preceding part of his Epistle, are actually meant by him, to be a description of " *all the world*," " *no flesh*" being excepted;—the whole reasoning of the Apostle is without force; his conclusion is broader than his premises; and the quotations he makes from the Scriptures are not only *no proofs* of what he wishes to establish, but have no kind of relation to it. The point he labors to establish is, that "*both Jews* and *Gentiles*"—that "*all the world*" have such a character, that they cannot be justified by law. But what is their character?—It is that which is first described in the preceding part of the Epistle, and then in the passages cited from the Old Testament. "We have before proved *both Jews and Gentiles*, that they are all under sin, *as it is written; There is none that doeth good, no, not one. They are all gone out of the way; they are together become unprofitable, &c.*" The Apostle manifestly cites these texts, for the very purpose of describing, still more particularly than he had done, the character of "*all the world.*"—It might indeed be thought from the first part of verse 19, "whatsoever the law saith, it saith to them who are under the law," that the Apostle meant to apply what he had just before said, to *Jews only*. But this would hardly agree with the scope of the passage, which was to establish a general truth respecting "*all the world.*" Besides, the first part of v. 19 will easily admit a construction perfectly corresponding with the scope of the whole passage. The Apostle would prove that *all* men are under sin. The *Jews* would naturally make an exception in their own favor. He tells them that there can be no exception; that what he has quoted from *the law*, that is, from their own Scriptures, must certainly relate to *Jews*, as well *as to Gentiles.*—The quotations cannot relate to Jews *exclusively* of Gentiles, because that would not agree with the manner, already noticed, in which the quotations are introduced;—" We have proved *both Jews and Gentiles*, that they are *all* under sin; *as it is written &c.*" Nor does it so obviously agree with the conclusion v. 19, which relates to "*all the world.*" Besides, it is difficult not to believe that the writer of some of the Psalms quoted, particularly of the xiv, extended his views beyond his own nation, though he undoubtedly referred to that primarily, and in a special sense. When he introduces that description of wickedness, which is quoted by the Apostle, his language is general. "The Lord looked down from heaven, upon *the children of men*, to see if there were *any* that did understand." The Psalmist then proceeds to give a description, not, one would think, of the posterity of Abraham *solely*, but of *the children of men, the human race*, and says, *they are all gone aside.*— But we shall come ultimately to the same conclusion, if we admit that the passages were originally intended by the Psalmist to relate merely to his own nation. For if such a character belonged to that highly favored nation, it must of course have belonged to the rest of the world. So the Apostle decides when, many ages after, he attributes that description of character to *all the world*. On the same principle the passages quoted by him are applicable to *us*, as well as to those who lived in the time of Paul, or of David; as applicable to us, as what the Apostle says respecting justification, salvation, duty, or any thing else.

This manner of quoting texts from the Old Testament is not peculiar to Paul. We find frequent examples of it in the instructions of Christ himself. The Prophet Isaiah, chap. xxix. 13, had given the following description of the hypocrisy of the people, who were contemporary with him; viz. " that they drew near to God with their mouth, and honored him with their lips, but had removed their hearts far from him." Jesus quoted this passage as *applicable to the Jews in his day*. " Well did Esaias prophesy of you hypocrites, as it is written, &c." In the same manner Christ repeatedly quoted Isa.

vi. 9, 10, as a true description of the obstinate impiety of those, who rejected his gospel.

Now this manner of quoting and reasoning from Scripture, so often employed both by Christ and his apostles, clearly involves the principle, which I stated in answer to the objection; viz. that *human nature,* in all ages and circumstances, is, *as to its grand moral features,* the same, and that the dispositions and actions, which mankind at any time exhibit, are real indications of what belongs to the *nature of man universally.* Unless this principle is admitted, how can the Apostle be justified in making such a use as he does, of his citations from the Old Testament?—And to bring the subject nearer home, how can we make use of any thing which was said of the character of man, either in the Old Testament or the New, as appertaining to those who live at the present day? Indeed, how can any of the declarations of the Bible, all of which were made so many ages ago, be of any use to us, except to gratify curiosity? Whether, therefore, we consider the nature of the case, or the reasoning of the Apostle in Rom. iii.; are we not warranted to receive, whatever the Bible in any part affirms respecting the dispositions or conduct of men, as applicable, *substantially,* to men in all ages? If we are not, what can we say to vindicate the Apostle? If we are, then the text I first quoted from Genesis, and those texts which are quoted from the Psalms in Rom. iii, and other similar texts in the Old Testament, do all illustrate the character, which now belongs to man. And when we read in the Bible, or elsewhere, the highest description of human wickedness in the old world, in Sodom, in Canaan, in Jerusalem, in Greece, Rome, or India, or of the wickedness of individuals, as Pharaoh, Saul, Jeroboam, Judas, or the Cæsars; it is perfectly just and natural for us to reflect, *such is human nature;—such is man.* So that Orthodox writers, though they may not, in all instances, have attended sufficiently to the groundwork of their argument, do in fact reason in an unexceptionable manner, when they undertake to show what *human nature* is, from the description which is given of the wickedness of man in the Old Testament; and the objection to this reasoning, which I stated above, and which is, briefly, the objection of Dr. Turnbull and Dr. John Taylor, cannot be considered as valid.

Let me detain your attention a few moments, while I hint at the confirmation, which may be given to the general principle, asserted above, by an appeal to the sober convictions of men. They who are in the habit of comparing their moral affections and conduct with the perfect law of God, will have no difficulty in acknowledging, that they find, in the various representations of human depravity, contained in the Old Testament, a true picture of themselves. I say not that they are conscious of having committed sinful actions in *the same form,* or indulged sinful passions *in the same degree,* with all those, whose crimes are recorded in the Bible. This is not the case. But they are conscious of having in their hearts a wrong bias, a want of what the divine law requires, of the *same nature,* with that moral depravation, which has been exhibited by the greatest sinners. The sacred writers impute to various societies and individuals, pride, selfishness, idolatry, covetousness, impurity, revenge, falsehood, blasphemy. Have we not discovered in ourselves the root of all these vices? Should we not be liable to actual excess in every one of them, if we should be freed from restraints, and should follow, without any counteracting influence, the desires which naturally spring up in our hearts? And have not the greatest proficients in self-government and holiness always been the most ready to make this humiliating confession? Even some of the heathen, who made serious attempts to improve their own character, were forced to acknowledge that the disorder of their nature was too stubborn to be subdued by them, without help from above.

It is certainly nothing conclusive against the principle contended for, that some men can be found, who are not sensible of its truth in relation to themselves. This may easily be accounted for, without in the least invalidating the principle. For they may be altogether inattentive to what passes in their own minds, and so may be ignorant of themselves; or if they are in some measure attentive to the operations of their own minds, they may fix their eye upon some of the wrong standards of duty which are set up in the world, and so may judge incorrectly. It is surely no uncommon thing for men to be insensible of the faults of their character, especially of the hidden affections of their hearts. This insensibility, so frequently described in the Scriptures, is a matter of common observation, and has always been regarded, as one of the greatest hindrances to the salutary influence of divine truth.

The argument from the Old Testament might be extended to great length, comprising all the positive declarations there made, and all the examples there exhibited, of human wickedness; all the confessions both of saints and sinners; all the means employed to subdue the moral corruption of men and hold them back from sin, and every thing else, which showed formerly, and which, consequently, always shows, *what is in man*. They who read the Old Testament with such views as the Apostles entertained respecting it, will be constantly improving their acquaintance with themselves,—their knowledge of their own moral degradation, and their desire after that gracious influence of the Holy Spirit, which renews and exalts the soul.

LETTER VI.

My respected friends,

In the last Letter, I confined myself almost entirely to the establishment of a general principle, and to the proof which, according to that principle, may be drawn from the Old Testament, in support of the doctrine of man's moral depravity. I might also refer to declarations which are general or universal, as Jeremiah xvii. 9, " The heart is deceitful above all things, and desperately wicked; who can know it?" " *The heart*," not of any man, or any society of men in particular; but of *man universally*. The next verse confirms this sense. " I the Lord search *the heart* ;"—the same heart, as the one spoken of in v. 9; so that if, when the Prophet says, the Lord searches *the heart*, we are to understand him as meaning, that the Lord searches *the heart universally*, or *the heart of every human being;* then also, when in the closest connexion with this, he says, *the heart* is deceitful and wicked, we must understand him as meaning that *the heart universally*, or *the heart of every human being* is deceitful and wicked.—This is the only sense which any man can give the text, v. 9, who attends to its connexion with the following verse, or considers what language we commonly use to express a general or universal proposition. Another passage containing a universal proposition of like character, is found in Eccles. ix. 3. " *The heart* of the *sons of men* is full of evil."

But in the New Testament every thing is invested with clearer light. Here we find evidence, exhibited in many different forms, that *man*, as a *species*, that the *human kind*, is sunk in sin, and while unrenewed, entirely destitute of holiness, and unfit for heaven. This evidence I shall now lay before you, though it must be with great brevity, and in reference only to a few passages.

The first passage, to which I would call your attention, is found in the discourse of Jesus with Nicodemus, John iii. 1—7. This conversation took place near the beginning of Christ's ministry. About four thousand years had passed away, from the fall of man. Those four thousand years had furnished no small evidence of the human character. The corruption and violence of the old world had been seen. And notwithstanding the tremendous purgation, which the world underwent by the general deluge, it had been seen, that the new race, descending from righteous Noah, pursued the same downward course with the generations before the flood. The same had been the case with the posterity of Abraham. Although various and powerful means had been used to restrain men from wickedness and induce them to serve God, they had in every nation, and in every age, shown themselves prone to evil. Jesus knew what display had been made of the human character in every period of the world. He knew what was in man. The grand result of what his all searching eye had seen, and then saw, of the affections and conduct of the human race, he expressed to Nicodemus; "Except a man be born again, he cannot see the kingdom of God." The moral renovation here spoken of, is represented as necessary for all men. Εαν μη τις γεννηθη ανωθεν. It is said of *any one*. The sense is, that *no man, no human being*, who is not the subject of this renovation, can be a partaker of the benefits of Christ's kingdom. The necessity of this renovation, as appears afterwards, arises from the character which man possesses, in consequence of his *natural birth.* Of course, it is necessary for every child of Adam. " That which is born of the flesh, is *flesh.*" " By *flesh*," says Rosenmuller, with evident propriety, and in agreement with commentators generally, " is meant the nature of man,—man with all his moral imperfection, subject to the dominion of his bodily appetites. And he who is born of parents, who have this moral imperfection, is like his parents." All the children of men are here represented as having, by their very birth, a moral nature, which renders them incapable of enjoying the blessings of the Messiah's kingdom, unless they are *born again.* This interpretation is confirmed by all those texts, in which the word σαρξ, or σαρκικος, *flesh,* or *fleshly,* is used to express the opposite of that which is spiritual or holy. The metaphorical expression, being *born again,* must denote a *moral* change, because it is a change that fits men for a *moral* or *spiritual kingdom.* If we view this passage in connexion with those, which represent repentance and conversion, as necessary to prepare men for Christ's kingdom, we shall see that being *born again* denotes a change of the same general character with *repentance* and *conversion.* It is then clear, that this passage of Scripture, interpreted according to just rules, contains the following sentiment ;—that *all men, without exception, are by nature,* or in consequence of their natural birth, in such a state of moral impurity, as disqualifies them for the enjoyments of heaven, unless they are renewed by the Holy Spirit.

Rom. v. 12. " Wherefore as by one man sin entered into the world, and death by sin, and so death passed upon all men, for that *all have sinned.*" Although this text must be allowed to be, in some respects, very obscure; two things are perfectly clear. 1. That the Apostle considered sin, as *the cause of death*, or the reason why God sent into the world the evils involved in the word *death*. 2. That as sin is the *cause* of *death*, the extent of the one may be measured by the extent of the other. Determine how far *death* extends, and you determine how far *sin* extends. If a part of the human species die, a part are sinners. If all die, all are sinners. " Death passed upon all men, *for that* all have sinned." Εφ ὡ, according to the judgment of the most eminent critics, and the use of the phrase elsewhere in the New Testament, means the same as διοτι, eo quod, quia,—*for that*, or *because*. The Vulgate renders it, in quo, *in whom;* from which some have thought the Apostle meant to assert, that it is *in Adam* that all men have sinned, so that his transgression becomes theirs by imputation. But I see nothing in the passage, or in the nature of the subject, which can justify such an interpretation.

On this particular point, our opinions have been often misrepresented. We are said to hold, *that God dooms a whole race of innocent creatures to destruction,* or *considers them all as deserving destruction, for the sin of one man.* Now when I examine the respectable writings of the earlier Calvinists generally, on the subject of original sin, I find nothing which resembles such a statement as this. It is true, exceptionable language has in some instances been used, and opinions, which I should think erroneous, have sometimes been entertained on this subject. But the Orthodox in New England, at the present day, are not chargeable with the same fault. The *imputation of Adam's sin to his posterity,* in any sense, which those words naturally and properly convey, is a doctrine which we do not believe. If any shall say, as Stapfer does, who refers to Vitringa and other reformed divines, as agreeing with him,—that " for God to give Adam a posterity *like himself*, and to *impute* his sin to them, is one and the same thing ;" I should not object to such an imputation. For I see not how any man, who has a serious regard to scripture, or to fact, or considers what are the laws of our nature, can hesitate to admit, that God has given Adam a posterity like himself.

But the word *imputation* has, in my view, been improperly used in relation to this subject, and has occasioned unnecessary perplexity. In scripture, the word, *impute*, signifies uniformly, if I mistake not, charging or reckoning to a man that which is his own attribute or act. Every attempt, which has been made, to prove that God ever imputes to man any sinful disposition or act, which is not strictly *his own*, has, in my judgment, failed of success. And as it is one object of these Letters, to make you acquainted with the real opinions of the Orthodox in New England; I would here say, with the utmost frankness, that we are not perfectly satisfied with the language used on this subject, in the Assembly's Catechism. Though we hold that Catechism, taken as a whole, in the highest estimation; we could not, with a good conscience, subscribe to every expression it contains in relation to the doctrine of original sin. Hence it is common for us, when we declare our assent to the Catechism, to do it with an express or implied restriction. We receive the Catechism *generally*, as containing a summary of the principles of Christianity. But that the sinfulness of our natural, fallen state consists, in any measure, " in the guilt of Adam's first sin," is what we cannot admit, without more convincing evidence. But we think we have the best reason for believing that, in respect of *character*, there is a connexion between Adam and the whole human race. Nor do we, as the Author of this Sermon seems to think, rest this opinion on " a few slight hints about the fall of our first parents," but upon the plain, and reiterated declaration of the Apostle Paul, Rom. v. Notwithstanding all the difficulty with which this passage is attended, one point is plain. The writer makes it known, in different forms of expression, and with the greatest perspicuity, that a connexion really exists between the father of the human race, and all his children. Unless Adam's transgression had, in the plan of the divine administration, such a relation to his posterity, that in consequence of it, they were constituted sinners, and subjected to death and all other sufferings, as penal evils; the Apostle reasons inconclusively, and entirely misses the end he aims at, in his comparison of Adam and Christ. Nothing can be more obvious, according to the common rules of interpretation, than that he meant to assert this connexion; so that, if no such connexion exists, he had the misfortune to publish a mistake.

Though it would not be consistent with the plan of these Letters to collect the various passages of the New Testament, which prove what man's native character is; I cannot willingly leave the subject without adverting again to the manner, in which the Apostle Paul was accustomed to treat it. From a great multitude of pertinent texts, I take one. Eph. ii. 3. " Among whom also we all had our conversation, &c. and were *by nature children of wrath, even as others.*" He says this of believing *Jews,* as is evident from the beginning and the close of the verse, in connexion with the context. To be *children of wrath,* according to Schleusner, Rosenmuller, Koppe, and others, is to be *worthy of punishment,* pœnis divinis digni. To be children of wrath, φυσει, *by nature*, is to be *born so*, or to be so in consequence of our birth, or in consequence of our *natural disposition.* "Ob naturalem nostram indolem." See Schleusner's Lex. on this text. Compare Gal. ii. 15, "We who are Jews *by nature,*" i. e. *born Jews,* or *Jews by birth.* Schleusner says that, according to the whole scope of the discourse, Ep. ii. φυσις, *nature,* signifies the *state of those who had not been instructed and reformed by the christian religion.* True. But why was that state called φυσις, *nature ?*—a word which points us to our *origin, nativity, birth.*—We shall see the reason of this, if we compare this text with the passage, quoted above, from John iii. "That which is *born of the flesh,* is flesh;" a declaration fairly capable of no meaning but this, that man possesses *by his natural birth a depraved disposition, corrupt desires,* as the word *flesh* signifies in the text now under consideration, Eph. ii. 3, and in every other place, where it relates to the moral character or conduct of men. That which is born of the flesh, or that which man has by nature, is such a temper or character, that according to the Apostle, he is a *child of wrath ;*—such, according to the representation of Christ, that he must be the subject of a *new birth by the spirit,* or he cannot see the kingdom of God.—This must be the meaning of these two passages taken together, unless we are driven by our dislike of the doctrine contained in them, to violate the plainest rules of interpretation. If similar phraseology should be found on any other subject; if, for example, it should be said, that which is born of *human parents* is *human,* or that which is born of *man* is *frail and liable to decay,*—and that every man is *by nature* the subject of various appetites and passions; who would not understand these phrases, as denoting what man is, or what he has, *by his birth,* or what is *inbred*, or *native*? Or if language should be used by an inspired writer expressing in the same way, that which is opposite to what we understand by this text; that is, if it should be said, that the children of men are *by nature pure*,—or that what is born of human parents is *virtuous and holy;* would not our opposers think such a passage a proof sufficiently clear, of the *native purity*, the *original, inbred virtue of man*? And would they not be greatly " amazed " at the attempt of any man to put a different sense upon it?

That the human species is universally, while unrenewed, in a state of entire moral corruption, is implied in the invariable practice of the Apostles, wherever they went, to call upon men, according to their divine commission,—" upon all men every where to *repent*." The duty, and necessity of repentance, which denotes a radical moral change, was inculcated on all, to whom the Gospel was proclaimed. If, in any part of the world, an Apostle found *human beings*, he instantly took it for granted, that they were children of disobedience, and children of wrath, and treated them accordingly,—just as he took it for granted that they were mortal.—All the provisions of the Gospel are adapted to those, who are polluted and guilty. If any can be found, whether old or young, who are not the subjects of moral depravity and ruin, they are evidently excluded from any concern with those provisions.—When we pursue the history of the christian religion through the days of the Apostles, we find wherever it produced its genuine effects, it produced *repentance and fruits meet for repentance* ;—it formed men, whoever they were, to a new character; so that it became universally true, that if *any man* was a Christian, he was *a new creature*, or in the language of of Christ, was *born again*. We find no instance of the contrary. The character, which St. Paul gives of the followers of Christ, implies that they had, without exception, been *renewed*. He often turns their thoughts to their former state of degradation and ruin. He paints that state in the strongest colors. He illustrates it by the most striking metaphors. He reminds believers, that before their regeneration, they were servants of sin, dead in trespasses and sins, enemies to God, impure, earthly. He speaks of this moral corruption, not as a fact, which was local, or of limited extent, but universal. And accordingly, he makes it a part of the general system of Christian doctrine.

There is a difficulty, I well know, in applying the description, given by the Apostle, of the character, which the first converts to Christianity originally possessed, to men of the present day, whose exterior character has been formed under the influence of a Christian education. But this difficulty disappears, when we attend to the principle, which the Apostle recognises in his reasoning, Rom. iii, and which I have already endeavored to illustrate; namely; that, whatever difference may exist, as to outward character, *all men have the same natural disposition, the same original ingredients of moral character*. In conformity to this principle, we pass by what is merely regular and amiable in the eye of the world; we pass by all the diversities of exterior character, and look to the grand moral affections of the heart, in which all are alike. Agreeably to this view, and agreeably to what our Savior says as to sin in the heart, Matt. v. 21, 22, 28, it would appear that, although men have not openly, or by formal acts, made themselves idolaters, thieves, adulterers, and murderers; they do, in a greater or less degree, possess those very passions, or desires, which, if indulged and acted out, would make them so. And thus we shall have the happiness of agreeing with the Author of the sermon now before us, who in another ordination sermon, gives the following just description of the character of the human species.— " To whom is the minister of the gospel sent to preach ? To men of upright minds, disposed to receive and obey the truth, which guides to heaven ? Ah no ! He is called to guide a wandering flock ;—he is sent to a *world of sinners*, in whose hearts lurk *idolatry, sensuality, pride, and every corruption.*"*

Men, who assert the native purity of human beings, insist much upon the harmlessness and tender sensibilities of little children, before they are corrupted by example, and also upon the existence of what are called the natural affections in mankind generally. But how can those things, which man possesses in common with irrational animals, or those, which necessarily appertain to his present mode of existence, and which remain the same, whatever character he sustains, be considered as evidence of the purity of his moral nature ?

The attempt, often made, to account for the universal prevalence of sin, by the influence of example, without supposing any native bias to evil, cannot afford satisfaction. For we are still pressed with the difficulty of accounting for it, that children, whose nature is untainted with moral evil, should be disposed to imitate bad examples, rather than good ones,—to neglect their duty, rather than perform it ; and that all discreet parents and instructers, who have any familiar acquaintance with the youthful mind, should be led to frame their whole system of instruction and discipline, upon the principle, that children are *prone to evil, inclined to go astray.* Any plan of education, whether domestic or public, which should overlook this principle, and involve the opposite one of man's *native purity*, would be regarded by

* Serm. at the Ordination of the Rev. J. Codman.

all men of sober experience and sober judgment, as romantic and dangerous.

But I must bring my remarks on this subject to a close. My object was to show that we receive the doctrine of man's native corruption upon its own proper evidence, as we receive any other truth; and that it is totally unphilosophical and unscriptural, to suffer this evidence to be obscured or perplexed by the inquiry, how the doctrine can be reconciled with the moral perfection of God. Both the moral perfection of God, and the doctrine of human depravity, rest upon evidence, which is, in our view, perfectly conclusive. We believe them both, and believe them entirely consistent with each other. Indeed, we see no peculiar difficulty attending their consistency. If any one asserts, that our doctrine of man's depravity and the moral perfection of God are inconsistent with each other; it will behoove him to show, in what respects, and for what reasons, they are inconsistent. He ought to show too, how it is any more inconsistent with the goodness of God, for men to be corrupt in the earliest period of their existence, than in any subsequent period; or for all men to be corrupt, than for any part of them; or for men to be corrupt in a higher degree, than in a lower degree. If, from a consideration of the divine goodness, or for other reasons, any should persist in denying the doctrine of man's *native depravity*; they will easily see what a task they take upon themselves. They must first make it appear, by a thorough investigation, conducted in conformity to just and allowed principles, that none of the texts of Scripture, which I have cited, and no others of a similar character, contain the doctrine. In addition to this, they must satisfactorily account for all the corruption and wickedness, which man has exhibited, from childhood to old age, in all nations and circumstances, and in opposition to all the means which have been used to restrain him, without admitting that his *nature is prone to evil*;—a task, I should think, of the same kind, with that of accounting for all the phenomena of the natural world, by which the Newtonian philosophy proves the law of gravitation, without admitting that law.

LETTER VII.

My respected friends,

Unitarian writers generally, as well as the Author of the Sermon before us, have appeared to think, that the commonly received doctrine of *Election* is totally incompatible with the goodness of God, and that our believing that doctrine is proof sufficient, that we do not believe in the divine goodness.

To this subject, though not a very popular one, I hope you will attend with that candor and unprejudiced judgment, without which, as you must have often seen in others, all inquiry after the truth is in vain. Against the doctrine of the Reformed Churches, now to be considered, there are strong prepossessions. And I am free to acknowledge, that Orthodox writers and preachers of high repute, but deficient in judgment, have, in some instances, exhibited the doctrine in a manner, which has given too much occasion for these prepossessions;—and too much occasion for this Author, and many others, to think that the doctrine is inconsistent with the moral perfection of God. I wish you, therefore, distinctly to understand, that it is not the doctrine of Election, as stated by some of its injudicious advocates, or as understood by its opposers, that I would now defend.

This subject, as it respects a principle of the divine administration, is not only a very important one, but one which obviously involves questions of difficult and profound investigation. It respects the administration of a Being, possessed of infinite understanding, and infinite holiness,—a Being, to whom we have no right to dictate, and of whom we have no cause to complain,—a Being, before whose supreme majesty, we are nothing, and less than nothing. Though I have a heart as lofty, and vain, and presumptuous as others; yet when I bring this subject before me, and consider that I have undertaken to inquire respecting the administration of the eternal, incomprehensible God, my Sovereign, and my Judge,—I stand in awe; I check my presumption; and resolve to hold my mind in a humble, docile frame, lest I should incur that appalling rebuke of the Apostle,— "Who art thou, O man, that repliest against God?" I bid myself remember, that neither my opinions, nor those of any mortal, are entitled to regard, any farther than they agree with the truths of revelation, and that, whatever my opinions or wishes may be, those truths will remain the same. I would devoutly cherish the impression that no opinions can be right, which would make any part of Scripture unwelcome to me; and that the greatest dislike of men, which may be incurred by defending the doctrines of revelation, is not worthy to be named, in comparison with the frown of my final Judge, for rejecting those doctrines.

It is generally acknowledged by Christians, that no opinion or reasoning respecting the divine character, or administration, can be relied upon, except that which rests on the declarations of Scripture. On this subject especially, not the least respect is due to any argument, however plausible, which, on careful inquiry, is found contrary to what God has taught us in his word, or to what takes place in his providence. The object of our present inquiry is then very simple. If it were put to my natural reason to judge, by its own light, respecting what is called the doctrine of Election; my judgment might agree with the judgment of those, who reject the doctrine. If the question were, what difficulties attend the doctrine; I might perhaps bring forward as many as others. And if the question were, whether the doctrine, as generally represented by its opposers, and even by the Author of this Sermon, is according to the word of God; I should answer, as they do, in the negative. But the proper question is, *what saith the Scripture?* What does God teach us, as to the manner in which he designates those, who are to be heirs of salvation?

I shall not go largely into a consideration of the evidence from Scripture, in support of the doctrine now under consideration; but shall merely proceed far enough to show, that we do not believe the doctrine without evidence, and that our believing it is not a proof of our denying the moral perfection of God, but a consequence of our reverence for his word.

Proof of the doctrine of Election.

I find that Jesus Christ often speaks of a part of mankind, as being given him of the Father. This he does several times in John xvii. As an example of the whole, verse 2 may be taken. " As thou hast given him power over all flesh, that he should give eternal life to as many as thou hast given him." The sense is, *that the Father has given to Christ a part of the human race, and that those, who have thus been given to Christ, are the persons who shall have eternal life.* As to the meaning of the passage, the only question that deserves a moment's consideration, is, whether it relates to all who shall finally be saved, or merely to those who were disciples of Christ at that time.—In favor of the larger sense, there are several arguments.

1. Christ is here speaking of his general commission and work, as a Savior. He tells us, that the Father has given him power over *all flesh*, without the least intimation of any limits. And for what purpose was he endued with this extensive power? " That he might give eternal life to *as many as the Father had given him.*" His work, as a Savior, and the power committed to him did in fact extend, not merely to those who were then his disciples, but to the whole number of the redeemed. But why should he speak of his *power* in this extensive sense, if he meant that the end to be accomplished by it should be understood in so limited a sense? No limits are suggested. Why then should we not understand the phrase, " as many as thou hast given him," to denote all, to whom Christ will actually give eternal life?

2. The context shows, that Christ, in the prayer here recited, had his eye upon all, who should be saved in future ages. v. 20. " Neither pray I for these alone, but for them also, who shall believe on me through their word." There can be no reason to doubt, that he had as large an extent of views in the second verse, as in the twentieth.

3. This interpretation receives additional confirmation from a similar passage in John vi. 37, 39. " All that the Father giveth me, shall come to me; and him that cometh to me, I will in no wise cast out.—And this is the Father's will who sent me, that of all which he hath given me I should lose nothing, but should raise it

up again at the last day." Those who *are given* to Christ, and those who *shall come* to Christ, are here identified. Indeed, the passage plainly signifies, that, in every case, a person's being given to Christ *secures* his coming to Christ; a circumstance which fixes one point; namely; that those, who will finally be saved, are given to Christ *before* they come to him.—From v. 39, we have additional proof that, when Christ speaks of those, who were given him of the Father, he includes the whole number that shall be saved. "This is the Father's will,—that of all which he hath given me, I should lose nothing, but should raise it up at the last day." The work of Christ, as a Savior, doubtless extends alike to all, who shall be raised to eternal life at the last day. But this work of his is here represented as relating to those, whom the Father had given him. From the whole it seems evident, that when Christ speaks so familiarly, in John xvii, of those who were given him, he refers to all who shall be saved.

But even on supposition, that the language related to those only, who were then his disciples; the argument would still be the same, because the principle would be the same. There could be no reason, why the Father should give Christ those, who were saved by him during his life, and not those who should be saved afterwards; and no reason, why being given to Christ should stand in certain connexion with salvation in one case, and not in the other.

If we should examine other texts of similar import. we should find still more abundant proof of what is so evident from the two passages above cited; namely; *that the Father has given a portion of mankind to Christ, in a peculiar sense, and in distinction from others, and that Christ will actually bestow eternal life on all who have been thus given him.* I see not how any man can give a different sense to the texts alluded to, without being conscious that he is driven to it, by his prepossession against this doctrine.

Pursuing the single inquiry, *what the scriptures teach*, we find several passages, which speak, with a remarkable emphasis, of *a purpose and choice of God* respecting those, who will be saved. My limits will allow me to consider only two.

The apostle says to the Ephesians, ch. i. 3—11, " Blessed be the God and Father of our Lord Jesus Christ, who hath blessed us with all spiritual blessings in heavenly things in Christ ; *according as he hath chosen us in him before the foundation of the world, that we should be holy, &c. ; having predestinated us unto the adoption of children by Jesus Christ to himself, according to the good pleasure of his will, to the praise of the glory of his grace,* —in whom also we have obtained an inheritance, *being predestinated according to the purpose of him, who worketh all things after the counsel of his own will.*" Here we are taught, that God has a *purpose, choice, will,* and *good pleasure*, respecting those who are saved. It is such a *purpose*, that when men are saved, they are saved *according to it.* It is a *purpose* or *choice*, which was in the mind of God, *before* they were *saved*, and *before* they *existed.* They were " chosen in Christ before the foundation of the world." And it is a *purpose*, which does not rest upon any personal merit in those, who are its objects. The *purpose* or *choice* is here repeatedly represented as a matter of *grace*, as *according to the riches of grace ;*—exactly in agreement with other passages, which exclude *all works of righteousness* from having any concern in this subject.

The other passage I shall particularly notice, is Rom. ix, 11—24. In verses 11, 12, 13, it is said ; " For the children," that is, Jacob and Esau, "being not yet born, neither having done any good or evil, that the purpose of God according to election might stand, not of works, but of him that calleth, it was said unto her, the elder shall serve the younger. As it is written, Jacob have I loved, but Esau have I hated." It is beyond all doubt in my mind, that this interesting passage was meant to be understood in a *national* sense; that is, that they respected Jacob and Esau, not personally, but as the heads of two tribes or nations; or, in other words, that they respected those two nations. It is apparent too, that what is quoted from Moses, v. 15; "I will have mercy on whom I will have mercy, and I will have compassion on whom I will have compassion," was said originally respecting a part of the Israelitish nation in the wilderness. But it is equally clear, that the apostle makes use of the divine conduct respecting the posterity of Jacob and Esau, mentioned in v. 11, 12, 13, and the declaration of God, quoted in v. 15, as illustrative of a general principle in the divine administration. This principle is brought into view, v. 16, as an inference from what preceded. "So then it is not of him that willeth, nor of him that runneth, but of God that showeth mercy." It is deduced, as a general principle, from what God said respecting the offending Israelites in a particular case. This mode of reasoning is repeated immediately after. First, a passage is quoted from the Old Testament; v. 17; "For the scripture saith unto Pharaoh, even for this same cause have I raised thee up, that I might show my power in thee, and that my name might be declared throughout all the earth." From this declaration of God respecting a single individual, a general conclusion is drawn, v. 18. "Therefore hath he mercy on whom he will have mercy, and whom he will he hardeneth." This is laid down by the apostle, as a general principle of the divine administration. And it is this general principle, that is asserted in the orthodox doctrine of Election, or sovereign grace.

Now take a brief view of this remarkable passage. What is it that the apostle takes so much pains to establish? Evidently this, that God makes distinctions among men, or bestows peculiar favors on some, and not on others, pro libitu, pro arbitrio, *according to his own will, or pleasure.** How does he prove this? From *particular instances* of the divine conduct, as made known by the Scriptures. It is for this purpose he quotes what God said respecting his treatment of Jacob and Esau, and of Pharaoh. Taken in any other view, the quotations have no relation to the subject, and the reasoning of the apostle from them is nugatory.

But how can the apostle infer a general truth from particular facts? How can he infer what the divine purpose and conduct will generally be, respecting the higher distinctions to be made among men in the concerns of religion, from what they were towards a few individuals in regard to other distinctions?—Plainly, because, as he evidently understands it, the same principle is involved in both. The truth asserted in v. 16, is *general.* "It is not of him that willeth, nor of him that runneth, but of God that showeth mercy." The sense is, that, in relation to the subject under consideration, "nothing is effected by the efforts of man, but that every thing depends on the mercy of God.† This general truth is inferred from what God said respecting his conduct in a particular case, because that case im-

---

* See Schleusner, Rosenmuller, and other Commentators, on the place.

† Rosenmuller.

plied the same principle. What objection can lie against this argument? If God proceeded in the manner described, in his treatment of two nations, that is, made a distinction between them by his own sovereign purpose and act; he may surely proceed in the same manner towards individuals. And if he has actually proceeded in this manner and on this principle, in his treatment of particular individuals; why may he not proceed in the same manner in his treatment of others generally? That the Apostle reasons thus, is undeniable.

It may be made still more certain, that we understand this passage correctly, by looking at the objection, which the Apostle supposed would be made. "Thou wilt say then unto me, why doth he yet find fault? for who hath resisted his will?" v. 19. The nature of the objection, proves, that it related to that very doctrine of God's sovereign purpose and agency, which makes a a part of our faith. It is the very objection, which is still made against that doctrine. The nature of the objection shows the nature of the doctrine, against which it was urged. And the nature of the answer, v. 20—24, shows, still more plainly, what was the nature of the objection, and the nature of the doctrine objected to. It is exactly the answer, which it is suitable to give to one, who urges just such an objection as this, against the Orthodox doctrine of God's sovereign purpose and agency. Such a striking correspondence would, in any other case, and must in this, be considered, as affording very satisfactory evidence of the scope and meaning of the discourse.

There is one more important inquiry respecting this passage; and that is, whether that general principle of the divine administration, which the Apostle establishes, relates to the eternal interests of men, or to something of less moment. Now I think nothing can be plainer, than the correctness of the common construction of the passage, viz.; that it relates to the difference which exists among men with regard to their spiritual and eternal state. This appears from the commencement of this particular part of the discourse, v. 6, 7, 8, in which the Apostle brings into view the essential difference between *real Israelites*, and those who are *of Israel*, that is, descended from him;—between the children of the flesh, and the children of God. The Apostle labors throughout the discourse, to illustrate the manner, in which this difference is made, drawing his illustrations, as was natural, when reasoning with Jews, from the Jewish Scriptures. That he refers to the difference which is made among men in relation to their religious character and salvation, is evident also from v. 22,23 &c, where, in pursuance of the selfsame subject, which was treated v. 6—18, he speaks of the vessels of mercy, prepared for glory, in contradistinction to the vessels of wrath; of those who were called, both Jews and Gentiles, of God's people, &c.

If still further confirmation of the correctness of the reasoning above exhibited were necessary, I could, as I think, make it appear, that the doctrine of God's sovereign Election is the only doctrine, which accounts satisfactorily for the actual difference, which exists between true believers, and the rest of the world.

But if, after all, any should be disposed to urge the common objections against this doctrine, that it makes God unrighteous, and that, if it is true, we cannot be blamed for our sins; I would, for the present, refer them to this chapter, to learn how the Apostle Paul would answer their objections.

The doctrine, we are now considering, is in my apprehension, clearly implied in the general doctrine of the divine purpose. That God has a wise and holy plan, and that all events take place in conformity to it, is not only taught, expressly and abundantly, in the Scriptures, but results from the absolute perfection of God, and from the necessary dependence of all created things on him, as clearly, as any mathematical truth results from its premises. But if God has a general plan or design respecting the events which take place, he must surely have one respecting so important an event, as the salvation of his people.

But I can proceed no further with the proof. This subject has been argued by the ablest writers, that have appeared since the christian era. The controversy has been wrought up to such a degree of warmth, and the doctrine is associated in the minds of not a few, with so many strange and absurd notions, that it has become a matter of difficulty and hazard for a man to offer any proof in its favor, or even to profess that he believes it. Indeed, a man in some instances, can hardly find himself at liberty simply to repeat the texts of Scripture, which support the doctrine, without being attacked with a score of common place reflections, intended to put down the doctrine at once, without discussion. I trust my readers will be sensible, that the state of mind, which is exhibited in such cases, is altogether at variance with Christian candor, and in a high degree unpropitious to the cause of truth.

LETTER VIII.

My respected friends,

Though I have detained you longer than I intended, on the doctrine of Election; I must beg your indulgence, while I express my thoughts without reserve, on various incorrect views and representations of the doctrine, and on some of the difficulties attending it.

Orthodox writers have not unfrequently made use of expressions which, at first view, may seem to furnish occasion for some of the heavy charges, brought against us by our opposers. But let it be remembered, that, for the rash, unqualified expressions of men, who have become hot and violent by controversy, we are not to be held responsible. We here enter our solemn protest against the language which has sometimes been employed, and the conceptions which have sometimes been entertained on this subject, or rather, perhaps, against the appendages which have been attached to it, by men, who have been denominated Calvinists. Though we embrace the doctrine, as one which is taught in Scripture, and which corresponds with enlightened reason and Christian piety; we do not embrace it in the form, and with the appendages, to which I allude.—But my present concern is chiefly with the representations of our opposers.

First. It is often represented, that we believe in an *arbitrary, unconditional, absolute decree of election.* These words are used abundantly by opposers of the doctrine, and are made the means of exciting many prejudices against it. This representation of the doctrine must receive particular attention.

The word *arbitrary* has acquired a bad sense; and is now understood to express the character of a master or ruler, who is tyrannical, or oppressive; who acts without regard to reason or justice, and is governed by his own capricious will. God's purpose respecting the salvation of men is, in our view, at the greatest distance from any thing like this. We consider the purpose of God to be altogether as just and reasonable, as his administration. If, in the actual *salvation* of the penitent and holy, God is wise and good; he is equally wise and good, in his *purpose* to save them,—his conduct being an exact accomplishment of his purpose. No objection, therefore, can lie against the previous purpose of his will, which does not lie equally against the acts of his government. The inquiry, then, respects a matter of fact. Does God *act* wisely and benevolently in saving sinners? Or does he act from a capricious, tyrannical will? If the actions of his government are capricious and tyrannical, so is his purpose. If his actions are wise and good, his purpose is so likewise. Now although in various respects, God's proceedings in saving sinners are inscrutable to us, and we are unable to see by what reasons he is influenced; we believe he has reasons, which are perfectly satisfactory to himself, and which, were they made known, would be satisfactory to us. It is utterly impossible, that a Being of infinite perfection should act under the influence of a capricious or despotic will. Though his administration may often be contrary to our judgment and our expectations; we confide implicitly in his wisdom and goodness. Nothing can be more suitable for us, than such confidence in our all perfect Creator.

I say then, we do not hold the doctrine of Election in any such sense, as implies, that the purpose of God is *despotic* or *capricious*. It is indeed often represented in Scripture to be the purpose of his *will*, and to be according to his *good pleasure*. But what can be more wise and reasonable, than the *will* or *good pleasure of* God? When the inspired writers declare the purpose of God to be according to *his own will*, they do, it is granted, signify to us, that it varies from the will of *man;* but they do this, to show its superior wisdom and goodness. If it were according to the will of *man*, it would be marked only with *human* wisdom. But as it is according to the will of *God*, it is marked with *divine* wisdom.

We inquire next, whether the purpose of God respecting the salvation of men is *unconditional and absolute*. I know that, in consequence of particular errors which have prevailed, it has been so represented by many of its advocates. But the language is certainly liable to be misunderstood, and ought not to be used without special care. Why should we employ words, which will not convey, truly and exactly, to the minds of others, the views which we ourselves entertain? Here, as before, I look at the divine conduct in saving sinners, considering that, as exactly corresponding with the previous divine purpose. And my inquiry is,—does God actually save sinners *unconditionally?* The first answer I give to this is, that God would never have saved them, had not Christ interposed, and made an atonement. This, then, is a *condition* of human salvation; it is the grand event, on account of which God forgives. But I inquire farther; does God actually save sinners, that is, forgive them, and receive them into his kingdom, without any condition *on their part?* The Bible furnishes the answer. " Repent and be converted, that your sins may be blotted out." He that believeth shall be saved." This is the uniform representation of the Bible. The condition of eternal life *to be performed by men,* is repentance, faith, obedience. They can no more be saved without these, than without the death of Christ. These conditions, it is true, are of a different nature from the atonement; but they are equally necessary. From this view of the subject, I come to a satisfactory conclusion. If God does not actually save sinners without conditions; he did not *purpose* to save them without conditions,—his purpose and conduct always agreeing exactly with each other. In his eternal purpose, he regarded *the same conditions,* and regarded them *in the same manner,* as he does now, when he saves. Clearly, then, the purpose of God to save men cannot, in this respect, be considered as *unconditional.* And as the word is apt to be understood as excluding all regard to these conditions, and being so understood, involves a palpable and dangerous error; the use of it ought, I think, to be avoided; except when the particular error to be confuted, or some other circumstances, will show plainly, that it is used in a sense agreeable to the truth.

But the principal object of Orthodox writers in using the word *unconditional* in this case, has been the *denial of a particular error.* Some men have asserted, that the divine purpose respecting the salvation of sinners, which is so often spoken of in Scripture, is grounded altogether on the foreknowledge of the good works of those, who are destined to salvation; and have, in this view, called the purpose of God *conditional.* Orthodox writers have denied *such a conditionality* as this, and have justified themselves by appealing to such texts, as the following; 2. Tim. i. 9, "God hath saved us and called us with an holy calling, not according to our works, but according to his own purpose and grace, which was given us in Christ before the world began." Tit. iii. 5.

"Not by works of righteousness which we have done, but according to his mercy he saved us." God's saving us according to his purpose and grace is here contradistinguished to his saving us according to our works; and the defenders of Orthodoxy have justly considered all such representations of Scripture, as opposed to the opinion, that the divine purpose is conditional in the sense above mentioned.

To remove all appearances of inconsistency between the two different views above taken, of the meaning and propriety of the word *unconditional*, in relation to this subject, it is only necessary to make two obvious remarks. 1. Those things, which are spoken of as conditions on the part of man, are not so, in any degree, in the sense of *merit*, and therefore take nothing from the freeness or riches of divine grace. 2. That which is referred to in the passages above cited, where all conditionality is excluded, appears evidently to be the act of God in the first renewal of the sinner, or in first saving him from sin. " Who hath saved us, and called us with an holy calling, not according to our works," &c. It was the *commencement* of the work of God in salvation. So in the parallel text, in Titus. " Not by works of righteousness which we have done, but according to his mercy he saved us, by the washing of regeneration and renewing of the Holy Ghost." The salvation here spoken of, as excluding all consideration of works, was the act of God in *regeneration,—the renewing of the Holy Ghost*. This point is made still clearer by Ephes. ii, 4 —10. Accordingly, we hold it as a fact, universally, that impenitent, unrenewed sinners do no good work, which God regards as a condition of their being renewed, or on account of which he has promised them regeneration;—that, in all cases, he calls and renews them, according to his own purpose and grace. Now if his merciful act in their renewal to holiness is, *in this sense, unconditional;* so is his previous purpose. That the one is so, is as certain and unexceptionable, as that the other is.

Such are my views, and, if I mistake not, of my brethren generally, respecting this part of the subject. But whenever we speak of the forgiveness of sin, the comforts of religion, or any other blessings, which God has promised to bestow, as tokens of his favor to his children, whether here or hereafter; we are led, by the tenor of Scripture, to understand them as promised, not only on the ground of the perfect atonement made by the Savior of sinners, but also in view of conditions to be performed by them.

After the foregoing explanations, and similar ones from others, I hope the doctrine we hold respecting the purpose of God in the election of his people, or his agency in their salvation, will no longer be represented as implying, that God, in this respect, bears any resemblance to a capricious, arbitrary, or despotic ruler. Although some Orthodox writers may have inadvertently used language, which might lead to such a view of the character of God; yet that view is totally repugnant to our feelings, and to every thing which our doctrine is intended to contain. God does, indeed, plainly possess the *uncontrollable power* of an absolute monarch; but his uncontrollable power is always directed by infinite wisdom and goodness. Like a despotic sovereign, he does indeed act according to *his own will;* but his will, be it remembered, is the will of a wise and benevolent ruler, a friend to his subjects; and his acting in all things according to his own will, instead of being a cause of dissatisfaction and alarm, is the greatest possible security to the interests of the universe. Like an absolute monarch, God may also frequently act, without any apparent reasons. But in reality there is no part of his administration, for which the highest and best reasons do not exist in his own mind.

Now the danger of representing the character and administration of God by the language, which is commonly applied to the character and administration of an absolute earthly sovereign, is, that the similitude, which is intended, and which really exists, will be carried too far; that instead of being restricted to those points in which a similitude would be honourable to God, it will be understood as reaching those, in which a similitude would be a stain to his perfect character. The words despot, monarch, absolute, and arbitrary were not originally and necessarily expressive of any bad qualities. *Despot* signifies a master, a prince who rules with unlimited power; *monarch*, one who exercises power or authority alone ; *absolute*, complete, unlimited ; *arbitrary*, according to one's own will. They all admit of a good sense ; and, in truth, they would never be understood by us in a bad sense, had they not become associated in our minds with the bad qualities of those earthly masters or rulers, to whom they have been applied. But in consequence of this association, we cannot safely apply them, or others like them, to God, without special care to limit the points of analogy, which are intended. And in most cases of the kind, even this precaution would not preclude all exposure to error; because the words having acquired a bad sense, cannot be applied to any one, not even to God, whatever care may be used, without danger of conveying more or less of that bad sense to our minds. I should therefore, think it unadvised, in any common case, to make use of such terms, as those abovementioned, in describing the character, or administration of God.

It is said by our opposers, that the doctrine we maintain on this subject, makes God *unjust*.

As to this charge of injustice, which is always meant to relate to those, who are not chosen to salvation, the views which we entertain, and which appear to me very satisfactory, are briefly these. The Scriptures teach, that all men are sinners, and, as such, children of wrath; that if God should be strict to mark iniquity, no man could stand before him; that salvation, in all instances, is of grace. Now suppose salvation is not granted to all. Suppose it not granted to any. Is God *unjust?*— unjust in not vouchsafing to men that, to which they have no claim? unjust in inflicting the evil, which they deserve? The divine *law* then is unjust. For how can the law be just in threatening an evil, which may not be justly inflicted? Further. If we should say, God cannot justly withhold the blessings of salvation in the instances here intended; this would be the same as saying, that justice requires God to save all. But the Scriptures represent it not only as an unmerited favor, that God saves any, but as a matter of fact, that he will not save all. Is God then chargeable with actual injustice? But if God is just in annexing such a penalty to his law, and just in executing it; it must be obvious that he is equally just in his *determination* to do so. For no principle of common sense can be more plain and certain, than that it is just for the omniscient God to determine beforehand to do that, which it is just for him actually to do. No imputation of injustice, therefore, can lie against the previous purpose of God respecting those who are not saved, which does not lie equally against his law, and his administration.

Here we find one of the principal sources of difficulty respecting this subject. It is not well considered, that the divine purpose is grounded on the same reasons, and conformed to the same views, with the divine conduct. When God punishes transgressors, he does it for sufficient reasons. When he previously determines to punish them, it is for the same reasons. When the Judge shall say to the wicked, "depart from me, ye that work iniquity;" the reason of the sentence is obvious, namely, that they had worked iniquity. With a perfect foreknowledge of that fact, and altogether on that account, he determines beforehand to pronounce that sentence against them. Thus the purpose of God perfectly corresponds with the acts of his government. Accordingly, his purpose to punish is no more absolute and unconditional, than his act in punishing. And the act of God in punishing those, who transgress his law, is no more absolute and unconditional, than the act of a magistrate in punishing transgressors of civil law. A good ruler punishes only for offences against the law; punishes only according to law; or, which is the same thing, according to the ill desert of offenders. And no good ruler can ever design or decree punishment on any other principles. I object as strongly, as any opposer of the doctrine of the divine purpose, against representing God as intending or appointing the destruction of sinners absolutely and unconditionally, without regard to justice, and goodness, and from a delight in seeing the misery of his creatures. Such a representation is infinitely distant from the truth. And whatever unguarded expressions Othodox writers may have sometimes used; I am persuaded they have really meant nothing contrary to the sentiments, which I have exhibited.

From the free remarks which I have made on this

subject, you will see what my views and those of my Orthodox brethren are, respecting what is called the divine purpose or *decree of reprobation*. It is, as we understand the subject, the determination of God, the righteous Governor of the world, to punish disobedient subjects *for their sins*, and according to their deserts. In one respect, therefore, there is an obvious difference between the purpose of God to *save*, and his purpose to *destroy;* a difference exactly agreeing with that which exists between the act of God in saving, and his act in destroying. He saves men as an act of grace, not out of respect to any thing in them, which renders them *deserving* of salvation. But he punishes the wicked purely out of respect to their sins, which render them *deserving* of punishment. He executes upon them simply an act of justice. That is, in a word; they, who are saved, receive a good which they do not deserve; but they who are destroyed, receive just that evil which they deserve. Accordingly, the *purpose* of God, in the former case, is a purpose to bestow upon men blessings, not deserved; but, in the latter case, it is a purpose to inflict upon men the very evil, as to kind and degree, which they deserve.

It has often been alleged, as an objection against the doctrine of Election, that it makes God *a respecter of persons;* or represents him, as influenced by *partiality.*

In order to determine, whether this objection is well founded, we must inquire what *respect of persons is.* The word, I think, has the same sense in Scripture, and in common discourse. Let us then see what its signification is.—Levit. xix. 15; "Thou shalt do no unrighteousness in judgment; thou shalt not *respect the person* of the poor, nor know the *person* of the mighty; but in righteousness shalt thou judge thy neighbor;" that is thou shalt not be influenced in judgment by any consideration of the poverty or riches, the weakness or power of those, who are to be judged, but by a single regard to justice and truth. In 2 Chron. xix. 5—7, Jehoshaphat inculcated strict justice and fidelity upon Judges from the consideration, that with God, whose servants they were, there was no iniquity, *nor respect of persons*, nor taking of gifts; that is, that he was never biassed in judgment by any corrupt passions, personal attachments, or bribes, but acted purely out of regard to justice. See also Deut. x. 17, 18, where the people were cautioned, by similar language, against supposing that God would feel any partial respect to the persons of men, or that he would not exercise a just and equal regard to the fatherless, the widow, and the stranger. Acts x. 34. Peter learnt from his vision at Joppa, and from subsequent events, that God was not a *respecter of persons*; that, in dispensing his blessings, he had not that partial and exclusive regard to the Jews, which had been attributed to him, but that, in every nation, he that feared God, and worked righteousness, was accepted. It referred to the special favor shown to Cornelius, a sincere worshipper of God among the Gentiles. So Rom. ii. 11, the same declaration is made, to show that, in his final judgment, God would treat all men on the same principle of impartial justice, without the least regard to any national distinction. See also James ii. 1—4, where *respect of persons* is explained to be a partial regard to the rich and splendid, and contempt of the poor.

Now if *respect of persons* is really what I have represented it to be; the doctrine of Election, which we hold, does not imply, that God is chargeable with it in any degree. It implies the contrary. For the doctrine asserts, that he is not influenced to make choice of those who are to be saved, by any respect to their persons, more than to the persons of others, nor by a regard to any thing in them, or in their circumstances, which renders them more pleasing to him, or more worthy of his favor, than others. We believe, that those, who are chosen of God to salvation, are not chosen because they were, in themselves, more worthy of this blessing, than others; that God looked upon their moral feelings and conduct with the same disapprobation, and had the same view of their ill desert, and that he chose them, as we may say, *for reasons of state,*—for general reasons in his government, which he has not revealed. He did it, as it is expressed by the inspired writers, " according to the counsel of his own will,"— " according to his good pleasure,"—or " because it seemed good in his sight." These phrases plainly denote that the purpose and administration of God are, in this respect, different from what our wisdom would dictate, or our affection choose; that they cannot be accounted for by any principles known to us, but result from the infinite perfection of God, and are conformed to reasons, which he has concealed in his own mind. These are our views. Accordingly, when, from the deep veneration we feel for the unsearchable wisdom of God, and an honest regard to what we conceive to be the obvious sense of various passages in his word, we assert the doctrine of Election; we are at the greatest possible distance from imputing to him any thing like partiality, or respect of persons. We believe he acts, and determines to act, altogether from different and higher reasons. And we are satisfied, that those reasons are perfectly wise and benevolent, not because we distinctly know what they are, but because we believe in the moral perfection of

God, and in cases the most profoundly mysterious, are sure, that his designs and actions are right.

Will any one still assert, that, if God chooses men to salvation, as the doctrine of Election implies, it must necessarily be from partiality, or respect of persons? Then it behooves him to prove, that God cannot choose them from any other motive;—that it is impossible there should be any other reason for making the difference. Unless this is made to appear by strong and conclusive arguments; we may still believe, that God does thus choose men to salvation, and, at the same time, believe that he is no respecter of persons, but that in this case, as in all others, he is influenced by reasons, which are perfectly consentaneous to his own eternal wisdom and benevolence, and which, if known to us, would appear in the highest degree honorable to his character.

Another objection, often urged against the doctrine of Election, is, that it *destroys free agency*, and *makes men mere machines*.

I reply; that, so far as our honest convictions are concerned, this objection is groundless; because we entertain no views of the doctrine, which seem to us inconsistent, in the smallest degree, with the most perfect free agency.

But it may be said that, whether we are aware of it or not, the opinion, which we entertain respecting the divine purpose, is *really* inconsistent with free moral agency.

In reply to this, I have time only to state, in few words, the reflections, which have been most satisfactory to my own mind.

The purpose of God, determining the salvation of his people, needs not to be supposed inconsistent with their moral agency, unless the purpose of God respecting the conduct or condition of men is so in every case. I make it then a *general inquiry*. Is it in all cases, repugnant to the notion of the free moral agency of men, that God should have any previous purpose or design respecting their actions? If any man, accustomed to thorough investigation, should assert this broad principle; I should be much inclined to ask for his reasons.—Are the acts of the understanding, the affection, or the will of man deprived of their own proper nature, because they are conformed to a divine purpose? Is any one thing, great or small, which goes to constitute moral agency, taken away or in any degree altered, by the simple fact, that it exists according to God's eternal plan? It would seem to me reasonable to suppose, that God's purpose, or will, if it has any influence, must make things what they are, instead of depriving them of their proper nature.—I first look at things, both in the natural and moral world, as they exist. I try to discover what they are. Then, as they are of necessity dependant on God, I conclude they must exist according to his purpose. I find myself a moral being; that is, I am conscious of those powers, and those actions, which give me the clearest notion of a moral agent, and which, to my perfect satisfaction, render me accountable to a moral law and government. I then conclude, as I am a creature of God, that I exist as I am, namely, a moral agent, according to his purpose. And if God's purpose, determining my existence as a moral agent, is consistent with my actually existing as such; why may not his purpose, determining the exercises of my moral agency, be consistent with the existence of such moral exercises? The following positions, which I think conformable to sound reason and philosophy, express my views in brief. God first determines, *that man shall be a moral agent,* and that in all the circumstances of his existence, he shall *possess and exercise all his moral powers.* And then God determines, that, *in the perfect exercise of all his moral powers,* he shall act in a certain manner, and form a certain character. The determination of God, thus understood, instead of being *inconsistent* with free moral agency, does in fact *secure* moral agency. In regard to this subject, it aims at nothing, and tends to produce nothing, but the *uninterrupted exercise of all our moral powers.*

But I drop all reasoning of this sort, and appeal to facts. There are numerous instances mentioned in Scripture, in which God is expressly declared to have *predetermined* the actions of men; and yet they had as much moral freedom, and felt themselves as worthy of praise or blame in those actions, as in any other. The examples of this, which every where occur in the sacred volume, prove incontrovertibly, that the purpose of God is consistent with moral agency. For in those cases, in which we certainly know that a divine purpose has existed, because it has been expressly declared, there has been, in every respect, as much evidence of moral agency, as in any case whatever, and as much, as we can conceive possible. Not the least thing, which can belong to the powers of a moral agent, or to the manner of exercising them, has been taken away, or obstructed, by the divine purpose. Nay, I should rather say, that those very powers of a moral agent, and the proper manner of exercising them, have been the true result of that purpose.

Now admitting in the cases referred to, even if they were much fewer than they are, that the purpose of God has consisted with the unimpared moral agency of man; I find no difficulty in admitting, that it may in any other case. And if so, the objection we have been considering, that the doctrine of Election destroys moral agency, and makes men mere machines, loses all its force.

I shall notice one more objection against the doctrine of Election, namely, *that it is inconsistent with the sincerity of God in the declarations of his word.*

The answer to this objection, which appears to me the most satisfactory, consists in assigning to the doctrine its proper form and relations. When I undertake to explain the purpose of God respecting those who are to be saved, I consider it essential to say, that it is to be so understood, as not to contradict his truth and sincerity in any of the declarations of his word. If, in connexion with God's purpose respecting the salvation of his people, the Bible teaches, that he commands men universally to repent, and invites them to accept eternal life, and that he is perfectly ready to grant them the blessings of salvation, on the most reasonable and gracious terms; our faith must receive the doctrine, as having this form, and standing in this relation. It is thus the doctrine is actually received by Orthodox ministers generally. While they believe the doctrine of Election, they do undoubtingly believe and expressly teach, the perfect sincerity of God in all his addresses to men, whether chosen to salvation, or not; and they present the invitations, of God's word to sinners, without any reference to that distinction, and with as much earnestness, and as much belief of the divine sincerity, as if they had no conception of any divine purpose. And my apprehension is, that all this is perfectly just; and that if we had a thorough acquaintance with the subject, we should see, that the purpose of God, and his corresponding agency are of such a character, that they occasion no difficulty at all respecting his sincerity. These two points of divine truth are entirely distinct. They relate to the character of God, and to the state of man, in different ways. And when they are proved, each one by its own proper evidence, we receive them both, exactly as we receive different truths, made known to us in different ways, in any of the sciences. As to the fact of their *consistency*, it is sufficient to satisfy us, to find, that they are both supported by conclusive evidence, and that neither of them palpably contradicts the other. If any man asserts that there is an inconsistency between these two doctrines, he must prove it. And in proving it, he must remember, that it will be difficult to satisfy thinking men, unless he can make it appear, that the evidence which supports one or the other of them is defective, or that the main proposition, contained in one of them, is, in the same sense in which it is there affirmed, contradicted or denied in the other.

In closing my remarks on this part of the subject, I am willing to concede, that *those views* of the doctrine of Election, against which Whitby, and many other respectable writers direct their principal arguments, are justly liable to objection. And if, in stating the doctrine, we should copy the example of some of its advocates, and call the purpose of God *an absolute, irresistible unconditional, unfrustrable decree*, using these epithets abundantly, and without qualification, and in such a manner, as would imply, that the divine purpose is unreasonable, or oppressive, or the divine agency in executing it, compulsory; we should really give the doctrine such a character, that it could never be received by men of rational and candid minds. This is the apology, which I have been accustomed to make for some Christians who exhibit marks of sincere piety to God, and heartfelt reverence for his word, who yet hesitate to admit, in so many words, the doctrine of Election. What they disbelieve is not the simple doctrine, as we understand it, but something which has been artfully, or injudiciously appended to it. Cases of this kind have led me to reflect on the importance of special caution, as to the manner of explaining and defending this profound and holy doctrine.

I have now done, as concisely as possible, what I thought necessary to explain the proper form and relations of this doctrine, and to guard it against misapprehension. I make these explanations a part of the statement of the doctrine. And it must, I think, occur to my readers, that, when I use such care to shape and limit the doctrine, and to guard it against misapprehension, I do but imitate what the Apostle Paul did in other cases. His opposers were inclined to put a wrong construction upon his doctrines, and to make wrong inferences from them. " If our unrighteousness commend the righteousness of God, what shall we say? Is God unrighteous who taketh vengeance? God forbid."—Again, he taught, in respect of penitent sinners, that " where sin abounded, grace did much more abound." He then reasons with objectors. " What shall we say then? shall we sin, that grace may abound? God forbid." We make use of the same caution on the present subject. The Scriptures teach that God has given to Christ a portion of the human race; that all, who have been thus given to him, shall come to him, and be saved, without any exception; and that they are saved according to God's eternal purpose. This is what we mean by the doctrine of Election. But is this purpose of God *absolute* and *arbitrary*, in the sense in which these terms are commonly applied to man? God forbid.—Is this purpose of God, in all respects, *unconditional*? By no means. For without the shedding of blood there can be no remission; nor can any be received into Christ's kingdom without repentance and faith.—But if God determines to save only a part of mankind, is he not *unjust*? God forbid. There is certainly no injustice to those who are saved; nor can there be any to those, who are not saved, if their sufferings are only what they deserve. But is not the purpose of God in this respect chargeable with partiality, or respect of persons? We say, God forbid. He makes the difference on principles, or for reasons perfectly agreeable to infinite wisdom and goodness.—But does not God's purpose to save his people, or his agency in executing that purpose, destroy their free agency, and make them machines? By no means. They are as free in this case as in any other; as free as they could be, were there no divine purpose. Finally; is not this immutable purpose of God inconsistent with the truth and sincerity of his proposals of mercy to sinners? We say here also, God forbid. His purpose no more interferes with his sincerity, than it does with any other divine attribute, or with any other truth. In his offer of salvation, he treats men as moral agents; and he always has bestowed salvation upon those, who have accepted his offer in the manner proposed; and he would have bestowed it upon those who perish, if they had in the same manner, complied with the conditions. Who then can impeach his sincerity?

You now see what we mean by the doctrine of Election, and in what manner we believe it. As the result of his own unsearchable wisdom and grace, and for reasons which relate to the great ends of his administration, God eternally purposed to save a great number of our race, and purposed to save them precisely in the manner, in which he does actually save them. Now every man, who duly weighs the subject, must perceive, that, according to this statement, the notion of a *previous* divine purpose is attended with no peculiar difficulty. If the divine purpose exactly corresponds with the divine conduct, our whole inquiry may properly relate to that conduct. For if the divine conduct in saving men is unobjectionable; the divine purpose, of which that conduct is the accomplishment, must be equally unobjectionable. Whatever it is proper for God to do, it is proper for him to determine to do. And whether that determination precede the action by a longer or shorter space, its character is the same.

After coming to this article of divine truth, concerning which so many mistakes have been entertained, and against which so many objections have been arrayed, I felt a desire to disclose to my readers, with the utmost frankness, my inmost thoughts upon the subject; being fully persuaded, that the doctrine, properly stated, is honorable to God; that it is abundantly confirmed by the scriptures, and has strong claims upon our faith. Indeed we should find it difficult to see, how any objection could ever be urged against it, were it not for the natural repugnance, which according to the word of God, exists in the heart of man, against the doctrines of divine truth, and which, to our great discomfort, and with a full conviction of its unreasonableness and criminality, we have felt in ourselves.—Were it not for this repugnance, which plainly shows the moral disorder of the human mind, no man, we think, could be found, who would not regard the doctrine with the most cordial acquiescence. For, my respected readers, the precious blessings of salvation must be ultimately, either in the hands of God, or of man. The extent, to which they shall be received, must be determined by God, or by man. The Scriptures teach, and facts teach, that God has reserved this great concern in his own hands; that he "saves men according to his own purpose and grace;" or which is the same thing, that he hath mercy on whom he will have mercy." I make the appeal to your impartial judgment, whether this momentous concern could be in better hands; whether we have not reason for unbounded confidence in the purpose and administration of a Being, who is infinitely wise and good; and whether any sentiment respecting this whole subject can be more reasonable in itself, or more suitable for us, than that, which was uttered with so much joy by the blessed Jesus, respecting this very doctrine; *Even so, Father, for so it seemeth good in thy sight.*

LETTER IX.

My respected friends,

If there is any one doctrine of revelation, which the Orthodox distinguish, in point of importance, from all others, it is the doctrine of the *Atonement*. My design in this Letter is, not to write a treatise on this subject, but to expose certain erroneous methods of reasoning respecting it, to clear away some of the objections and difficulties, which have been supposed to attend it, and so to prepare the way for a fair consideration of its truth and importance. This is all which the nature of my undertaking requires.

Here, as in other cases, a regard to truth obliges me

to say, that Unitarians have greatly misrepresented our opinions. The Author of the Sermon before us gives it as a part of the Orthodox system, that "God took upon him human nature, that he might pay to his own justice the debt of punishment incurred by men, and might enable himself to exercise mercy." He undertakes in another place to express our opinion in still stronger terms; "that God took human nature, that he might appease his own anger towards men, or make an infinite satisfaction to his own justice;" and after giving our opinion this shape, he asks very earnestly, for one text where it is taught. We reply, that an opinion, *thus shaped and colored*, is taught nowhere in the Bible, and believed by no respectable Trinitarians. It is an essential part of our faith, that there is a real distinction between the Father and the Son, and that the distinction is of such a nature, that they are two, and are in Scripture represented to be two, as *really*, as Moses and Aaron, though not in the same sense, nor in any sense inconsistent with their being one. In consequence of this distinction, we consider it perfectly proper to say, that the Father sends the Son to die for sinners, and accepts the sacrifice he makes; that the Son obeys the Father, seeks his glory, &c. We find that the Scripture does thus represent them; and though in our view they both possess the same divine perfection, we believe that, in consequence of the distinction between them, this representation of Scripture is just. We pretend not, with minds so limited as ours, to be able to know the intrinsic nature, or the ground of this distinction; but its *results* we know, because the Bible reveals them; and we believe the distinction to be correspondent with what is thus revealed. So that it is something quite diverse from the form of sound words, which we adopt, and quite diverse from our belief, to say, that "God sent himself,"—" that God took human nature, that he might appease his own anger, and enable himself to exercise mercy." And if any writer should still say that, if the Son shares divine perfection with the Father, it is impossible there should be any such distinction, as the Scripture makes between them; he would indeed repeat that which has been said by a succession of writers from the Fratres Poloni down to the present day, but which, so far as I know, has had little better proof, than strong affirmation.

But it is not to my purpose to go into any argument in proof of the personal distinction in the Godhead; but merely to say, that the passages, above quoted from the Sermon, and a multitude of other passages, which might be quoted from Unitarian writers, are far from being a true and impartial representation of our faith. They are indeed calculated to slur the Orthodox doctrine of the Atonement. But with every sober, honest man, the question will be, *are they just?*—It is as plain to us, as to this writer, that God, as God, cannot be a sufferer, or bear a penalty. And hence we infer the necessity of the incarnation. "The Word," the divine Redeemer, "was made flesh," and thus was put into a capacity to suffer and die.

The Author of this Sermon, and other Unitarian writers seem to think, that the idea, which is conveyed to common minds by the Orthodox system, is "that Christ's death has an influence in making God placable or merciful, in quenching his wrath, and awakening his kindness towards men." This representation demands particular attention.

I observe, then, that it is uniformly the sentiment of the Orthodox, that *the origin, the grand moving cause of the whole work of redemption, was the infinite love, benignity, or mercy of God;* and that it is purely in consequence of this love, that he appointed a Mediator, and adopted every measure, which he saw to be necessary for the salvation of man. The goodness, mercy, or placability of God, considered as an attribute of his character, could then be neither produced nor increased by the atonement of Christ; as the atonement itself owed its existence wholly to that eternal, immutable goodness. This view of the subject, which we derive from John iii. 16, and many other texts of similar import, we inculcate with more than ordinary frequency and earnestness. We believe that it is essential to the honor of the divine character, and to the sincerity and comfort of christian devotion. If we have ever made use of language, or indulged opinions, in the smallest degree unfavorable to this sentiment, we deplore the error we have committed. And whenever we find a fellow creature, who has entertained a different sentiment, we will vie with the Author of this Sermon, in our efforts to correct a mistake, which we regard with so much horror.

But how happens it, that Unitarians have so often, and so materially misapprehended our opinions on this momentous subject? The only occasion we have given for their misapprehension has been, the use of *strong metaphorical language*. It has been common for Orthodox writers and preachers, especially when they have aimed to move the affections of men, or to impress the truth upon them deeply, to represent Christ, as rescuing sinners from the vengeance of God, or shielding them from the arrows of his vengeance; as appeasing, or turning away his anger, staying his fury, quenching his wrath or vengeance, divesting his throne of its terrors, satisfying his justice, delivering men from the demands of his dreadful law, &c.

Now I pretend not that this language is exactly like the language of the Scriptures. But the resemblance is so great, that no objection can possibly lie against the one, which does not lie equally against the other. To make this perfectly clear, I shall give a few examples of the manner, in which both the Old Testament and the New frequently speak of God. Psalm xc. 7. "We are consumed by thine anger." Isa. v. 25. "His anger is not turned away;"—xxx. 30. "The Lord shall show the indignation of his anger;"—xl. 25. "He poured on him the fury of his anger;"—lxvi. 15. "The Lord will come to render his anger with fury." Hosea xi. 9. "I will execute the fierceness of mine anger." Deut. xxix. 30. "The anger of the Lord and his jealousy shall smoke against that man." In other places the anger of the Lord is said to be kindled. It is said, that he is angry with the wicked every day; that he hath whet his sword; that he hath bent his bow, and made it ready; that he revengeth and is furious; and that he will meet his enemies, as a bear bereaved of her whelps. The writers of the New Testament sometimes use similar phraseology. They speak of the indignation and wrath of God, and represent vengeance as his prerogative.—The Scriptures also represent God as turning or being turned from his anger, from the fierceness of his anger, and from his hot displeasure. This was the familiar language of history and devotion under the former dispensation. And we well know that the God, whom Moses, David, and the prophets worshipped, was the God and Father of our Lord Jesus Christ.

It will be said, that the language above cited is *metaphorical*. Undoubtedly it is. And so is the language, which is used by Orthodox writers on the subject of the atonement. The Scripture metaphors, which I have brought into view, are drawn from the same sources, and are of the same nature with those, which are objected to in the writings of the Orthodox. And I am sure that no advocate for Orthodoxy, how great soever the warmth of his natural temperament, and how glowing soever his imagination and his style, has ever, even in poetry, used bolder metaphors respecting God, than are found in the sacred writers. Where shall we find imagery more terrific, than in those passages of Scripture, in which God is represented as full of anger and vengeance, even the fierceness and heat of anger, so that his wrath smokes and burns against the wicked;—in which his fury is represented to be like the fury of a bear bereaved of her whelps;—in which too he is set forth, as a terrible executioner, or warrior, with his sharp sword, or with his bow and arrows, ready for the work of destruction? And what advocates for the Atonement have employed language more highly figurative, than we find in those passages, in which God is said to cause his anger to cease, or to be turned, by prayer, from the fierceness of his wrath? Even if we should familiarly speak of the Atonement in the language, which the Author of the sermon thinks so exceptionable, and should represent it as designed to "render God merciful, to quench his wrath, and awaken his kindness towards men;" we might very safely rest our justification for the use of such metaphorical language, on the example of men, who spake as they were moved by the Holy Ghost.

Will it be said, that the bold metaphors, above cited from the Scriptures, were peculiar to the idiom of the Eastern language, especially the language of the ancient Hebrews, and that they are inadmissible under the dispensation of the Gospel? I grant that they belonged to the idiom of the Eastern nations, especially of the ancient Hebrew writers. But it must be remembered, that Christ, in the most unqualified terms, recommended the Scriptures of the Old Testament to his disciples; and also that the writers of the New Testament thought it proper to quote, without palliation or explanation, some of the metaphorical passages referred to, and sometimes, with similar metaphors, to enliven their own style. And surely it cannot be thought strange, that a Christian minister, who is accustomed to entertain so high a reverence for the Holy Scriptures, and to look to them, as containing every thing pure and excellent, both in matter and form, should infuse into his preaching or writing the same kind of metaphor, as that which abounds in them. It has generally been considered best by Unitarians, if I mistake not, as well as by others, to *keep as near, as may be, to the peculiar phraseology of the Scriptures.* Why, then, are we blamed for doing it here? It is not very easy to account for the manner in which Unitarian writers have treated this thing. If they acknowledge that the language of Scripture, above cited, is to be understood as *highly metaphorical;* why should they suppose that similar language in our sermons and books of divinity is meant to be understood *literally?* The moment they interpret our language, as they interpret the figurative language of the Bible, the difficulty vanishes.

But what is the *meaning* of the metaphorical language now under consideration? To satisfy ourselves on this subject, it is only necessary to consider the nature and design of metaphors, and the manner in which we learn their signification. In metaphorical language, words are taken out of their proper, literal sense, and for the sake of illustration or impression, are used to denote other things, which are conceived to have some resemblance to what is denoted by the literal sense. It is essential to a metaphor, that there should be, in some respect, a real or apparent resemblance between the *proper* sense of the word, and the *metaphorical*. How, then, are we to interpret the metaphorical language of Scripture, above cited? Does it imply that God himself is really like an angry, fierce, revengeful man, who is impelled by his outrageous passions to inflict pain, and commit acts of violence? Infinitely otherwise. What the Bible makes known respecting God, and all our best conceptions of his character forbid it. *Every divine perfection forbids it.* And common sense forbids it. Nor is it the least objection to the use of this species of metaphor, that the literal sense would be contrary to truth, and would violate the plainest principles of religion. This is the case with respect to some of those metaphors, which are considered most unexceptionable; as when God is called a rock, and when he is said to walk, or ride, or sit. In all such instances, common sense, properly enlightened respecting the nature of the subject, is competent at once to determine the import of the metaphorical language. If a metaphor is taken from an object familiarly known, and is used with any degree of judgment, or taste; we perceive instantly the point of similitude which is intended, and the meaning of the metaphor is perfectly obvious.

We say, then, that the texts above quoted, do not imply, that the *character* of God is in any degree like the character of a man, who is impelled by his angry, malignant passions, to acts of violence. They do not imply that any thing like the feeling of revenge in a man, can ever belong to the God of love. The analogy intended is between the *effects* of anger and revenge in man, and the *effects* of what is called anger and revenge in God. But even here, careful restriction is still necessary. For the evils, which God inflicts upon sinners, spring from *motives* totally different from human anger and revenge. Nor do the effects of the divine displeasure resemble the effects of human anger, as to the *manner* in which they take place. But as to the *certainty* and *dreadfulness* of the effects, there is an obvious resemblance. In order to set forth how fearful and how inevitable is the punishment of the wicked, it is the custom of the inspired writers to resort to the most terrific objects in nature. To illustrate the dreadfulness of the displeasure of God against sinners, they point us to a man, whose anger is fierce, and consumes all before it; and, to make the illustration still more impressive, they point us to a raging bear bereaved of her whelps. So terrible are the effects of the divine displeasure.

If we have taken a correct view of the metaphors above cited, we are prepared to understand the representations of Scripture on the other part of the subject. When God is spoken of as turning or being turned from the fierceness of his anger, or causing his anger to cease; the sense must obviously be, that the dreadful *effects* of his righteous displeasure are prevented, or removed. A man whose anger abates, and whose mind becomes tranquil, ceases to inflict evil. It is with a view to this, that, when the effects of God's holy displeasure are prevented, or removed, he is said to turn or be turned from his anger; and, if those effects were very dreadful, from the fierceness of his anger. And on the same ground, if any being in heaven or earth, should do any thing, which, according to the principles of the divine government, would have an influence to prevent or remove the evils, that would otherwise result from the displeasure of God; that being might be said to turn God from his anger, or render him merciful; and if the evils, thus prevented or removed, were great and dreadful, he might, by a still bolder figure, be said to "quench the wrath of God, and awaken his kindness towards men."

Now as this kind of metaphor is so abundantly used in the Scripture, why may it not be used by those, who make the Scripture their pattern and guide? And when, in conformity to their perfect pattern, they do use it, why should they not be understood, as using it in the same manner with those inspired writers, from whom they borrow it? Why should not the same principles of common sense, and candor, and good taste be applied to the interpretation of it in the one case, as in the other? If this were done, no objection could remain in the minds of Unitarians, certainly not in the mind of the Author of this Sermon, against the language of Orthodox writers, respecting the influence of the Atonement. For he says, that many Unitarians, clearly meaning to include himself, "think that the Scriptures ascribe the remission of sins to Christ's death, with an emphasis so peculiar, that we ought to consider this event as having a special influence in removing punishment, as a condition or method of pardon, without which, repentance would not avail us, at least to that extent which is now promised by the gospel." I am glad to find this development of scriptural views; although there is a sinking phrase at the close of the sentence, which the Apostle Paul would never have written. It is then admitted as a fact, and certainly it must be regarded as a fact of vast moment, " that the death of Christ has a special influence in removing punishment;" that it is an indispensable condition of pardon, and the only consistent method, in which salvation can be granted. This important fact is described by Orthodox writers in various ways. It is the representation of some, particularly of those, whose ardent temperament, or vivid fancy, makes them fond of glowing imagery, that the death of Christ quenched his Father's wrath, caused him to lay aside his thunder, and to look upon sinners with a smiling face; that it turned a throne of fiery vengeance into a throne of mercy, &c. In such metaphorical language as this, the just punishment of sin is likened to the effect of human wrath, of thunder, and of irresistible power in a king, who rises, in frowning majesty, to inflict condign punishment upon rebels; and the language teaches, that the punishment of sin, illustrated by such images, is prevented or removed by the mediation of Christ. The language, taken literally, would impute a character to God, which would excite universal horror. But if understood according to the legitimate principles of interpreting metaphors, it teaches the simple, but allimportant truth, that the death of Christ was the means of procuring pardon, or the medium, through which salvation is granted.

Another representation which is frequently made, and which is borrowed from Scripture, is, that Christ *bought* us, or *redeemed* us from destruction by the price of his own blood. This figure is drawn from the practice of redeeming captives from bondage, by paying a price. The similitude, when exactly expressed, is this; as captives or slaves are released from bondage and restored to liberty, by the payment of a satisfactory price; so sinners are delivered from just punishment, and made heirs of heaven, by the atonement of Christ. Sometimes this same thing is spoken of by Orthodox writers, as the payment of a debt. This figure is also derived from Scripture, which represents us, as God's debtors.

Matt, vi. 12. "Forgive us our debts." Spiritual concerns are familiarly represented in the parables of Christ, by what takes place between debtors and creditors. As sinners we deserve punishment; that is, we owe it to the righteous Governor of the world, to suffer evil in proportion to our sins. When Christ is said to pay our debt, it is signified simply, that by means of his sufferings, he delivers us from punishment. This similitude does not relate particularly to the mode of deliverance, nor to the nature of the evil which is escaped, nor to the nature of the good secured; but merely to *the fact* of his procuring deliverance by means of his death. As the debtor, who has nothing to pay, and is confined to prison, is freed from imprisonment by the generosity of a friend, who steps forward in his name, and pays his debt; so sinners are freed from punishment by the kindness of the Savior, who interposed and shed his blood for them.

It is said, that Christ redeemed us from the curse of the law, by being made a curse for us. The law denounced a punishment. This was its curse. Christ delivers us from that punishment, by being made a curse; that is, by suffering an evil, which, so far as the ends of the divine government are concerned, was equivalent to the execution of the curse of the law upon transgressors.

When Christ is said to have *satisfied divine justice*, or the demands of justice, the sense is the same. In civil governments, if justice is satisfied; in other words, if that is done which perfectly answers the ends of justice; there is no further necessity of punishment. So, when Christ has done and suffered that which answers the ends of justice in the divine government, the necessity of punishment, so far as those ends are concerned, is superseded. And if any of us should say, that *our sin was imputed* to Christ, our meaning must be, that Christ suf fered on account of our sin,—suffered, in some sense, as he would have suffered, if our sin had been imputed to him; though a real imputation of our sin to Christ, in a *literal* sense, would have been a palpable inconsistency in a government founded in justice and truth.

I might mention other forms of figurative language, which have been employed by respectable divines, to set forth the design and influence of Christ's death; and might say respecting them all, that if they were interpreted according to the same principles, which govern us in the interpretation of the metaphorical language of Scripture, a very satisfactory sense might be given to them, so that no difficulty would remain. I would therefore appeal to all those, who have duly considered the nature and just interpretation of metaphors, whether it is a mark of judgment, or good taste, to overlook the metaphorical sense of the phraseology now under consideration, and to persist in treating it, as though it could have no other than a literal sense. Against the literal sense, there are indeed many objections. And there are as many against the literal sense of the texts of Scripture, above recited. But against that metaphorical sense, which I have suggested, there are no objections in either case.

But respecting these metaphors, I have two additional remarks. The first is, that some men, who profess to hold the general principles of Orthodoxy, have evidently been led into error by mixing a degree of the literal sense with the metaphorical. Though they seem to interpret the phrases referred to, as figurative; it is soon made apparent by their reasoning, that they still retain some impression of the literal sense. To this I think we can trace the notion, that, if Christ has made a perfect atonement, and satisfied divine justice, those, for whom he has done this, are no longer under the same obligation to obey the law, and punishing them for their sins would no longer be just. This would indeed follow from understanding some of the representations of Scripture, and of Orthodox writers, in a literal sense. For if Christ paid our debt, or the price of our redemption *literally*, i. e. just as a friend discharges the obligation of an insolvent debtor, or purchases the freedom of a slave by the payment of money; it would certainly be an unrighteous thing for us to be held to pay our own debt, or to suffer the evils of servitude.

To the same cause I am disposed to ascribe it, that so many men have thought the doctrine of the atonement, or of salvation through the blood of Christ, unfavorable to the cause of morality. If the atonement be literally and exactly like the payment of what is due from an insolvent debtor; if it have such an effect, as to release the sinner from his obligation to render obedience to the law,—such an effect as to take away or diminish his ill-desert, or to make it less just in God to punish; the doctrine would indeed be unfavorable to morality. But we deny that the atonement has any such analogy, as is here implied, to pecuniary transactions; and we deny that the metaphorical language, which is taken from those transactions to illustrate the subject, indicates any such analogy. The atonement, as a means, and we believe the only consistent means, does indeed deliver sinners from punishment. But its influence is such, and operates in such a way, that the righteous authority of the law is confirmed, and that the undiminished obligations of sinners to obedience, their ill-desert, and the justice of their punishment are all set in the clearest light.

Another hurtful notion, which seems to spring from the same source, that is, from attaching something of a literal sense to figurative language, is, that

God's requiring perfect satisfaction to his justice in order to the forgiveness of sin, or his determination not to save sinners, unless their debt is fully discharged by another, shows less benevolence, than if he should forgive and save by his own unpurchased goodness, without any satisfaction rendered by another. This notion often lurks in the minds of those who believe the doctrine of atonement, but whose faith is mixed with obscurity of knowledge, and easily perplexed with difficulties. By those who reject the doctrine of atonement, the same thing is urged, as an objection against it. They contend, that the doctrine represents God to be mercenary, selfish, inexorable; and so makes his character much less amiable, than if he should forgive his disobedient but penitent children, by free mercy, without requiring any satisfaction from another. "How plain is it, according to this doctrine," says the Author of the Sermon before us, "that God, instead of being plenteous in forgiveness, never forgives; for it is absurd to speak of men as forgiven, when their whole punishment is borne by a substitute." Unitarians have often made the same allegation against our doctrine. Now this would be a real difficulty, and might be urged conclusively against the doctrine, if the language, employed in describing the atonement, were to be taken literally. For surely a rich creditor, who imprisons a poor insolvent debtor, and refuses to release him, till every farthing is paid by him or by his surety, shows much less kindness and generosity, than if he should give up the debt and release the poor debtor *freely*. And a father, who deals out to an offending child the full measure of justice, and withholds every token of paternal kindness, till he receives the most perfect satisfaction, exhibits a much less amiable character, than if, from the ardent love of his heart, he should be inclined to hail the first opportunity of showing favor to his child; to meet him, while yet a great way off, and, on seeing marks of penitence, to embrace him, to cover his faults, and load him with kindness. But here the analogy fails. For God's refusing to forgive without satisfaction, is an exercise of his infinite goodness, as the guardian of his kingdom. His requiring full satisfaction to his justice, or a full atonement for sin, and his appointing that such an atonement should be made, resulted wholly from benevolence. "God so *loved* the world, that *he gave his only begotten Son.*" It shows higher love for God to save in this way, than if he should save without an atonement, by an act of unpurchased mercy; which is only saying, that it shows greater benevolence in God, as moral governor, to save sinners in a way, which will vindicate the honors of his violated law, and secure from injury the interests of his kingdom, than in a way, which would expose his law to contempt, and the interests of his kingdom to injury. And this view of the subject, I think, must be obvious to every enlightened christian, who is disentangled from the literal sense of metaphorical language, and who attends to the whole account, which the Bible gives, of the love which God has exercised, and the measures he has pursued, in the salvation of men.

It would lead me beyond my intention, to point out all those errors, which may be traced to the habit of giving something of a literal sense to the metaphorical language of the Holy Scriptures, and of other writings, on the subject of the atonement. Having suggested instances of this, sufficient to excite proper attention to the subject, I shall proceed to my second remark; namely; *when there is an evident tendency in the minds of men to understand any part of the metaphorical language, which has commonly been used respecting the atonement, in a literal sense, and when we perceive that this occasions hurtful misapprehensions; it is the dictate of christian wisdom, to be sparing in the use of such language, and, when used, to guard it with some special care against its liability to be understood literally.* This caution I think should be applied to the language, which illustrates the atonement by pecuniary transactions, as the payment of a debt, which a poor man owes; cancelling his obligations; or purchasing his release from imprisonment. Nor should I think it the part of wisdom, at this day, and on this subject, to make a very copious use even of those Scripture metaphors, which represent God as having the passion of anger, or wrath, and the atonement as the means of quenching it, or turning him from it. An abundance of this species of metaphor is not expedient, because it is not so consentaneous to the genius of our language, as to that of the Hebrew; and especially, because the endless controversies, and extravagant fancies, which have prevailed in the world, have perplexed the minds of men, and exposed them to erroneous impressions on this subject. The object of language is to communicate useful truths to others. If it comes to be the case with any particular words or phrases, that they do not in fact communicate such truths, though the words or phrases may be proper in themselves, and even though they may be authorised by Scripture; it becomes expedient to explain them clearly, or to adopt new ones.

Socinian writers seem to suppose, that we overlook those numerous texts, which, without any reference to the death of Christ, declare the free mercy of God towards penitent sinners, Here I think it easy, by a few connected remarks, to remove all misapprehension, and to present the subject in a light which cannot fail to be satisfactory.

The doctrine now before us, divides itself into two parts; first, the *simple fact, that God is merciful*, and *will forgive* penitent sinners; *second*, the particular *way* or *method* of forgiveness. These two things are perfectly distinct in their nature, and may, if God pleases, be subjects of distinct revelations. He may, if he sees it to be best, reveal to mankind, at one period of time, or in one part of his word, the *simple fact* of his mercy, or his readiness to forgive the penitent, without giving at that time, or in that part of Scripture, the least intimation of any medium, through which his mercy flows. And it is clear, that the knowledge of this *simple fact*, without any other information, would be of vast importance. Now this *simple fact*, so important to guilty men, is made known in a great multitude of texts, both in the Old Testament and the New, where nothing is said of the *method*, in which mercy is exercised. If this had been the case universally, and God had nowhere revealed any thing, but simply that he would forgive the penitent; our faith must have been confined to that simple truth. As to the *way*, or *method*, in which the divine forgiveness would be exercised, we should know nothing, except that it must be a way consistent with the perfections of God, and the safety of his moral government. I grant, that our faith, even if thus limited, might be a powerful principle of action, and an inexhaustible source of comfort. And in such a case, it would certainly be our duty to check the impatience of a prying curiosity, and to wait quietly, till God should see fit to give more light. But he has given more light. He has taught us, by a revelation, additional to what I have just supposed, that his mercy, which is so often declared in the Scriptures, is exercised towards penitent sinners, *through the blood of Christ;* that forgiveness comes in this way, and in no other. Thus our faith is extended, just in proportion to the greater extent of the revelation.

With regard to this last point, it is the opinion of some writers, who admit the doctrine of the Atonement, that nothing is revealed, but the single truth, that forgiveness comes through the mediation of Christ; and that we are wholly incapable of knowing what particular bearing the death of Christ has upon the moral government of God, or *how* it secures mercy to penitent sinners. But careful attention to a few texts of Scripture must, I think, lead to a different conclusion. I shall name only two. Gal. iii. 13. "Christ hath redeemed us from the curse of the law, being made a curse for us." The text, and what immediately precedes it, clearly teach, that men, as transgressors, are under the curse of the law, which they have transgressed; that Christ delivered them from that curse, that is, from the evil, which the law denounced against them for sin; and that he did it, *by being made a curse for them.* A literal and exact substitution was impossible. But the Apostle's language must signify, that the curse, which Christ was made, or the evil he endured, had respect to the same law, from whose curse sinners were redeemed. It had respect to the same law; not that it was literally and exactly the penalty of the law, or the punishment which the law threatened against sinners; but it had such a relation to the law, and such an influence upon it, that sinners, on account of it, might be consistently released from its curse; whereas, had not Christ been made a curse for them, that is, suffered and died for them, they themselves must have endured the curse. Thus, although the curse of the law, falling on Christ, is, in various respects, different from what it would be, if it should fall upon sinners; yet, in relation to the ends of the law, or of the divine administration, it is substantially the same. And as those benevolent ends are secured, by the curse falling upon Christ; it becomes consistent with the order of God's kingdom, for penitent sinners to be delivered from the curse.

The other passage I shall quote is Rom. iii. 24, 25, 26. "Being justified freely by his grace, through the redemption that is in Jesus Christ: Whom God hath set forth *to be* a propitiation through faith in his blood, to declare his righteousness for the remission of sins that are past, through the forbearance of God; To declare, *I say*, at this time his righteousness; that he might be just, and the justifier of him which believeth in Jesus." Here the immediate object of Christ's being set forth is represented to be, to *declare, or make known the righteousness of God*. Notwithstanding the authority of Schleusner and Rosenmuller, I am clearly of opinion, with most Commentators and Divines, that δικαιοσυνη, in this place, has its primary and common sense, and signifies that attribute of God, which leads him, as moral Governor of the world, to render to every man according to his deeds, and of course to inflict the curse of the law on sinners. The object of the death of Christ is then, to declare, or manifest, that God is righteous, and that in the salvation of sinners he will support the honors of his law, and " the interests of virtue."

In contemplating this subject, I ask myself, what hinderance there is in the way of God's showing the same favor to transgressors, as to the obedient. The answer is obvious. His law, and his character, as Lawgiver, forbid it, and the interests of his moral kingdom forbid it. If, in the common course of his administration, he should show the same favor to transgressors, as to the obedient, he would set aside the authority of his law, and leave no visible distinction between virtue and vice. Any ruler, who should proceed in this way, would soon bring to an end the order and happiness of his subjects. The expedient, which the wisdom of God has adopted, prevents this consequence of extending favor to transgressors. The cross of Christ makes known the righteousness or justice of God, as moral Governor. It shows that he does make, and will forever make a distinction between holiness and sin. It has such an influence upon his moral administration, that he can be just, and the justifier of him that believeth; that is, can forgive sin without degrading the majesty, or surrendering the claims of justice. To express the same in other words; the influence of the atonement is such, that it has become consistent with justice to do, what would otherwise have been totally inconsistent. It is in this way I come to a similar conclusion with the author of the Sermon; namely; that Christ's death, " has an inseparable connexion with forgiveness, that it has a special influence in removing punishment, as a condition or method of pardon, without which repentance would not avail us."

Correspondent with this is the practical view which devout Christians generally take of this subject. When they behold Jesus, who was holy, harmless, and undefiled, suffering and dying for sinners, they see the honors of God's righteousness vindicated, and the principles of his moral government established. They consider what ends are accomplished in the divine administration by the just punishment of transgressors. All these ends they see accomplished, in the highest degree, by the death of Christ. And thus it becomes clear, that God can forbear to punish penitent transgressors, on account of Christ's death, without any injury to his moral government, or any sacrifice of the interests of virtue.

Against our scheme, Unitarians urge one particular objection, which may deserve a few moments' special notice. The objection in short is, that the Trinitarian scheme lowers down the value of Christ's sacrifice, and "robs his death of interest." The alleged ground of this objection is, that we believe Christ to be God and man, united in one person, and that, as divinity could not be the subject of pain, the *sufferer* must have been merely a man.

This objection entirely overlooks an important article in our system. We believe, that all the divine and human perfections, which the Scriptures ascribe to Christ, constitute but *one person;* and consequently that all his actions and sufferings belong to him, *as* one person; much as all the actions and sufferings of any man, whether mental or corporeal, belong to him, as one man. It results from this view of the subject, that the value or significancy of any action or suffering in Christ must be according to the dignity or excellence of his whole character. Whether the action or suffering takes place particularly in one part or another of his complex person, it is attributable to his whole person; and it derives its peculiar character from the character of his whole person, constituted as it is. The suffering of Christ was therefore of as high importance or value, in making an atonement, as if it could have been, and in reality had been, in the most proper sense, the suffering of the Divinity. So that whatever may be the conceptions of Arians or Socinians, as *we* view the subject, the fact that Christ endured suffering in his human nature, and not directly in his divine, occasions no difficulty as to the preciousness, which we ascribe to his atonement. And I think the views of the Orthodox in this case are capable of being defended in the most satisfactory manner.

The rejection of the doctrine of the Atonement, with which some, who call themselves Christians, are chargeable, is not to be regarded merely as a speculative error. It plainly indicates the disposition of the heart. For, after God has sent his Son to be a propitiation, and has told us, that we must rely upon his atoning blood, as the sole ground of forgiveness; if we disregard that provision, and hope for heaven on the footing of our own virtue or good works, we give proof of a temper of mind, which is in total contrariety to the humble spirit of christian faith. We signify that we think ourselves entitled to future happiness, on our own account, and that we have no need of the merit or intercession of another to recommend us to the favor of God. Some Socinians boldly use language like this. They have the audacity to bring forward a personal claim upon the favor of God. The same spirit appears in all, who rest their hopes of heaven on their own goodness. Although God has provided a perfect righteousness, as the foundation of their hope; and has taught them, that the salvation of sinners depends wholly on Christ crucified, and that no works of righteousness, which they have done, and no accomplishments or dispositions, which they possess, must ever be named in his presence; they still persist in spurning this provision of infinite mercy; in counting as foolishness, the grand plea, with which a Savior's death has furnished them, and in obtruding their own virtue upon his notice, as a better reason for their acceptance, than all the worthiness and all the grace of Christ crucified.

Thus far I have thought it necessary to proceed in order to remove misapprehensions, and to give a just, though brief view of the real sentiments we entertain on this momentous subject. It has, I trust, been made evident that our scheme of faith is far from sullying the glory of God's moral perfections, or impugning the principles of either justice or benevolence. On the contrary, it has for its foundation the immutable perfection of God's moral character, and the inviolable principles of his righteous government. And it is, if we know our own hearts, the strong attachment we feel to his glorious character and government, and our earnest desire, that they may have the honor of a perfect and eternal vindication, which creates in us such an interest in the doctrine of the atonement.

LETTER IX.

My respected friends,

The design I wish to execute in these letters, requires me particularly to bring into view one more doctrine of the Orthodox, namely, the doctrine of *divine influence*. To those, who entertain the same views with us of the character of man, and the nature and necessity of holiness, this doctrine must appear of the highest worth. But here, as in former cases, instead of giving a regular treatise on the subject, it is my intention to correct mistakes, to expose the weakness of objections, to solve difficulties, and to do all I can to induce those, who have rejected, or half believed this doctrine, to inquire with a candid, unprejudiced mind, into its truth and importance.

It has been the general representation of Unitarians, that we believe there is an invincible, overpowering, irresistible influence of the divine spirit on the minds of men, which is totally repugnant to their moral agency and accountability, and which makes them entirely passive,—mere machines.

In order that you may be under advantages to judge, whether this representation is just; I shall here offer you a brief statement of our doctrine, with the leading topics of argument, which we urge in its support, and the explanations we are accustomed to give it in relation to other obvious truths.

Our doctrine of divine influence results, as we conceive, from the nature and condition of created beings, who are and must be dependent on their Creator and Preserver. This necessary dependence of an intelligent creature, relates to the acts of the mind, as well as to outward circumstances. But we infer the doctrine more directly from the fact, that men are universally sinners; that their moral nature is the subject of a most woful disorder. We think it the dictate of sound experience, that men will not in fact cast off the dominion of their corrupt affections, and render to God the homage of a sincere obedience, without special divine aid.

But the argument, on which we rest without any wavering, is the testimony of the sure word of God. I need not give the proof in detail. They who attentively peruse the Scriptures, will not fail to perceive, that this doctrine is there taught with great clearness, and in a great variety of forms. If God, by his spirit, produces no good affections in our hearts; if he vouchsafes no spiritual illumination; if he does nothing to cleanse us from sin, and form us to holiness; what can be the import of those texts, which teach, that God works in his people both to will and to do; that he creates in them a new heart & a new spirit; that he opens their eyes, draws them, turns, renews, strengthens them, and helps their infirmities? And what can be the meaning of the language, which christians universally use in prayer, when they ask God to subdue their sins, to purify their hearts, and to work in them all the good pleasure of his goodness; and when they ascribe to God all the good they possess? We understand the language of Scripture on this subject in its most obvious sense; and on this obvious sense we found our belief, that all virtue or holiness in man is to be ascribed to the influence of the divine spirit, and that without the effectual agency of the Spirit, man would have no holy affections, and perform no acts of holy obedience. This is a general statement of the orthodox doctrine.

But we do not stop here. The doctrine has relations to other subjects,—relations which are of great moment. We are sensible we cannot do justice to the doctrine, without attending to those relations, and giving the consideration of them a proper influence in regulating our conceptions of the doctrine.

This doctrine has a relation, first, to the attributes of God. In view of this relation, we say, the influence, which God exerts in or upon his creatures, is such as agrees with his infinite perfections,—such as results from them, and is suited to make a just exhibition of them. It is prompted by divine benevolence, as the influence is to accomplish a good end. It is regulated by divine wisdom, which renders it perfectly suited to accomplish that end. Secondly, the doctrine of divine influence has an immediate relation to the human mind. In view of this relation, we say, that the divine influence is adapted to the nature of the mind; that the Holy Spirit operates in such a manner, as to offer no violence to any of the principles of an intelligent and moral nature; that it always produces its effects in the understanding, according to the essential properties and laws, which belong to the understanding, and in the will and affections, without interfering with any of the properties and laws, which belong to them. We consider this peculiar agency of the divine Spirit in producing and continuing holiness in men to be just as consistent with every thing, which belongs to an intelligent and moral nature, as the general agency of God in preserving and governing his rational creatures. Nor do we apprehend, that there is any thing more incompatible with the nature, and properties of the mind, in the influence, which *God* exerts upon it, than in the influence which *we* exert upon it. It is a matter of fact, that we have an influence, often a controlling influence, over the understanding and will of our fellow creatures. The influence which others have upon us, be it ever so great and effectual, may operate, as we certainly know, in a way perfectly correspondent with our moral nature. We are so constituted, that we may be influenced by others to do good, in consistency with our own freedom, and virtue, and praiseworthiness; that is, we are none the less voluntary in doing good, and none the less deserving of approbation, because we are induced to do it by the rational, moral influence, which others exert upon our minds. I pretend not that the two cases are exactly parallel. But it is natural to suppose, that the divine influence is, at least, as consistent with our free agency and accountableness, as any human influence can be. For surely God, who made us, can have access to our understanding and heart, and produce any effects there, which he pleases; and surely he must know how to do this, without infringing any of the principles of our intelligent or moral nature. This, in our view, cannot be denied, without implicitly denying the dependence of moral beings on God, and taking away his power to control their actions, and to execute the plan of his own government. For if any man maintains that the special operation of the Holy Spirit, is incompatible with the moral freedom of man; how can he consistently maintain that agency of God in his providence, which is denied by none, but Atheists? And who that admits the Bible to contain truth unmixed with error, can doubt the constant agency of God in every part of the creation, and especially in the souls of his redeemed people?

It is in the manner above mentioned, that we explain the doctrine of divine influence. It has been explained substantially in this manner, from time immemorial. These relations of the subject to the moral government of God, and to the moral agency of man, and the qualifications which necessarily arise from them, have been insisted upon with no ordinary zeal, by the Orthodox Divines in New England. We assert neither the special agency of God in the kingdom of his grace, nor the common agency of God in his providence, without asserting or implying that the agency is such, as secures to man the unimpaired exercise of all his rational and moral powers, —such as preserves his moral freedom entire. We treat the whole subject in such a way, as evinces to every man of reflection, that we understand it with these qualifications. We speak of man, as being in the highest sense *active* in repenting, believing, and obeying. We represent repentance, and obedience, as his duty, and labor to persuade him to perform them. We urge motives to influence him, as a moral agent; we present to him the rewards of obedience, and the punishment of disobedience; we exhort and reprove him, and in all respects treat him in such a manner, as shows, that we believe the doctrine of man's moral agency, as firmly, as we believe that of the divine influence.

If our opponents can prove, that our views of the divine influence certainly lead to the denial of man's freedom and accountableness, as a moral agent, they may justly charge us with holding principles, from which such consequences do in fact follow; though they cannot charge us with holding those consequences.—But why should our views be considered as involving such consequences? Is it because we assert the divine influence to be *powerful and effectual*? But how does it appear, that an influence upon the mind, which is perfectly suited to its nature, and its faculties, has any more tendency to make man a machine, or to destroy his agency, when it is powerful enough effectually to accomplish its design, than when it fails of accomplishing it? Is it so with us? When we exert a powerful and effectual influence over a person, persuading him to relinquish some sinful indulgence, to which he was addicted, or to perform some virtuous action, to which he had a strong reluctance; do we, on that account, look upon him, as any the less a free moral agent? Do we regard that determination of his mind, and that conduct, to which we persuaded him, as having no virtue, because he was led to it by our persuasive influence? Even if he should tell us, what is often a matter of fact, that the influence of our arguments was *overpowering, and irresistible;* we should consider this as a proof, not of the loss of his free agency, but of the strength of our arguments; and we should regard his ready submission to such arguments, as evidence of a sound understanding, and of a commendable disposition.

The mode, in which we exert our influence, is indeed widely different from that, in which the divine influence is exerted. But the consideration of this difference will furnish a new argument in favor of our doctrine. For surely he who made intelligent creatures, and who unerringly knows the powers and properties of the mind he gave them, and all its laws of action, must be able to adapt his influence to the nature of their mind more perfectly, than we can. These brief remarks are sufficient to show, how utterly they misconceive the subject, who think, as many seem to do, that the agency of God can extend only so far, can rise only to such a degree of efficacy, without interfering with the agency of man. The fact is, that the highest point of energy, to which the divine agency, thus exerted, can rise, interferes not in the least with the proper exercise of our rational and moral powers. The whole design and tendency of the influence, which the Holy Spirit exerts over us, is to unshackle the mind from corrupt passion and prejudice, and, instead of encumbering and destroying moral agency, to conform its free exercises to the rules of virtue, and so to improve and elevate all the moral faculties.

I ask again; is it supposed that the divine influence, which we assert, is incompatible with moral agency, because God exerts it upon us in a way so different from that, in which we exert our influence; that is, without the use of language, or any outward signs; or because we do not perceive its operation upon us, as distinct from the acts of our own minds? To this I would reply; that the invisibleness of the divine influence no more proves that it is not real and efficacious, than the invisibleness of the Creator, or the act of creative power, proves that the Creator does not exist, or that his creative power was never exerted. Could we stand, as spectators, to witness the creation of a world; we should only see the *effect produced*. The cause would be *invisible*. But would this occasion any doubt, as to the *reality* of that cause?—As to the use of language and other outward signs; it shows our imperfection, that we can have access to the mind in no other way. The direct access, which our Creator has to the mind, is, in all respects superior to what we are capable of, and of course *his* influence, whatever might be said of *ours*, can never be supposed in the smallest degree to infringe moral agency.

But though we allow ourselves in the unfettered use of reason on this momentous subject, our ultimate reliance is on the oracles of truth. The inspired writers speak of the influence of the Spirit, as being in the highest degree *powerful* and *efficacious*, without the least appearance of apprehending that it is incompatible with human activity, or that there is any occasion to defend the doctrine against the objection above stated. Indeed they view the doctrine in a very different light, and make use of it, as a motive to activity. " Work out your own salvation with fear and trembling; for it is God who worketh in you, both to will and to do." In this practical use of the doctrine, there is the most evident propriety. For what can be a more animating encouragement to a man, who is struggling against the power of moral corruption, and is ready to sink under a sense of his weakness, than the assurance of that divine Spirit, which will help his infirmities, and render his efforts successful? As the end of the Spirit's influence is to subdue sinful affection, and excite that which is holy; the more powerful and efficacious that influence is understood to be, the more encouragement to diligence does the christian derive from it.

The grand difficulty, which attends this subject, seems to arise from the supposition of some analogy between the power of God upon the human heart, and that exercise of power among men, which overcomes or supersedes voluntary agency; in other words, that which shows itself in cases of *coercion* or *force*.

If they who object to our doctrine, as incompatible with man's free agency, will examine their own thoughts carefully, they will find, I think, that their objection arises chiefly from the supposition of this analogy;—that it arises from the habit of comparing the effectual operation of the divine power on the mind and heart, with instances, in which men are constrained by superior force, to do or suffer that, which is against their choice. Such analogy we deny altogether; and we deny every conclusion drawn from it.

I cannot leave this part of the subject, without remarking on the unfairness of our opponents, in going to such an extreme, as they generally do, in giving a construction to the words, *irresistible, overpowering, invincible,* &c. when applied to the divine influence. Although I am by no means fond of a very copious use of such terms; yet I owe it to those who employ them more freely, to say, that these words are in good use, in relation to this general subject, and, all prejudice aside, will bear a sense perfectly unexceptionable. This I say, *first,* from a consideration of *the nature of the case.* Whenever these words are used, they are to be understood *relatively;* and the subject generally shows, to what they relate. If I speak of an irresistible or overpowering *argument,* I speak of it with reference to that, which might be supposed to make resistance, or to that which is to be overcome; i.e. I speak of it with reference to some reason or objection, which has been urged against the point to be proved, but which is now made to appear without force, or yields to an argument of *superior* force. Or the terms may relate to some opposing prejudice or passion, which is now weakened and subdued by the strength of the reasoning, or the persuasiveness of the eloquence, directed against it. In a manner like this, we are always understood, when we speak of an *irresistible* or *overpowering argument*. The terms, in such a case, are never supposed to imply, that the understanding, or the conscience is the thing that is overcome, or subdued; and for the plain reason, that the force of an argument, however great, cannot produce such an effect. In many cases, the direct tendency of the *irresistible* argument is to illuminate and strengthen the moral faculties of the mind, or to subdue that by which they were blinded and weakened. Now who was ever so weak as to imagine, that an *irresistible, overpowering argument* had any tendency to break the mental faculties or to prevent the freedom of their operation in any movement of moral agency? We are accustomed to use these terms freely, and without fear of being misunderstood, in relation to any influence, which a man exercises over the minds and moral actions of others, either by his eloquence, his generosity, or his superior wisdom and piety.

I would have it remembered, that, by this illustration, I mean only to evince, that the words irresistible, unconquerable, &c. when applied by Calvinistic writers to the influence of the Holy Spirit in the hearts of men, are not justly liable to the objection commonly urged against them; because the nature of the case shows, to what they must relate. When we represent the influence of the Holy Spirit in sanctifying the hearts of men, as *irresistible*, or *overpowering*, we speak solely with reference to that, which is supposed to make resistance, or is to be overcome. Now in the divine work of sanctifying the hearts of men, or causing them to love God, is it possible to suppose, that *moral agency* is to be overcome? If their moral agency should in fact be overcome, would that help to make them holy? And can any think that we mean to assert this? The thing to be overcome by the divine influence, is sinful inclination, corrupt affection. Men naturally love the creature more than the Creator. They are earthly in their desires, and have a disrelish for divine things. This is their disorder,—the disease of their souls. The influence of the Spirit bears upon this moral disease. When we say, that influence is *irresistible*, and *overpowering*, our meaning is, that this disease of the soul, though very powerful and stubborn, is made to yield to the merciful agency of the divine Physician;—that the remedy becomes *effectual*. The question really is, whether the *successful* operation of the divine Spirit,—in other words, whether the *efficaciousness* of the remedy, applied to the spiritual disorder of man, is destructive of his moral agency? There is, in my view, just as much reason to ask, whether the efficaciousness of the remedy, which is applied for the cure of a *fever*, is destructive of moral agency. I take it as an admission of all, who call themselves Christians, that the moral disease of man is *capable* of a *cure*, and that it is most desirable, that it should be cured. If it is cured, it must be by a remedy suited to the nature of the disorder. What the nature of the disorder is, God perfectly knows; and is perfectly able to apply a *suitable* and *efficacious* remedy. Now when this almighty Physician kindly undertakes the cure of our souls, the obstinacy of the disorder yields; its resistance is taken away; that is to say, the heart is effectually cleansed from its pollution; love of sin, enmity to God, pride, ingratitude, and selfish, earthly desires are *subdued*, and man is induced to love God, and obey his commands. In other words, the sinner is so influenced by the Spirit of God, that he *freely* forsakes his sins, and, with all readiness of mind, devotes himself to the service of

Christ. And this is the same as saying, that, instead of exercising his moral agency *wrong*, he now exercises it *right*. The nature of the case shows, that this is and must be the meaning of the words under consideration, when applied by intelligent Christians to the influence of the Holy Spirit. I say therefore, that they will bear a sense perfectly unexceptionable; and that this is the sense, which naturally occurs, and which, for this very reason, every man is obliged, by the rules of candor and sound criticism, to put upon them.

I have a second reason for thinking that those, who use the terms under consideration, mean to use them in a sense, which does not infringe moral agency; and that is, that they uniformly speak of man, even when he is supposed to be the subject of that very irresistible influence, as exercising an unimpaired freedom, and agency; as *choosing* holiness, *refusing* sin, *loving* God, *obeying* the gospel. These are certainly acts of a free, moral, accountable creature, and, as clearly as any thing, can show the properties of a *moral agent*. The plain meaning of those, who speak of the influence of the Spirit, as irresistible, or overpowering, must therefore be, that the divine influence not only is *consistent* with moral agency, but actually produces, as its proper effect, the free exercise of moral agency, in all those modes of it, which are required by the commands of God.

Now considering that the terms, which have been thus freely examined, are commonly used in cases somewhat similar to that of the divine influence, without ever being supposed to imply any thing repugnant to the most perfect moral agency; considering also, that, when they are used in reference to that influence, the nature of the subject shows to what they must relate, and in what sense they must be taken; and considering, finally, that those, who use them, make it perfectly manifest by other language respecting the same subject, that they mean nothing, which can interfere with any of the principles of moral action; I appeal to you, my respected readers, whether the outcry, which has been made against what is called the *resistless, overpowering* influence of the Holy Ghost in the conversion of sinners, is consistent with candor, or with justice? I have long been convinced, that there is a palpable unfairness and violence in the treatment, which the Orthodox have received on this subject. If, in describing the gracious influence of the Holy Spirit, any of us use language, that is strong and impressive,—language which points to the power and obstinacy of the evil to be overcome, and to the certain efficaciousness of the remedy applied; our opposers labor to put upon that language the most unfavorable construction possible. Instead of kindly and fairly inquiring whether our words will admit of an unexceptionable meaning, and whether that unexceptionable meaning is the one which we aim to express; do they not, in many instances, make it their object to find out, if possible, some meaning, which shall be marked with absurdity, and which shall, at any rate, expose to contempt the sentiment they wish to confute? This is a heavier allegation than I am fond of bringing against any respectable men. But I cheerfully leave it to others to decide, whether the attempts which have frequently been made to decry this most precious doctrine of the effectual operation of the Holy Spirit in renewing and sanctifying the hearts of sinners, together with the want of candor, the heat of feeling, and the vehemence of expression, which have been exhibited by at least some of our opposers, do, or do not prove the allegation just.

I cannot close this letter without expressing my astonishment, that any who profess to be Christians, should set themselves against the doctrine of the divine influence. For if we see a moral disorder in ourselves, which we wish to be subdued; it would be reasonable to suppose, that we should set a high price upon any thing, which would assist us in subduing it. And if the word of God reveals a divine agent, whose almighty energy effectually subdues the power of sin; those who have any right feelings, must prize this, as a most precious discovery. They must seek this heavenly influence, as the most important blessing, earnestly desiring, that it may be exerted upon their hearts. The greater its energy, the more highly do they value it. Instead of feeling any objection against the notion of its being *irresistible* and *overpowering*, they most sincerely pray that it may be so. They know it is directed to the one grand work of subduing sin, of purifying the heart, and guiding into the truth. They wish this work to be done effectually. Every thing in them, which makes resistance, they wish may be overcome. Their prayer is, " let the influence of the Holy Spirit be too powerful to be resisted. Our own efforts must be unavailing, unless aided from above. May God work effectually in us both to will and to do. We crave the operation of that efficacious, invincible power, which will subdue every corrupt affection, and sanctify us throughout in body, soul and spirit."—Such must be the cordial prayer of every one, who knows himself, and has a desire to be like the blessed Jesus. And I am constrained again to express my astonishment, that any can be found, who calumniate or despise that doctrine of divine influence, which is one of the most distinguishing and most attractive features of the Christian religion.

LETTER X.

My respected friends,

In the foregoing letters, I have endeavored to arrange my remarks on the principal doctrines embraced by the Orthodox, with as much regard to order and connexion, as possible. In consequence of this, I find I have omitted several passages in the Sermon before me, to which particular attention seemed to be due. It has not been my object to animadvert on every sentence, which I might deem exceptionable. But there are in the Sermon a few passages of a general character, which I have not yet brought into view, but which cannot justly be suffered to pass unnoticed. To these I would now for a short time invite your attention.

I have already remarked on what I consider a palpable instance of injustice in many Unitarian writers; namely; that they represent certain opinions to be peculiarly and exclusively theirs, when in reality they are embraced and inculcated by the Orthodox. The Sermon furnishes some examples of this, in respect to the mediation of Christ, besides what I have before noticed. The author, in pursuance of his general design, gives a summary account of the views, which he and his brethren entertain on this subject, and which, according to his representation, distinguish Unitarians from the Orthodox. But with respect to these views *substantially*,—I must say, they form no such distinction. If Unitarians hold them, there is, thus far, no controversy between them and us. And the agreement of the two parties in these views, should have been asserted; just as we assert that they are agreed in believing the existence of a God, and the doctrine of a resurrection. So that if, by professing these views, the Author gets any credit to himself and his brethren, exclusively of the Orthodox, he gets it unfairly.

The principal of these views respecting the mediation of Christ, I shall now quote from the Sermon; and as I wish to make all convenient despatch, I shall take the liberty at the same time to repeat them, as belonging to myself and my brethren.

"We believe, that Christ was sent by the Father to effect a moral, or spiritual deliverance of mankind; that is, to rescue men from sin and its consequences, and to bring them to a state of everlasting purity and happiness. We believe, too, that he accomplishes this sublime purpose by a variety of methods; by his instructions respecting God's unity, parental character, and moral government, which are admirably fitted to reclaim the world from idolatry, and impiety, to the knowledge, love, and obedience of the Creator; by his promises of pardon to the penitent, and of divine assistance to those, who labour for progress in moral excellence: by the light which he has thrown on the path of duty; by his own spotless example, in which the loveliness and sublimity of virtue shine forth to warm and quicken, as well as guide us to perfection: by his threatenings against incorrigible guilt; by his glorious discoveries of immortality; by his sufferings and death; by that signal event, the resurrection, which powerfully bore witness to his divine mission, and brought down to men's senses a future life; by his continual intercession, which obtains for us spiritual aid and blessings; and by the power with which he is invested of raising the dead, judging the world, and conferring the everlasting rewards, promised to the faithful."——"We believe, that Jesus, instead of making the Father merciful, is sent by the Father's mercy to be our Saviour; that he is nothing to the human race, but what he is by God's appointment; that he communicates nothing but what God empowers him to bestow; that our father in heaven is originally, essentially and eternally placable, and disposed to forgive; and that his unborrowed, underived, and unchangeable love, is the only fountain of what flows to us through his Son. We conceive, that Jesus is dishonoured, not glorified, by as-

cribing to him an influence, which clouds the splendour of divine benevolence."——" Whilst we gratefully acknowledge, that he came to rescue us from punishment, we believe, that he was sent on a still nobler errand, namely, to deliver us from sin itself, and to form us to a sublime and heavenly virtue. We regard him as a Saviour, chiefly as he is the light, physician, and guide of the dark, diseased, and wandering mind. No influence in the universe seems to us so glorious, as that over the character; and no redemption so worthy of thankfulness, as the restoration of the soul to purity. Without this, pardon, were it possible, would be of little value. Why pluck the sinner from hell, if a hell be left to burn in his own breast? Why raise him to heaven, if he remain a stranger to its sanctity and love?"
——" We believe, that faith in this religion, is of no worth, and contributes nothing to salvation, any farther than as it uses these doctrines, precepts, promises, and the whole life, character, sufferings, and triumphs of Jesus, as the means of purifying the mind, and of changing it into the likeness of his celestial excellence."

These views are all ours; and we are happy to express them in the simple, elegant, and forcible language of this Sermon. And we would indulge the hope, that the injustice of representing them as *peculiar* to Unitarians, in distinction from the Orthodox, will not soon be repeated.—We have, indeed, other and higher views, as you may have already perceived, respecting the mediation of Christ; but none incompatible with these. And let me say, it is very evident to us, that those other and higher views, which are peculiar to the Orthodox, respecting the atonement and mediation of Christ, invest all the practical views, above exhibited, with new beauty and force, and render them, in a higher degree, effectual in promoting a devout and holy life.

I now proceed, with increasing surprise, to notice the same species of injustice, respecting *the nature of christian virtue, or holiness.* The injustice, which I now charge against this Sermon, lies in this;—that Orthodox ministers and Christians, especially those in New England, are held up to public view, as rejecting the sentiments here referred to, respecting the nature of holiness, when, in fact, all that is particularly valuable in these sentiments, is insisted upon, and abundantly illustrated by various Orthodox writers, whom we hold in the highest estimation. Those, who are acquainted with the writings of the most respectable Divines in New England, and those who have statedly heard the preaching of Orthodox ministers of the present age, and who know the general sentiments of Orthodox Christians, will have no difficulty in determining, whether impartial justice is here rendered us. I speak in the name of my brethren generally. Do not *we* believe, as well as Unitarians, " that the moral faculties of man are the grounds of responsibility, and the highest distinctions of our nature, and that no act is praiseworthy, any farther than it springs from their exertion?" When we speak of the influence of God's Spirit on the mind of man, do not we, as well as Unitarians, " mean a moral, illuminating, and persuasive influence, not physical, not compulsory?" Do not we, as well as they, " give the first place among the virtues, to *the love of God?*" Do not we believe, " that this principle is the true end and happiness of our being; that we were made for union with our Creator; that his infinite perfection is the only sufficient object and true resting place for the insatiable desires and unlimited capacities of the human mind;—that the love of God is not only essential to happiness, but to the strength and perfection of all the virtues; that conscience, without the sanction of God's authority and retributive justice, would be a weak director; that benevolence, unless nourished by communion with his goodness,——could not thrive amidst the selfishness and thanklessness of the world;

———and that God—is the life, motive and sustainer of virtue in the human soul?"

Do not we believe, as well as this Author and his brethren, "that great care is necessary to distinguish the love of God from its counterfeits?" Do not we "think that much, which is called piety, is worthless?" Should not we be as ready, as they are, to say, that, "if religion be the shipwreck of the understanding, we cannot keep too far from it;"—and "to maintain that fanaticism, partial insanity,—and ungovernable transports, are any thing rather than piety?" Is it not as favorite an opinion with us, as with them, "that the true love of God is a moral sentiment, founded on a clear perception, and consisting in a high esteem and veneration of his moral perfections?"—This Author says in the name of his brethren; "We esteem *him*, and *him only*, a pious man, who practically conforms to God's moral perfection and government; who shows his delight in God's benevolence by loving and serving his neighbor; his delight in God's justice by being resolutely upright; his sense of God's purity, by regulating his thoughts, imagination, and desires; and whose business, conversation and life are swayed by a regard to God's presence and authority. In all things else, men may deceive themselves. Disordered nerves may give them strange sights, and sounds, and impressions. Texts of Scripture may come to them, as from heaven. Their souls may be moved, and their confidence in God's favour be undoubting. But in all this there is no religion. The question is, do they love God's commands,—and give up to these their habits and passions? Without this, ecstacy is a mockery. One surrender of desire to God's will is worth a thousand transports. We do not judge of the bent of men's minds by their raptures, any more than we judge of the direction of a tree during a storm. We rather suspect loud profession; for we have observed, that deep feeling is generally noiseless, and least seeks display."

To all these views we most cordially subscribe. A man, who should undertake to exhibit elegantly, and in a few words, what Edwards wrote on Religious Affections, could not do it better, than in the language of this Author. Edwards, and Bellamy, and many other authors, most beloved, and most frequently perused, among the Orthodox in New England, have labored with great assiduity and success, to distinguish true religion from its various counterfeits, to put down all the excitements and transports which spring from human imagination or passion, and to recommend that religion, which consists in conformity to God's moral character, and obedience to his law. And if the Author of this Sermon should call to mind all the theological works, with which he was once conversant, he would not improbably find, that in regard to these very sentiments, which he represents as peculiar to Unitarians, he is under no small obligation to Orthodox writers. No writers have ever shown better than those above mentioned, " that religious warmth is only to be valued, when it springs naturally from an improved character; when it comes unforced;—when it is the warmth of a mind, which understands God by being like him; and when instead of disordering, it exalts the understanding, invigorates conscience, gives a pleasure to common duties, and is seen to exist in connexion with cheerfulness, judiciousness, and a reasonable frame of mind."—This Sermon simply asserts these just and important sentiments ; but the writers above named, have largely illustrated and confirmed them. And with Orthodox ministers in New England, this distinction between true piety and its counterfeits is, more than almost any thing else, the subject of preaching and conversation. Probably however, we still fall short of our duty. And we ought to deem it a favor, if any one shall come forward to chastise our negligence, and to excite us to greater seriousness and fidelity in this momentous concern, even though we may be conscious that he does it, by denying us the credit of sentiments, which we hold precious as our life.

This Author proceeds. "Another important branch of religion, we believe to be love to Christ. The greatness of the work of Jesus, the spirit with which he executed it, and the sufferings which he bore for our salvation, we feel to be strong claims on our gratitude and veneration. We see in nature no beauty to be compared with the loveliness of his character; nor do we find on earth a benefactor, to whom we owe an equal debt." —Does all the honor and happiness of entertaining such views as these, belong exclusively to Unitarians? Do these sentiments respecting Christ distinguish them from the Orthodox?—I would ask the same questions respecting most of the observations, which this Author makes on the *benevolent virtues?* Is it a *peculiar, distinguishing* mark of Unitarians, to attach great importance to these virtues? Let any man read the books, or hear the preaching, which we most admire, and then say.

Without proceeding any farther, it could not but be evident to my readers, that they cannot unhesitatingly, and without examination, repose full confidence in the representations, which are found in this Sermon, respecting the sentiments of the Orthodox.—On such a subject as this, and with respect to such a writer, I should have preferred silence, had not justice required me to speak.

But I knew it could not be made consistent with truth and propriety, that those ministers and Christians, who are denominated Orthodox, should lie under the reproach of rejecting a great number of the most obvious principles of religion;—principles, which they believe to be of vital importance to the system of Christianity, and which they maintain with a seriousness and ardor, which bear ample testimony to the sincerity of their faith.

On this particular subject, as well as on every other, which is introduced into these Letters, I feel happy, in addressing myself to those, who have chosen *candor and liberality*, as the honorable badge of their party. Let me ask you, then, my respected friends, whether it can detract any thing from the *value* of those truths, which you believe, that they are believed also by the Orthodox; and whether the *honor* of believing such truths would be any the less to you, if it should be shared equally by us?— What end, then, can this Author seek to accomplish, by making a selection of some of the most unexceptionable, most amiable, most attractive truths of religion, and representing them as belonging peculiarly to Unitarians, and as distinguishing them from us,—when in fact we believe them, to say the least, as sincerely as they do? Possibly credit and influence may, by such means, be secured to Unitarians. But there are men, who will inquire, whether they are secured *justly?* Possibly reproach or disgrace may, by the same means, be cast upon us. But is it *deserved?* And pray tell me, what good end can be answered by possessing credit, which is unjustly acquired, or by inflicting disgrace, which is not merited?—This Author advances much, to which we most cheerfully subscribe, in praise of candor and charitable judgment toward those, who differ from us in religious opinion. Referring to this, he says; "There is one branch of benevolence, which I ought not to pass over in silence, because we think that we conceive of it more highly and more justly, than many of our brethren." And he shows how strongly he reprobates the conduct of a Christian, who is "covered with badges of party, who shuts his eyes on the virtues, and his ears on the arguments of his opponents, *arrogating all excellence to his own sect*, &c." I wish there were less appearance of inconsistency between these charming passages in the Sermon, and those others, on which I have thought it necessary to animadvert.

Though I intend not by any means, to enumerate all the instances of misrepresentation, which occur in this Sermon; there is one passage, respecting moral government, upon which I would detain you a few moments. "If there be any principle of morality," says this Author, "it is this, that we are accountable beings, only because we have consciences, a power of knowing and performing our duty; and that in as far as we want this power, we are incapable of sin, guilt, or blame. We should call a parent a monster, who should judge and treat his children in opposition to this principle; and yet this enormous immorality is charged on our Father in heaven."—The author would evidently impute this gross impiety to the Orthodox. And yet I must say, in their behalf, that the principle for which he contends, is *ours*, as well as *his*. We believe that this principle is inwrought into our moral nature; that every man feels its truth; that every judgment he passes upon his own actions, and every conviction of duty, implies a practical acknowledgment of it; in a word, that it is one of those principles, which need no arguments to prove them, because they are themselves plainer, than any thing which can be adduced as proof.

The views, which we entertain of the moral corruption of man, whether original or superinduced, and in whatever degree it may exist, are perfectly consistent with the principle, " that we are accountable beings, only because we have consciences, and a power of knowing and performing our duty." Indeed, such are our notions of the nature of an intelligent, moral being, that we conceive it to be utterly impossible, that any degree of depravity should take away his conscience, or his power of knowing and doing his duty. These, as we think, are inseparable properties of an accountable creature, in all stages of his existence, and whatever may be his circumstances, or his character. He cannot be subject to law, or accountable for his actions, without these properties, any more than he can, without a soul.—It is with these views, we hold the doctrine of man's depravity. We believe it, not in such an unrestricted, absolute sense, as is sometimes supposed, but with all the limitations, which result from its connexion with other acknowledged truths. Explanations, like those above suggested, ought always to be considered, as making a part of the declaration of our faith; and, in this case they are peculiarly necessary, on account of the facility, with which the doctrine comes into alliance with various hurtful errors.—Let it therefore be remembered, that if any one represents us as believing, that men are depraved in such a sense, that their conscience, or their power of knowing and doing their duty is taken away, or any principle of free moral agency infringed;—in other words, if any one represents us as believing the doctrine of depravity, whether innate or acquired, in such a sense, as makes it any less fit and proper, that God should place men under a moral government, and address to them commands, promises, and threats, than if they were perfectly free from corruption; they give a representation of our views, as really incorrect, as if they should accuse us of holding, that, in consequence of men's depravity, they have no eyes to see the light of the sun, and no ears to hear the noise of thunder.

If there is any principle respecting the moral government of God, which the Orthodox clergy in New England earnestly labor to inculcate, it is this; that, as accountable beings, *we have a conscience, and a power of knowing and performing our duty.* Our zeal in defence of this principle has been such, as to occasion no small umbrage to some, who are attached to every feature and every phraseology of Calvinism. On this subject, there is, in fact, a well known difference between our views, and those of some modern, as well as more ancient Divines, who rank high on the side of Orthodoxy. I urge it, therefore, as a matter of justice, that how earnestly soever the Author of this Sermon might have been disposed to censure the opinions of others, he ought to have made an express exception in *our* favor. And considering what advantages he has had of being acquainted with the modes of thinking and preaching, which generally prevail among the Orthodox ministers of New England, I hardly know how christian candor ought to shape its apology for this oversight.

It is readily admitted, that some men may be found among us, whom we venerate and honor, as advocates for true religion, who yet have preached or written obscurely, or confusedly, on the subject of depravity, free agency, and a moral government. But surely, we are not, as a body, to be charged with entertaining all the opinions, and with justifying all the expressions of every man, who believes generally the principles of Orthodoxy. I am confident, that you would strongly condemn us, if we should treat you in such a manner as this. Should I, in these Letters, impute to you, as a Society of Unitarians, all the extravagancies of opinion, which some German, English, or American Unitarians have held, and all the rashness and violence of language, which they have employed; you would doubtless think me guilty of acting contrary to fairness and equity. I have endeavored to avoid the most distant approach to this species of unfairness; and therefore have purposely refrained from associating passages in this Sermon with passages from those Unitarian writers, against whom the greatest public odium has been excited.—Now on the other hand; suppose you find in an author, or hear from a preacher, reputed Orthodox, an unguarded expression on the subject of depravity, or moral agency, or on any other subject,—an expression liable, at least, to misconstruction, and suited to excite prejudice against Orthodoxy; will you impute that expression, or the opinion conveyed by it, to the Orthodox generally? We may perhaps consider the expression, and the opinion, as exceptionable, as you do; and it may be as really contrary to truth, for you to impute them to us, as for us to impute them to you.—The question is, have we authorised that writer, or that preacher, to speak in our name, and publicly to make known our faith? Or have we ever, in any form, declared our unqualified assent to his opinions, or professed those which are like them? If not, why should every speculation and every expression of his be charged to our account? Infidels may just as well charge upon the whole community of Christians, the irregularities and vices of every individual, who is regarded as belonging to that community. There have been, within a few years, some instances of this kind of unfairness towards the Orthodox generally, and particularly towards some of the subdivisions among them, which cannot but be reprobated by all men, who possess common justice, or common sense.

LETTER XI.

My respected friends,

I have reserved, as the last subject of discussion in these Letters, *the practical influence,* or *tendency* of the system, embraced by the Orthodox.

To my mind, it is exceedingly obvious, that representations are often made on this subject, which are radically erroneous, and that, by these means, an impression is produced on the feelings of many, hostile at once to their personal welfare, and to the interests of religion. Such representations ought to be corrected, and the subject, which must, by both parties, be considered as highly important, to be set in a true light. The salutary influence of the Orthodox system has been often illustrated, and has appeared to me so perfectly clear, that it has been a matter of astonishment, that any intelligent man should entertain a doubt respecting it. The most candid construction, which I have been able to put upon the opinions and representations of our opponents, as to the practical tendency of Orthodoxy, is, that they take an erroneous view of the system itself. They behold it in a false light. They overlook its genuine features, and see, or think they see deformities, from which it is wholly free. Now admitting that the system does appear thus in their view, I can easily account for it, that they should believe its moral tendency to be so mischievous. If the system of the Orthodox were, in truth, what Priestley, and Fellowes, and Belsham, and even the Author of this Sermon have represented it to be; its consequences would indeed be *pernicious*. So I might say, if Christianity were, in truth, that monstrous thing, which infidel philosophers have represented it to be; the opposition and hatred, which have risen up against it, would have been just. But it is not so. And the Advocates for Christianity have a right to say, and are bound to say, and to prove, that it is a system of consummate excellence; that the enmity of its opposers against it, has been altogether unjust and criminal; that it merits the highest attachment, and that, to all its friends, it is fraught with inestimable blessings. I would not make a reproachful comparison. But we know, that the Orthodox system is not what Unitarians have declared it to be. Its genuine features are not seen at all in the picture, which they have drawn of it. Now the question to be discussed in this Letter, is, not whether such a system of doctrines, as Unitarians impute to the Orthodox, is mischievous in its tendency; but what is the influence of *that system*, which we *really believe, and teach*?

The Author of this Sermon thinks, that it is " unfavorable to devotion;"—" that it takes from the Father the Supreme affection which is his due, and transfers it to the Son;"—" that it awakens human transport, rather than that deep veneration of the moral perfections of God, which is the essence of piety;"—" that it robs Christ's death of interest,—weakens our sympathy with his sufferings, and is, of all others, most unfavorable to a love of Christ, founded on a sense of his sacrifices for mankind;"—" that it discourages the timid, gives excuses to the bad, feeds the vanity of the fanatical, and offers shelter to the feelings of the malignant;"—" that it tends strongly to pervert the moral faculty, to form a gloomy, forbidding, and servile religion, and to lead men to substitute censoriousness, bitterness, and persecution, for a tender and impartial charity;"—that it is a " system, which begins with degrading human nature, and may be expected to end in pride."—Priestley, Belsham, and others, in perfect accordance with this Author, have represented the system of Orthodoxy to be *rigorous, gloomy, and horrible,—the extravagance of error,—a mischievous compound of impiety and idolatry.*

It would be a sad case, if the Unitarians above named, had no better proof to offer of a candid, liberal spirit, than what they have given in these heavy, but unsupported charges,—these harsh and causeless censures. I might very safely leave such censures as these, without any remark,—trusting that their extreme violence would be sufficiently visible to counteract any unfavorable effect, which they might be likely to produce.—But I have another object in view, which requires me not to pass over this subject lightly. I wish, in as comprehensive a manner as possible, to give a direct elucidation of the salutary influence of the system, which the Orthodox believe. The confutation of particular charges, as far as necessary, may be found in this general elucidation.

I shall first inquire, whether the grand and obvious properties of that system of religion, which we believe, are not adapted to produce a good influence in a general view, on those who embrace it. After this, I shall advert to some particular parts of Christian virtue and duty, and inquire in what way they are likely to be affected by the Orthodox system.

What then are the grand, obvious properties, which a system of religion must have, in order to produce a good influence on the character and practice of those who embrace it?

First. It must exhibit *a Being of infinite perfection, as the object of worship*. If there is any thing faulty in the character of him, whom we worship, it will, according to a well known principle, have a bad effect upon our character. But the God whom *we* love and adore, must not be described by our opposers. Or if they do describe him, their description must not be received, instead of ours. The Orthodox have described the character of God, as infinite and immutable in every divine perfection, both natural and moral; as amiable and glorious in the highest possible degree. Is not such a God worthy of supreme love and adoration? And can the sincere worship of such a Being fail to promote moral purity in us? Can it be otherwise, than that the habit of affectionately and devoutly contemplating the perfect justice and benevolence, which we ascribe to God, must have a powerful tendency to make us just and benevolent? I know we are accused of worshipping a Being, who is unjust, partial, and malignant. And it is a matter of course that we should be accused of imitating that injustice, partiality and malignity, which are thought to belong to the character of him, whom we worship. But it remains to be proved, that such attributes do in fact belong to the character, which is the object of our adoration. It has often been affirmed by our opponents; but the unsupported affirmation, that we worship an unjust, malignant Being, cannot surely be admitted as proof, in opposition to the most sober declaration on our part, that we ascribe to God infinite justice and benevolence. But there can be no occasion to enlarge on this topic, after what I have written, in Letter III. To that I refer you. And if you have carefully attended to the views there expressed, of the character of Jehovah, and can have confidence enough in me to believe, that they are indeed the views, which I and my brethren entertain; I will add nothing, but an appeal to your judgment, whether the worship of such a God can be otherwise than salutary to the cause of virtue?

Secondly. A scheme of religion, in order to have a good moral influence, must exhibit *a moral government, marked with holiness and righteousness throughout.* There must be a holy and benevolent Sovereign, who, by a system of wise and good laws, requires of his subjects that conduct, which is necessary to the order and happiness of his kingdom. In his administration, he must show a constant regard to the principles of his government, and an invariable determination to give them support and efficiency. The authority of the law, and the character of holiness and justice in the Lawgiver must be sustained, by the influence of a penalty;—a penalty, the execution of which shall spread an impression of awe through the universe, at the sight of God's high displeasure against sin. Now does not the system of religion, which the Orthodox maintain, exhibit a moral government possessing all these properties? Does it not constantly hold up to view, a Supreme Ruler, perfectly holy and benevolent? Does it not inculcate upon all men, a wise and holy law, in all its extent, as of immutable obligation? Does it not constantly teach, that the Governor of the world loves holiness, and abhors sin, and that he manifests an invariable determination to support the principles of a righteous moral government? Does it not exhibit with tremendous force, the sanctions of the law,—that is, the everlasting happiness of the obedient, and the everlasting punishment of transgressors? Is not the penalty of the law, as we represent it, awful in the highest degree, and so fitted, as far as any thing of the nature of penalty can be, to prevent transgression? So far as men are to be influenced by *fear*, will they not be prompted to a careful obedience, according to their impression of the certainty and the greatness of the evil, which will be consequent upon sin? In this respect, has not the Orthodox system most obviously the advantage over its opposite? Have we not always been reproached by those, who would gladly lower down or disannul the sanctions of the law, for displaying in too strong colors the certainty and the dreadfulness of future punishment? And is it not true, that those, who soberly admit the views, which we give, of the displeasure of God against sin, and the punishment with which he will recompense it, find it more difficult, than others, to keep their minds in a state of inconsideration, and sinful repose?—I am willing to make the appeal to all attentive observers, whether there is not, in fact, the greatest and most sensible repugnancy between a life of ungodliness, and the representation we make of the divine government? And, in truth, does not this fact account for much of the opposition, which our views of religion have always had to encounter among men, who are too proud to bear reproof, too fond of quiet, to submit willingly to what would disturb and alarm them, and too earthly, to yield to the attractions of a devout and spiritual life?

That the interests of virtue may be secure, *the exercise of mercy towards offenders*, whenever it takes place, must be so regulated, that the divine law shall be magnified, and its sanctions exercise all their power over the consciences and hearts of men. This is one of the *grand points* in the Orthodox system. I shall not now enter on the particulars, which make up the system in this respect, but shall merely state, what we conceive to be fairly its practical result, and on account of which, more than for any other reason, we feel so much interest in its support.

According to our views of the intervention of Christ, the salvation of sinners reflects no dishonor upon the character of God, as a moral Governor. He appears to his subjects, as just and true, and awakens as deep an awe in their minds, when he *forgives*, as when he *punishes*. In consequence of this, God's rational creatures find in his administration as powerful motives to deter them from transgression, and induce them to obedience, as if they saw in fact, that the penalty of the law was, in all its dreadfulness, inflicted upon every transgressor. So that, while rebels against God are pardoned, his law loses none of its authority or influence; the interests of virtue are not sacrificed; and the glory of justice and truth is in no degree tarnished. Nay, all the attributes of God acquire the lustre of a higher display, and all the principles of his benevolent and righteous government, a more powerful ascendency. Accordingly, those who are placed under this dispensation of mercy, are moved to repentance and obedience by the high authority of a perfect moral government, and by all the attractions of infinite compassion and grace. Thus our system of religion, in regard to the work of redemption, is calculated, in our view, to promote the cause of holiness in the highest degree. It is stamped with perfect holiness throughout. It exhibits a holy God, who is constantly engaged in administering a holy government. It proclaims a pure and holy law, and enforces it with the most weighty sanctions. It brings to our view a holy Redeemer, who gave a perfect vindication and support to that law. It presents a holy salvation, to be obtained through the influence of a holy Intercessor, and by the persevering efforts of a holy faith. Every thing, with which we have to do in this great concern, bears the stamp of holiness, and tends to promote holiness in us.

Now tell me candidly, my respected friends, whether the system of Orthodoxy, some features of which have now been portrayed, is not of as holy a nature, and of as purifying a tendency, as the system which Unitarians adopt? Do we not exhibit as holy a God, as righteous a law, and as high sanctions to enforce it, as they do? Is not the tribunal to which we point men, as just, and the sentence, of which we forewarn them, as momentous and decisive, as that which Unitarians teach us to expect? Do we not hold forth a blessedness of as great worth, and a punishment as dreadful, as they?

In regard to the work of redemption; does not our scheme present as complete a vindication of the violated law and government of God, as theirs? Does it not show as much regard to the interests of virtue? Does it not demand holiness with as commanding an authority, and allure men to it by as melting a display of kindness? Does it not present as many and as bright examples of moral excellence, divine and human? What then is wanting to give the religious system, which we embrace, the most salutary influence upon the character and conduct of men?

As to practical influence, any religious system is, in reality, what it is to those who cordially embrace it, not what it is, or what it appears to be, to those who reject it. I doubt not, that a trial of the Orthodox system by this rule, would end in its favor. Enlightened Christians, who seriously believe this system, do, if I mistake not, find in it motives, in great variety, and of powerful efficacy, to universal holiness.—I should however feel a strong reluctance, in reasoning on this subject, to do what some writers have done ; that is, to institute a comparison between the Orthodox and Unitarians, in respect of character. For although Orthodox believers have in different periods, especially in these last days, achieved much for the welfare of man, and have, in many instances, exhibited an elevation of christian virtue, which has been an honor to the grace of God ; instances enough of a contrary character occur, to make us blush ; and even those, who have reached the highest point of goodness, have fallen far short of the attainments they ought to have made, under the influence of such powerful motives. Instead, therefore, of making any boasting comparisons, I would join with those who are humble and contrite in heart, in the deepest lamentations over that astonishing perverseness, which counteracts the influence of the most holy motives,—over that obstinate disease of our nature, which renders the best means of cure in so great a measure ineffectual.

But the fact, that the remedies, which physicians apply to the sick, are not always, and in the highest degree, efficacious, does not prove, that their *tendency* is not salutary, or that there is any thing more salutary.

In the case now under consideration, notwithstanding all the instances, in which the system of the Orthodox has failed of producing a salutary effect, we are still carefully to inquire into the *practical tendency* of the system, or the *moral influence* which it is *suited* to have, and in this respect, to compare it with the opposite system.

I shall proceed therefore, to the second thing proposed,—viz., to advert to particular parts of Christian virtue, and duty, and to inquire what influence the Orthodox system is likely to have upon them.

1. *Love to God.* The more exalted our conceptions of his natural and moral attributes, the more likely are we, other things being equal, to abound in love. Certainly, clear and elevated apprehensions of his glorious character have a stronger tendency to excite love, than those which are low and obscure. Now it is as evident to me, as the light of noon, that the system of Orthodoxy clearly exhibits the perfections of God, and invests them with the highest glory. It teaches us to acknowledge his infallible wisdom, and his unlimited benevolence in all his works. In view of all the evils, which fall to our lot, or to the lot of others, it teaches us not only to submit to his sovereign power, but to admire his paternal goodness. Those very measures of government, which our opponents think irreconcileable with his moral perfection, appear to us bright illustrations of it. In every point of view, the faith we embrace, is suited to excite love to God, and to give to that love the character of constancy and ardor.

2. *Gratitude to God.* In proportion to the impression we have of his kindness to us, will this affection be excited. If we believe that God, from the impulse of his own compassion, has bestowed upon us a favor of infinite value, and wholly undeserved; we shall feel a stronger motive to gratitude, than if we consider the favor bestowed, of inferior value, or suppose that we have any personal claim to it. According to this principle, those views of redemption, which we have been taught to consider, as the dictates of Scripture, are fitted to

raise gratitude to the highest pitch. We look upon ourselves to be in such a state, in consequence of our apostacy from God, that it is the greatest achievement of infinite benevolence, to save us. We see from what an abyss of guilt and wretchedness God delivers, and what an exceeding great and eternal weight of glory he bestows. And we see that this deliverance from guilt and wretchedness, and this eternal glory were purchased by the precious blood of Christ. With these views, we are constrained to anticipate that song, which is prompted by the gratitude of saints in heaven; " Unto him that loved us, and washed us from our sins in his own blood, —to him be glory and dominion forever and ever."

With respect to gratitude, it is perfectly easy to make a comparison between the influence of our system, and that of our opponents. Unitarians may gratefully acknowledge the goodness of their Creator in forming and upholding them, and in the common bounties, with which his providence blesses them. They may admire his benevolence too, in providing, as they conceive he has done, for their happiness in a future state. And they may set a high price upon the various means of moral improvement, which they enjoy. But their system does not tend like ours, to excite those high and tender emotions of gratitude, which spring from a consciousness of deep criminality and unworthiness. It is easy to compare the sensations of a man, who has been rescued from the danger of perishing in the ocean, by some heroic effort of benevolence, with the sensations, which are produced by the common acts of kindness. It is easy to conceive too, how those sensations of the drowning man would be heightened, if his deliverance was effected by the disinterested kindness of one, whom he had often wounded by injuries, and especially, if the danger, from which he was rescued, was the immediate consequence of an act of unprovoked hostility. Such a generous effort of compassion, heightened too by circumstances like these, would do all that an act of human kindness could do, to turn a heart of stone into a heart of flesh, to call forth all the tenderness of gratitude, and to fix a sense of obligation, never to be obliterated.

The principle of this comparison, with respect to the excitement of gratitude, is inseparable from our nature; and the result of the comparison will show, that the religious sentiments, which we entertain, are adapted not only to produce gratitude, but to give it the greatest degree of strength and tenderness, of which the human mind is capable. According to our scheme of faith, we are sinners without excuse. We have lifted up our hand against our Maker, and in instances too many to be numbered, proved ourselves his enemies. In consequence of this, we have brought ourselves upon the brink of hopeless destruction. Our Father in heaven has interposed, and by an act of love, unparalleled in strength and purity, and at an expense, which the creation could not pay, has delivered us from that hopeless destruction, and given us an inheritance in the heavens. Compared with this act of divine love, the noblest exploits of benevolence, ever performed by man, lose all their splendor, and all their power to move the heart. The kindness and grace of God, exercised towards us in this glorious work, will create a holy gratitude, which will swell the hearts of the redeemed forever, and transfuse a celestial ardor, inexpressibly delightful and pure, into their everlasting songs. Nor are those, who cordially yield themselves up to the influence of these views, strangers to this holy affection, even now. It often glows in the heart of the young disciple of Christ. It often cheers the spirits of Christians, in every stage of their progress towards heaven, and prompts them to bless God for his goodness, even in affliction. It kindles a celestial light in their souls on the bed of languishing; and in the hour of death, it awakens in them sensibilities, which, amid the weakness and agonies of dissolving nature, struggle to utter themselves in, "thanks to God for his unspeakable gift."

3. *Love to Christ.* The bare mention of this virtue will lead at once to the obvious result of the comparison, which I have instituted between the two systems. For surely that system must be admitted to have the strongest tendency to excite love to Christ, which ascribes to him the highest excellence of character. The different systems of Unitarians ascribe to him various degrees of created and limited excellence. The Orthodox system clothes him with eternal and infinite excellence. Those who embrace this system, feel it to be their duty and privilege, to love Christ with the most exalted affection, —an affection without any limits, except those which arise from the finiteness of their capacities. But Unitarianism, in every form, forbids this high and unlimited affection to Christ. It tells us we are in danger of overrating his character. It begets a fear of regarding him with too high a veneration. When we have hearts, which wish to express their sacred ardor in the adoring language of Thomas, "my Lord and my God;" it thrusts itself before us, and tells us to forbear. Whereas the system of Orthodoxy calls us to raise our love to Christ to a higher and higher degree. It tells us he has an excellence and glory, which our affection can never reach. It makes our blessedness in a future world to consist

very much in clearer discoveries of his divine perfections, and in exercising towards him a more exalted, more uninterrupted love.

4. *Faith in Christ.* The same general remarks apply to this point, as to the last. Believing or trusting in the Savior is represented, as one of the grand, comprehensive duties of the Christian religion. But surely that faith or trust in Christ, which results from the principles of our opponents, must be a very different thing, from that which our system inculcates. Under the influence of the doctrines which we believe, we repose a confidence in his atoning blood, which relieves us from the agitations of guilt, and inspires us with humble, joyful hope; a confidence in his power, and wisdom, and goodness, which puts our hearts at rest respecting the most important concerns of the creation. Our own interests, temporal and eternal, we commit, cheerfully and entirely, to his care. We trust in him for all that is necessary to purify our hearts, to guide and protect us during our pilgrimage, to comfort us in affliction, and to give us peace and triumph in the prospect of death. And when the time of our departure draws near, we hope to look up to our merciful, condescending Redeemer, and, with that confidence in his infinite grace, which quells every fear, to say, " *Lord Jesus, receive my Spirit.*"—Does the Unitarian system teach any thing like this? Does such a faith spring from the principles, which it inculcates?

5. *Dread of sin, and watchful care to obey the divine precepts.*

The importance of the doctrine of rewards and punishments is insisted on by Unitarians, as well as by the Orthodox. The question is, does their scheme, or ours, exhibit the doctrine in the form best adapted to impress men with a dread of sin, and excite them to obey the divine precepts? Now I think it must be obvious to those, who are acquainted with the most respectable authors on both sides, that the heaven which we are taught by our system to contemplate, is a state of higher perfection, and of purer and more elevated enjoyment, than that, which our opponents describe. Unitarian authors represent the future condition of Christians, as being much less removed from their present condition, than what we suppose to be fact. Accordingly they look upon us, in relation to this subject, as overstepping the bounds of sober truth, and attempting to set off the joys of heaven with too high colors. Read what they have written on this subject, and you will be satisfied, that the views they exhibit of the heavenly felicity, are less adapted to excite a deep interest in the mind of man, and less adapted to sway his active powers, than those which are exhibited by the best writers on the other side. If this is in fact so, then, whatever may be said as to reason and argument in the case, the Orthodox system has certainly the advantage, as to *moral influence.* For the contemplation of a future reward, to be obtained by virtuous efforts, must evidently tend to excite those efforts, very much in proportion to the greatness and excellence of that reward.

If any hesitate to admit what I have advanced on this part of the subject, I will not stop to contest the point, but pass to the consideration of *future punishment*, on which our reasoning can be attended with no difficulty. Here my first inquiry is,—does the threat of punishment tend to deter men from sin? Is the penalty of any law, divine or human, fitted to have an influence to prevent transgression? If so, it must be by moving the passion of *fear.* The evil threatened is addressed to this passion, and can produce an effect upon no other principle of action. The next question is, whether the prospect of an evil, that is great and insupportable, has a tendency to excite a *stronger* sensation of fear, than the prospect of an evil, comparatively small and easily endured? I appeal to common sense. I appeal to common practice. When legislators find, that the penalty of any law does not work upon the fears of men powerfully enough to prevent the commission of crimes, they increase its severity. And this they do upon the general principle, that the penalty of a law will be likely to awaken the fears of men, and influence their conduct, other things being equal, very much in proportion to the greatness of the evil, involved in that penalty. Upon this obvious principle, I wish you to examine the practical tendency of our doctrine respecting future punishment. We believe that the future punishment of the wicked will be *inexpressibly great*, and will *endure forever*. We bring that great and endless punishment into view, in order to illustrate the evil of sin, and the displeasure of God against it. We believe that such a punishment is just; that it is no more than commensurate with the illdesert of sin; and that it shows no more displeasure against sin, than is necessarily prompted by the perfect love which the King Eternal feels for the welfare of his kingdom. Now will not any man be powerfully held back from the commission of sin, by the serious apprehension, that it is a great evil, that God is greatly displeased with it, that it tends to produce extensive injury to the creation, and that it will be followed with inexpressible and hopeless misery? If you would weaken the power, which hinders a man from sin, weaken his apprehension of the greatness of the evil of it; weaken his apprehension of the displeasure of God against it, and of the dreadfulness and the duration of the misery to which it will lead. Now is not this what the system of Unitarians actually does, so far as it opposes the views of the Orthodox respecting future punishment? I have nothing to say here, as to the arguments used on one side or the other. I speak simply, as to *practical tendency*. And I am not anxious what conclusions any man will adopt, who will allow himself, on rational principles, soberly to investigate the two systems under consideration.

I might say, were it necessary, that the powerful influence of the doctrine of future punishment, as we hold it, is illustrated by numberless facts. Men strongly inclined or tempted to sin, have been deterred from the commission of it, by the fear of endless punishment. By the same fear, many have been roused from spiritual lethargy, and excited to make that most important inquiry, " what shall we do to be saved?" How many have been excited by this doctrine, to such reflections as these;—" is that sin, which I indulge in my heart, so great an evil in the sight of a just and benevolent God, that he has threatened everlasting punishment, as its recompense? Am I, while impenitent, exposed to that recompense? And shall I, by the momentary pleasures of sin, bring hopeless ruin upon my immortal soul?"—Such reflections as these, naturally occasioned by the doctrine of endless punishment, have, in instances too many to be enumerated, led, through the mercy of God, to a thorough reformation of character.

6. *Reverence for the word of God*. The grand maxim of the Polish Socinians was, that *reason is our ultimate rule and standard*, and that whatever in religion is not conformed to this, is to be rejected. This maxim, as they understood it, gave them perfect liberty to alter or set aside the obvious sense of the Bible, whenever it

did not agree with the deductions of reason. Unitarians in general have, with more or less decision, adopted the same maxim. I do not say, that all, who are called Unitarians in New England, treat the word of God with the same irreverent license, which some English and German Unitarians have shown. But I think no candid and competent judge can doubt, that the *general aspect* of Unitarianism does less honor to revelation, than the contrary system. Unitarianism bows with less veneration to the word of God, and receives its instructions with a less implicit confidence. It has lower views of the nature and degree of that inspiration, which the writers of Scripture enjoyed, and is proportionably less inclined to receive their word, as infallible. In forming our opinions, we inquire simply, *what saith the Scripture? and what was the sense, which the inspired writers meant to convey?* When we learn this, we are satisfied. Our reason receives its doctrines from the word of God. It sees the objects of religion, not in its own light, but in a light borrowed from revelation. As soon as our reason discovers what God teaches, we suffer it to go no farther. The Bible, we believe, contains a harmonious system of truth, eternal truth, unmixed with error. If our reason seems to see inconsistencies, we charge not the appearance of those inconsistencies to any fault in the Scriptures, but to the weakness and obscurity of reason, and we have no doubt it will entirely vanish, when our reason acquires a higher degree of improvement. I must refer it to the christian public to determine, whether Unitarianism teaches its disciples to treat the word of God with this kind of reverence and submission.

Our system gives us liberty to pass over no part of Scripture, as unworthy of regard. What is said on one part of a subject, we charge ourselves to receive with as much confidence, as what is said on another part; and what is opposed to our prepossessions, as readily, as what is agreeable to them. I might show this to be our practice, with regard to the doctrine of the Trinity, the moral corruption of man, the divine purposes, and the divine agency. But, in my apprehension, the Unitarian theory is so constructed, as to set aside one part of Scripture entirely. That is to say, the faith of Unitarians, certainly of that class of them, who believe in the simple humanity of Christ, is the same, as it would be, if those texts, which ascribe the highest perfections to Christ, were expunged from the Bible. There are texts, which assert that the Word was God,—that all things were made by him and for him,—that he is over all, God blessed forever. But these texts, and others of similar import, make no alteration in the faith of Socinians. Their opinions are founded on other representations of the Scriptures *exclusively*. These texts have no influence at all upon them. The Orthodox have a belief in the inspiration and authority of the Bible, which prevents them from treating any part of it in this manner. If the Bible teaches, that Christ is a man, they believe he is a man. If the Bible teaches, that he is divine, they believe he is divine. If it teaches, that he created all things, they believe it. If it teaches, that he prayed to the Father, that he suffered, and died, and rose from the dead, they receive all this as a matter of fact. So of the rest. Whatever the Bible declares respecting Christ, they regard as infallible truth. They extend the limits of their faith far enough to comprise all parts of the testimony of God. They do not come to the Bible with such a bias of mind, that, if they believe Christ to be *man*, they will believe this *only*, and whatever the Bible may say, will not believe that he is also *God;* or that, if they believe the divine *unity,* they will believe this *only,* and whatever the Bible may say, will not believe a divine Trinity. They have such liberality of faith, that, on the simple authority of God's word, they will believe both. I mention this merely to show, that their system, or their habit of thinking, leads them to entertain so profound a reverence for the Bible, that, as soon as they know what it declares, they are satisfied. They suffer not their reason to set itself up, and claim authority, as a teacher, or guide; but require it to submit to the authority of Revelation, and to exercise itself only to receive instruction from God, with the humble docility of a child. Now even admitting, that the system of the Orthodox contains a mixture of error, it is very apparent, that they have made it what it is, from sincere reverence for the word of God. *The high authority and infallible truth* of the Scriptures, is the principle, which controls their reasoning and their faith.

I could extend these remarks, and show, that on the subject of man's moral depravity, the atonement, regeneration, and other controverted points, the reasoning of Unitarians manifests less reverence for the word of God, than that of their opponents. I could illustrate this, as before, by the simple fact, that there are many passages of the Bible, which the writers seem to have thought very important, which yet are of no account with Unitarians, and have no influence whatever upon their faith. It would be easy for Unitarians themselves, by a little inquiry, to perceive, that their faith would be just what it now is, were the texts referred to, erased from the sacred pages. All the effect, produced upon their minds by any one of those texts, is, to occasion them perplexity and trouble, and to put them to the wearisome labor of explaining away its obvious sense, and making it appear consistent with their views.

I might cite many observations of English and German Unitarians, expressive of their low ideas of inspiration, and their want of reverence for the word of God. But I intended merely to direct the eye of the reader to what seems to me exceedingly obvious, and lead him to inquire, whether the *general aspect* of the system embraced by Unitarians, and the general style of their reasoning on religious subjects, is not indicative of less reverence for the sacred oracles, than what is manifested by the Orthodox. But whether the result of a comparison be or be not the same in their minds, as it is in mine; the uniform declarations and conduct of the Orthodox, and the general character of their writings, will, I hope, leave no man in doubt, as to the reverence which they entertain for the word of God, or as to the tendency of their system of religion to promote such reverence.

7. Let us finally consider the subject, in relation to *benevolent action*, particularly that highest kind of it, which is directed to *the spread of the gospel, and the salvation of men*.

The views, which our religious system exhibits of the eternal love of God, and especially of the condescension and grace of Jesus Christ, have a manifest tendency to beget the sincerest and most active kindness towards mankind. Under the influence of such examples of goodness, as we are taught to contemplate in the providence of God, and in the life of Jesus, we cannot be indifferent to the wants, or the sufferings of our fellow creatures.

But the grand influence of Orthodoxy relates directly to the spiritual and eternal condition of men. We believe,—and it is a distinguishing mark of our religion,—that the world lieth in wickedness; that all men are the subjects of a total alienation of heart from God, and justly exposed to everlasting punishment. This view of mankind, especially when we look upon ourselves as partners with them in the same guilt and ruin, must produce the tenderest emotions of sympathy. And when with a temper of mind, which is in any measure what it ought to be, we consider their moral degradation and misery in connexion with that grace of God, which has provided salvation; how deeply must we be affected; and how powerfully must we be stirred up to benevolent exertion in their behalf. Look abroad into various quarters of the world, where mankind are in a state of the profoundest ignorance and wretchedness, and see the efforts which are made for their reformation, and their happiness. Then look into Christian nations, and see, who are the most active in promoting these benevolent efforts. See what is the spring of all these remarkable movements, which really present the only prospect we have, of the salvation of the world. What is it that rouses the exertions of those, who are giving their substance or offering their prayers, or of those, who are exposing themselves to hardships, and suffering and death, in the cause of human happiness? 'Tis simply this. They see that the children of men have destroyed themselves; that their immortal souls are ready to perish. This touches the pity of their hearts, and kindles all the fervor of benevolent desire. They see that a Savior is provided, and that self-ruined sinners may obtain eternal life. This awakens their hope, their zeal, and their efforts. The reason they have to expect, that the grace of God will abound in the salvation of sinners, gives them alacrity and patience in their labors. If souls, precious as their own, and equally the objects of the mercy which the gospel proffers, may obtain the salvation, which is in Christ Jesus, with eternal glory; they have a reward like that, which Jesus himself enjoys, when he sees the travail of his soul, and is satisfied. I say then, that the doctrine of the utter ruin of man, and of the grace of God which bringeth salvation, is the spring of those animated exertions for the good of the world, which mark the present era.

To try the natural tendency of the doctrine of man's depravity, and his redemption by Christ, as we hold it, I will suppose the following case.—There is a certain Unitarian, who, though a very benevolent man, yet, with his present views of religion, makes no particular exertions, by the contribution of money, or by personal labors, for the conversion of sinners, either at home, or abroad. He is content that men in Christian and in heathen lands should remain as they are, except what may be done for them by the gradual progress of knowledge, and the arts of civilized life. But this same Unitarian alters his religious opinions, and becomes well satisfied, that mankind are, every where, in that very state of moral corruption and ruin, which the Orthodox system asserts, and that just such a salvation is provided, and may be obtained in just such a way, as that system teaches. Of this he becomes deeply convinced. What will be the consequence? Will not his heart be touched with compassion for sinners? Will he not long to see the grace of God displayed in their conversion? Will he not join himself to the company of those, who are laboring and praying and giving of their substance, for the salvation of those, who are perishing? Is not this the natural consequence of such a change in his religious views? Do not facts, as well as the nature of the case, show it to be so?

Now invert the supposition.—A man, who feelingly embraces the common Orthodox system, and who is led, by his views of the ruined, miserable condition of the human race, to unite with those, who show the highest degree of zeal in promoting the conversion of sinners at home, and in sending the gospel to the heathen;—such a man changes his faith, and comes to entertain the views of Unitarians, respecting the state and the prospects of human beings. Is not his zeal for the conversion of sinners, and for evangelizing the heathen, extinguished? And does he not forsake the society of those, who are active in promoting the benevolent enterprises of this auspicious day? Do not facts, as well as the nature of the case, show this to be the natural consequence of such a change in his opinions?—Unitarians, as it seems to me, act with perfect self-consistency on this subject. Their opinions and their practice correspond; and with the sentiments they now indulge respecting the nature of the gospel, and the character and condition of man, what powerful motives can they have to labor, or make sacrifices for the conversion of sinners? Have we any reason to expect, that Unitarians will so far imitate the holy Apostles, as to become preachers of the gospel among the heathen, and to be willing to spend and be spent, to suffer persecution, and to die, in the cause of human salvation? Possibly they may be accessible to the influence of motives, which we have not duly considered. If we are chargeable with a mistake, or with ignorance, on this subject, or if we indulge views, which can be considered, as in any measure unjust or injurious, we must refer to the writings and the conduct of Unitarians, as our apology. What exertions have they made to promote the spread of the gospel in pagan lands? What heathen tribes or nations are now receiving the words of eternal life from their missionaries, or experiencing, in other ways, the salutary effects of their religious charities, and their prayers?—For myself, I know not how it is, that any, who have a heart to feel for the woes, or to desire the eternal happiness of man, can be indifferent to the benevolent operations of this day, in behalf of those who are destitute of the gospel. But are not Unitarians, generally, chargeable with this indifference? Are they not chargeable with more than indifference? Instead of uniting with the multitude of good men, who devote themselves to works of Christian benevolence; do they not look with pity or contempt, upon the most fervent prayers, and the most earnest, faithful, and successful labors of the church of Christ, in the cause of human salvation? And is not all this a dark and forbidding characteristic of their system?

The views I have expressed, as to the practical tendency of Orthodoxy and of Unitarianism, are such, I apprehend, as must result from a due consideration of the character of these two systems.—I am aware it may be difficult for those, whose minds have strong prepossessions against Orthodoxy, to conceive that it should produce such effects, as I have ascribed to it. But certainly such effects do naturally result from it, as it is understood and embraced by the Orthodox. Such must be my apprehension, till some one shall take the doctrines of Orthodoxy, just as *we* hold them, not as represented by our opponents, and make out, by fair reasoning, that they have an opposite tendency.

I intended to proceed farther under this general head, and to consider the tendency of our religious system, compared with the opposite one, to promote a spirit of humility, and of prayer. But it will be perfectly easy for the reader to apply to each of these subjects the principles, which have been applied to the other subjects, treated in this Letter.

I shall now finish what I have to say on the important subject of *practical influence*, by one remark; namely; that the advantage, which the Author of the Sermon has, in setting forth the practical influence of Unitarianism, is derived, almost entirely, from those views of religion, which really belong to the Orthodox. These, generally, are the views, which he makes prominent in his Discourse, and by which he gives plausibility to his system. I leave the propriety of this mode of treating the subject, to the consideration of others.—To those of my readers, who understand thoroughly what the Unitarian scheme is, I must also refer the decision of another question; that is; whether this Author has not, in some instances, been silent respecting certain opinions, which are common among Unitarians, when the importance of those opinions, as well as the express design of his Sermon, required him to speak of them without reserve. If, on every important topic, he has been perfectly explicit in giving *his own* views; it must be that he differs very widely in opinion from the generality of Unitarians. And if so, then I should doubt, whether some man, who was of the same mind with them, might not have been more properly employed, as their agent and representative before the public. Though he may have given a true and unreserved account of his own religious faith, I cannot think he has given a just account of the general faith of those, for whom he undertakes to speak. Thus in my apprehension, he fails essentially as to both systems. As to Orthodoxy, he does not show a feature of it in its true light. What he has written would enable no man on earth correctly to understand any one article of our faith. As to Unitarianism,—I think he has as really failed of giving a just and complete account of it, though not in the same way, nor in an equal degree.

Although I have, in these Letters, spoken frequently of the injustice, which the Orthodox have been accustomed to suffer from their opposers, I would not have you imagine that I have meant to complain of any *personal* injuries, or wished to excite feelings of commiseration towards the Orthodox. I have complained of injustice in the treatment, which our religious faith has received from our opponents, because it tends to bar their minds and the minds of others, against the most salutary truths, and to perpetuate the evils of controversy.

I am conscious of no disposition and of no temptation, to reproach or injure those, whom I have here addressed. On the contrary, I have strong inducements to respect and honor them,—especially those of them, who were among my beloved Instructors and fellow students at the University, and many others, to whom I have particular personal attachments. But I have wished to cherish the influence of still higher motives, toward those, from whose religious opinions I dissent. I would regard them, as fellow creatures, whom God requires me to love, as I love myself,—who are destined to the same immortal existence, and capable of the same immortal joys with myself,—who are to appear, a few days hence, before the same high and holy tribunal, and whose final sentence is to come from the lips of the same infallible Judge. Under the influence of these considerations, suffer me to say, I have found it easy, not only to guard my mind against every feeling of animosity, but to exercise love and tenderness. In executing the business, which I am now closing, I have charged myself, first, to do as much as possible, to promote the cause of Christ; and then, as little as possible, to inflict a wound upon the feelings of my opponents. Indeed I have written with the desire and the hope of contributing, through divine mercy, to their eternal welfare.—I have also endeavored to keep in mind, that the feelings, which are apt to agitate the minds of contending parties, will shortly vanish, and that the controversy, which has made its way into New England, and the conduct of all those, who take a part in it, must be subjected to review, before Him, who cannot err.

And now, my respected friends, I desire freely and affectionately to inquire, what Unitarians expect to gain, by the efforts they are making in their pamphlets, periodical publications, and sermons, to disseminate the peculiarities of their religious system? Do they expect that Unitarianism will have a more powerful influence to promote good morals in society, or that it will produce better men, or better civil and literary institutions, than that religion, which brought our forefathers to New England, and which has given to all our institutions, to our ministers and churches, to our rulers, and to our community at large, a character of preeminence, which has been universally seen and acknowledged among us? As to this subject of practical influence, our system most evidently possesses every thing which is valuable in that of Unitarians. Whatever motives to goodness can be drawn from the "paternal character of God," or from any of his moral attributes, from the "loveliness and sublimity of virtue," from the example of Christ, from the precepts of the Gospel, or from the doctrine of a resurrection, and a future state of retribution; our system inculcates them at least as forcibly, and turns them to as good account, as that of our opponents. And our system has much in addition, which we consider of infinite worth, but of which theirs is wholly destitute. I ask then, what they expect to gain by the efforts they are making,—which are, in reality, efforts to diffuse among men, lower conceptions of the glory of Christ, and of the honor due to him from his people,—lower conceptions of the disorder of the human mind, and of the evil of sin,—lower conceptions of the value of Christ's atonement, and of the necessity and worth of divine influence to renew men to holiness,—lower conceptions of the recompense, which sinners deserve, and of the obligations of those who are pardoned, to the grace of God? Let the thing be varnished over ever so artfully, this is the real tendency of their efforts. And what good to themselves or to others do they expect from such efforts? Why should they wish to promote a system, which lets down the standard of Christianity, so that it meets, half way at least, the wishes of the irreligious;—a system, which does, in fact, find a place in the hearts of those, who are living to the present world, without giving them any disquietude, and which is likely to be embraced by thousands, in preference to the opposite, for the very reason, that it relieves them from being disturbed by the warnings of conscience, and allows them to live in the neglect of those things which are unseen and eternal;—a system, which never can coalesce with the feelings of those, whose hearts are warm with benevolence to the souls of men, and with zeal for their conversion;—a system, which, if it should prevail, would prevent forever the pious efforts, which our blessed Lord and Redeemer requires his followers to make, to convey the gospel of peace to the ends of the world? This general aspect of Unitarianism appears very portentous. It excites my fears. And it is sufficient, by itself, to produce in my mind an honest and serious apprehension, that whatever plausible arguments may be used to give the system support and currency,—it is indeed *another gospel.*

LETTERS

ADDRESSED TO

TRINITARIANS AND CALVINISTS,

OCCASIONED BY

DR. WOODS' LETTERS

TO UNITARIANS.

BY HENRY WARE, D. D.
Hollis Professor of Divinity in the University at Cambridge.

CAMBRIDGE:
PUBLISHED BY HILLIARD AND METCALF.
Sold also by Cummings & Hilliard, Boston.
1820.

DISTRICT OF MASSACHUSETTS, TO WIT:

District Clerk's Office.

BE it remembered, that on the twenty-eighth day of August, A. D. 1820, and in the forty-fifth year of the Independence of the United States of America, Hilliard and Metcalf, of the said District, have deposited in this office the title of a book, the right whereof they claim as Proprietors, in the words following, viz.

"Letters addressed to Trinitarians and Calvinists, occasioned by Dr. Woods' Letters to Unitarians. By Henry Ware, D. D. Hollis Professor of Divinity in the University at Cambridge."

In conformity to the Act of the Congress of the United States, entitled, "An Act for the encouragement of learning, by securing the copies of Maps, Charts, and Books, to the Authors and Proprietors of such copies, during the times therein mentioned;" and also to an Act, entitled, "An Act supplementary to an Act," entitled, "An Act for the encouragement of learning, by securing the copies of Maps, Charts, and Books, to the Authors and Proprietors of such copies during the times therein mentioned; and extending the benefits thereof to the Arts of designing, engraving and etching historical and other prints."

W. S. SHAW,
Clerk of the District of Massachusetts.

CONTENTS.

LETTER I. p. 4—9.

Occasion of the following letters.—Controversy useful.—Importance of the points at issue.

LETTER II. 9—17.

Propriety of a creed.—Charges of misrepresentation considered, as to the unity of God,—as to his moral perfection.

LETTER III. 17—53.

Natural character of man.—Doctrine of the Orthodox changed.—Imputation.—Total depravity.—The writer's view on the subject.—Defence of it—from observation and experience,—character of children,—scripture.—General views from scripture.—Particular texts from the Old and New Testament considered.—Depravity not a humbling doctrine.

LETTER IV. 53—80.

Election.—Alleged misrepresentation considered.—Westminster Confession.—Dr. Woods' explanations,—inconsistent with the moral character of God,—with scripture.—General scope,—particular texts considered.—Reprobation.

LETTER V. 80—109.

Atonement.—Alleged misrepresentations.—Language of the Orthodox not to be understood literally.—Redemption.—Sacrifice.—Atonement.—Two natures and one person in Christ.—Ground of forgiveness.—Value of good works.—Salvation of grace.

LETTER VI. 110—124.

Divine influence.—That which is peculiar to Calvinism to be distinguished.—General doctrine.—Indirect influence by instruments and means.—Irresistible grace.—Objections.—Unitarian views.

LETTER VII. 125—150.

Tendency and moral influence of Unitarian and of Trinitarian views,—generally,—as respects piety to God,—regard for Jesus Christ,—reverence for the Scriptures,—benevolent exertions,—spread of the Gospel.—Motives to activity.—Conclusion.

LETTERS

ADDRESSED

TO TRINITARIANS AND CALVINISTS.

LETTER I.

CHRISTIAN BRETHREN,

The Letters of the Rev. Dr. Woods to Unitarians, which have now been for some time before the public, suggest to me the propriety of addressing the few following pages on the same subjects, to Trinitarians and Calvinists. I feel the greater readiness to do it, and enter upon the task the more cheerfully, as the discussion of the interesting subjects, about which they are concerned, seems to be taking a character of moderation, temperance, and urbanity, which promises a favourable result. It assures us, that the great end, which, on each side, we propose to ourselves, will not be lost sight of in the ardour of debate, and the desire to maintain subordinate opinions, in which we differ from each other; and that we are not going to sacrifice the spirit of religion to any of its forms, or its dogmas.

I am far from thinking religious controversy to be universally an evil. It becomes so, only when it is improperly conducted. It is bad, and produces bad effects, only when the discussion of interesting questions of faith or duty is carried on with an intemperate spirit, or with sophistry; and when the disputants, ranged on each side, manifest more of a spirit of party, than of the love of truth. So far indeed is the public discussion of those questions, about which Christians hold different opinions, from being a thing, that should be discouraged as hurtful; that we ought rather to rejoice in it, as an evidence of a prevailing interest in the subject of religion in general, as a symptom of religious life in the community, and as a means of preserving that life, of awakening a deeper interest, of turning the public attention still more to the subject, and thus furnishing opportunities for impressing upon the minds of men a sense, which they might otherwise not have, of its high value and importance. These desirable effects it may produce in a considerable degree, however imperfectly and defectively the controversy may be conducted, and although great faults of manner, and even of temper, may mingle themselves in the debate. But if there be a reasonable degree of exemption from bad passions, party views, the arts of controversy, and offensive personality; the effect of bringing the subject into view, in the various lights in which it may be presented, can hardly fail to be highly favourable to the cause of Christian truth.

The book, which has given occasion to the present pamphlet, and upon which some remarks will be made in the course of the discussions which follow, is entitled to more than common attention on several accounts. The subjects of which it treats are in themselves highly important; and being those, about which the Christian community is at the present time much divided, they have excited a peculiar interest of late by being brought more frequently than common before the public mind. It comes from a gentleman of acknowledged talents and learning, and of high standing among his brethren as a scholar and a theologian. It professes to speak with authority, as it speaks in the name of that part of the Christian community, for whom it claims the very honourable distinction of "the Orthodox of New England," and is designed to explain and defend the opinions, by which they are distinguished, for the purpose of guarding them against misapprehension, and in order to do away the effects of misrepresentation.

The writer of the following sheets hopes to perform the duty he has assigned himself, whatever may be its defects in other respects, in a spirit, which shall not be liable to exception. It is his design to make such remarks, as occur to him, on the opinions and reasonings of the pamphlet before him, and to give a free exposition of his own views upon the several subjects treated of by Dr. Woods, together with the reasoning by which he has been led into those views. But he wishes it to be understood, that they are his own views only. He is not authorized, nor does he profess, to speak in the name of any party or body of Christians. How far his opinions on the subjects in controversy, and his manner of explaining and defending them, may agree with those of his friends, he knows not. He is willing to avail himself of this opportunity of appearing before the public on these subjects, believing that the cause of christian truth cannot fail of being promoted by unreserved freedom in the discussion of controverted doctrines; and by individuals communicating the result of their study and thought, without any reference to the opinions of the party or sect, to which they may be considered in general as belonging.

With respect to the points at issue between those, who are called Unitarians on the one hand, and Trinitarians and Calvinists on the other, it is of some importance that you should know in what light they are viewed, and what degree of importance is attached to them by Unitarians. Upon this subject, there is probably with us, as with you, some diversity of opinion; though I am persuaded that no intelligent Unitarian can think them unimportant, and practically a matter of indifference. It cannot be imagined, that the constitution of things is such, as to render truth and error on any subject perfectly indifferent, and equally salutary. And it is believed, as I shall have occasion to show in the sequel, that the doctrines for which we contend, and which are the subject of controversy between us, are calculated, as far as their effects are not prevented, nor counteracted by other causes, to have a better moral influence in forming the character, than the opposite doctrines; and that their reception and prevalence cannot fail to have great influence on the reception and spread of christianity in the world. At the same time, it is not maintained, that any one of the doctrines, about which we differ, is fundamental in such a sense, that the opposite is incompatible with the Christian character, and forfeits the Christian name for him who maintains it. It is not doubted that all the best influences of Christian faith may be felt, and the Christian life acted out, and the consolations and hopes of the Gospel enjoyed by those, whose speculative opinions upon each of the several points of controversy, which lie between us, are in opposition to each other.

LETTER II.

I shall confine myself to a few passing remarks on what is contained in some of the first letters of Dr. Woods, wishing to draw your attention chiefly to the important articles of doctrine, which are discussed in the remaining ones; since, with the exception of the doctrine of the divine Unity, they involve the most interesting questions, that lie between us and you.

With respect to what is implied in no equivocal manner in the beginning of the second letter, I would only observe, that as to the propriety of *having* a creed, no doubt, I believe, has ever been entertained. Unitarians have always claimed the right of every individual to have his own particular creed. What they have sometimes had occasion to object to is, not that each of the several sects and denominations of Christians should have its own creed, nor, that any individual should have one; but that any, whether an individual or a body of Christians, should insist upon their creed being the creed of others; either as a title to the Christian name, or as a condition of their being admitted to the participation of any Christian privileges.

In the concluding part of the same letter, and in the two following, Dr. Woods proceeds to charge Mr. Channing with a gross misrepresentation of the opinions of the Orthodox upon two points, the Unity of God, and his moral perfection; and of injustice in claiming these as distinguishing articles of the Unitarian Faith. Now, in respect to the first of these, the Unity of God, it is to be recollected, that the question is not, whether the Unity of God be *asserted* by Trinitarians. This is not denied them; but the true question is, whether opinions are or are not held by them in relation to this subject, which cannot be reconciled with the divine Unity. It is with this, and not with the other, that they are charged by Unitarians. Full credit is given to their word, when they declare their belief in the Unity of God, and when they tell us "it is asserted in all their systems of Divinity, and all their Confessions of Faith." Nor is there any thing that I can perceive in Mr. Channing's Sermon, that contradicts this. But until more than this is done, and until something more satisfactory, than. has yet been said, can be alleged by them to show, that the commonly received doctrine of the Trinity is reconcileable with the proper Unity of God, we must be allowed to consider the charge as still lying in its full force.

Of this the most respectable Trinitarian writers seem not to be insensible. How much they are pressed with this difficulty, and how impossible they find it to extricate themselves from it, appears in the variety of explanations which have been successively resorted to, and the dissatisfaction expressed with every attempt that has been made for the purpose. The last expedient, indeed, that of rejecting the use of the phrase " three persons," as applied to the Deity, and substituting for it that of " three distinctions," if by distinctions be meant any thing short of separate persons or agents, may be considered as restoring the divine Unity. But it reduces the Trinity to a mere unmeaning name, and were it not an abuse of language of mischievous tendency, would leave nothing on the subject, that need be thought worth contending about.

Professor Stuart (p. 23) expresses regret that the term *person* had ever come into the symbols of the churches, sensible, as it appears, that it cannot be used in any intelligible meaning, without infringing on the Unity, and running into palpable Tritheism; and the late President Dwight, though he contends for the propriety of the term, (vol. ii. p. 137,) as a *convenient* one for expressing the things intended by the doctrine, yet confesses, that if he is asked *what* it means, he must answer, I know not. But what is the particular convenience of the use of a term, which expresses no meaning, not even in the mind of him that uses it, we are left to conjecture.

Upon the other charge, which relates to the moral

perfections of God, the course which Dr. Woods has pursued seems to me liable to objection. In his fourth Letter, in stating what was necessary on his part, and the mode of reasoning proper to be pursued, in order to relieve the system he has undertaken to defend, from the charge of inconsistency with the moral perfections of God, he says, " we have nothing to do with the inquiry, whether the common doctrine of depravity can consist with the moral perfection of God, nor with any difficulty whatever in the attempt to reconcile them." This is certainly a very extraordinary thought, that in defending his system against an objection to which it is thought liable, he should have nothing to do with the very objection itself, nor with the difficulty it involves. Did the question relate to the simple fact, whether the doctrine of depravity, as maintained by the Orthodox, were a doctrine of scripture or not, its consistency or inconsistency with the moral perfections of God would indeed make no part of the ground, on which the argument should proceed. But the question he had to consider was a different one from this. The doctrine of depravity, together with the associated doctrines, has a place in the system of Orthodox faith. It is upon the ground of these doctrines, as Dr. Woods expressly admits, (p. 25,) that Mr. Channing has used the language, which he understands as implying the charge under consideration, viz. " that the Orthodox deny the moral perfection of God." Now it certainly does belong to him, who would relieve the system from that imputation, to show, not only that the doctrine of depravity, but that all the other doctrines connected with it in the Calvinistic system, are consistent with the moral perfection of God. This is the very point at issue, and the only point, so far as relates to this charge, with which he had any concern; and all that he has said to show, that he maintains many views respecting the divine government and purposes in common with Unitarians, and which are consistent with the moral perfection of God, will do nothing toward proving that he does not maintain other opinions, which are not reconcileable with it. He was required, therefore, in undertaking to repel this charge, not only to prove, which I shall afterward show he has not done, that the scheme of doctrine, which he defends, is taught in the scriptures, but also to prove that it is in itself consistent with the moral perfection of God. But this he has not attempted to do. He has, on the contrary, said that, which implies, that whatever the fact may be, the consistency demanded cannot be seen to exist. Now if he, who believes the doctrines in question to be taught in the scriptures, is yet unable to perceive *how* they are reconcileable with the moral perfection of God; ought he to be greatly surprised, or much disturbed, that another, who cannot find them taught in the bible, and who sees them therefore only as human opinions, without authority, should represent them as irreconcileable with that moral perfection, which he does find there clearly and constantly taught?

There is another consideration also, not to be overlooked, to show that he had something to do with this inquiry. If the doctrine of depravity, as it is maintained by the Orthodox, cannot be perceived by us to be consistent with the moral perfection of God, the presumption is very strong, that it is not true; since, if it actually be inconsistent, it certainly cannot be true. In proportion then to the difficulty of reconciling it, the proof of it from scripture and our experience ought to be clear, and not liable to objection. The neglect, therefore, to remove this fundamental objection to the whole system, you perceive, must have its influence upon all the reasoning employed in the direct proof of its several parts. Nothing but the most clear and satisfactory proof will be sufficient for the support of a doctrine, which labours under the weight of so much intrinsic incredibility, confessedly incapable of being removed.

I have one other remark to make in this place. Dr. Woods has stated correctly, (p. 26,) " That independently of revelation, and well known facts, we are incapable of judging, what the goodness of God will require, as to the condition of man ; or what man's character and state must be under the government of a being infinitely wise and benevolent." But the inference he would draw from this, I think you will perceive, is not warranted by the premises. For although it be conceded, that from the limitation of our faculties, we are incapable of saying what the goodness or justice of God would require; we *have* faculties capable of deciding with certainty, what they will *not admit.* We can pronounce without hesitation with respect to some things, that they are absolutely irreconcileable with those attributes. To say that we have not faculties for this, is to say, not that our knowledge is limited and imperfect, but that it is actually nothing. There may be a thousand cases, like those stated by Dr. Woods, which, previous to experience, we could not have foreseen, nor should have expected, which when first proposed present difficulties, but which are yet capable of being accounted for in a satisfactory manner, and reconciled with that justice and goodness, with which they seem at first to be at variance. But other cases, it is evident, may be supposed, which would admit of no such explanation. And what I contend is, that the orthodox doctrine, as to the natural " character of man, and the manner in which God designates the heirs of salvation" (p. 25) is of this kind ; and that Dr. Woods' assertion (p. 27) " that the facts he has there stated, and which are known to all, are as far from being agreeable to what we should naturally imagine the infinite goodness of God would dictate, as the fact that men are subjects of moral depravity," cannot be supported. There is no such analogy between the cases, as to warrant the conclusion. For we can see, with respect to the former, how they *may* be consistent with the moral perfections of God ; but we can make no supposition, upon which we shall be able to perceive, that the latter *can* be so. The reason is, that, with respect to all the former cases, such as the promiscuous suffering and ruin brought upon men by plagues, hurricanes, and earthquakes,—the cruelties and horrors of the slave-trade,—and the darkness and ignorance to which so large a portion of the human race are by the inevitable circumstances of their condition subjected,—the evil is not final and remediless, but is partial or temporary, and may be considered as inflicted for the purpose of discipline; and the single consideration, that it makes a part of human probation, and that the subject of it may yet, by the manner in which he conducts under it, be an infinite gainer in the whole of his existence, relieves it from all objection arising from any supposed inconsistency with the justice or goodness of God. But the doctrine of the native depravity of man, taken in its connexion with the whole scheme of which it is a part; personal unconditional election, a complete atonement made for those, who are thus ordained to eternal life, and their regeneration by a special irresistible influence of the spirit of God; and what is the necessary and infallible consequence of all this, the equally unconditional reprobation and final and everlasting ruin of all the rest of the human race, certainly admits of no such reconciliation with any notion we can have of the moral perfection of the Author of our being.

As Dr. Woods, however, makes no attempt to show how they are capable of being reconciled; as he has virtually admitted that they are incapable of being perceived by us to be consistent with each other; and has contented himself with endeavouring to prove the several doctrines as matters of fact, upon the principle, that if he can clearly prove them to be doctrines of scripture, he is not bound to show how they can be consistent with the divine perfections, it is unnecessary to say any thing more to show, that the imputation of which he complains is not removed. I shall therefore proceed directly to the consideration of the evidence upon which the several doctrines in question rest, as matters of fact.

LETTER III.

The discussion introduced by Dr. Woods in his fourth Letter, and pursued through the fifth and sixth, relates to " the natural character of man." As the question, " what is the natural character of man," lies at the very foundation of the controversy between Unitarians on the one hand, and Trinitarians and Calvinists on the other, it will prepare us for a fair discussion of it, to examine in the first place, what is the precise difference of opinion between them on the subject.

Heretofore, those who claimed the title of Orthodox, and professed to follow the doctrine of Calvin, were satisfied with the language used by the Westminster divines in the Catechism and Confession of Faith, in which the doctrines of that reformer are expressed with remarkable precision and distinctness. In them the doctrine, which respects the natural state of man since the fall, and in consequence of that event, has two parts. They represent the first sin of our first parent, as *imputed* to all his posterity, who are said *to have sinned in him, and to have fallen with him;* and they teach the entire corruption of man's nature, *that he is utterly indisposed, disabled, and made opposite to all that is spiritually good, and wholly inclined to all evil,—under the displeasure and curse of God, and liable to all punishments in this world and that which is to come.*

It seems that the first part of this account, though it was formerly reckoned one of the principal tests of Orthodoxy, more zealously maintained than any other, is now given up. It is wholly omitted in the Creed adopted by the Theological Institution in Andover. It is expressly given up by Dr. Woods. "The Orthodox in New England at the *present day*," he tells us, p. 44, "are not chargeable with the erroneous opinions held by their predecessors. The imputation of Adam's sin to his posterity, in any sense, which those words naturally and properly convey, is a doctrine which we do not believe." This change in the opinions of the Orthodox, and advance toward what we believe to be right views, we are glad to witness; and have no doubt that the same correct mode of thinking and reasoning, which has led to it, will lead also to the rejection of the other part of the doctrine, which has heretofore been considered as inseparably connected with it. We think that further reflection will convince them, that they *are* inseparably connected—that if the imputation of Adam's guilt is a solecism, and inconsistent with the moral character of God, it is equally so, that, in consequence of it, all his posterity should come into being with a nature so totally corrupt and inclined to sin, as to be incapable of any good.

I could have wished that Dr. Woods had given a more distinct and compact definition of the doctrine he meant to defend on this point, that there might be no mistake of the question between us. From scattered expressions, however, and from his having made no exception with respect to this part of the doctrine, I think we are to conclude, though he chooses to express it in somewhat softened and qualified language, that he holds it in its full extent. By such expressions as the following, (p. 31,) " by nature men are subjects of an innate moral depravity ;"....." while unrenewed, their moral affections and actions are wholly wrong." (p. 43,) " All without exception by nature, or in consequence of their natural birth are in such a state of moral impurity, as disqualifies them for the enjoyments of heaven, unless they are renewed by the Holy Spirit." And (p. 46) " Adam's transgression had such a relation to his posterity, that in consequence of it, they were constituted sinners, and subjected to death, and all other sufferings, as *penal evils ;*" he means all that is meant by the following expressions in the Assembly's Catechism and Confession of Faith. " The corruption of his nature by which he is utterly indisposed, disabled, and made opposite to all that is spiritually good, and wholly inclined to all evil, and that continually—and that men are thus by nature, as they are born, under the displeasure and curse of God; justly liable to all punishments in this world, and that which is to come."

I am fortified in this by recurring to the Creed of the Institution with which he is connected, in which I find the following passage. "That in consequence of his [Adam's] disobedience all his descendants were constituted sinners: that by nature every man is personally depraved, destitute of holiness, unlike and opposed to God, and that previously to the renewing agency of the Divine Spirit, all his moral actions are adverse to the character and glory of God; that being morally incapable of recovering the image of his Creator, which was lost in Adam, every man is justly exposed to eternal damnation."

The doctrine respecting the natural condition of man, which I shall now state, and endeavour to maintain in opposition to this, may be expressed in the following manner.

Man is by nature, by which is to be understood, as he is born into the world, as he comes from the hands of the Creator, innocent and pure; free from all moral corruption, as well as destitute of all positive holiness; and, until he has, by the exercise of his faculties, actually formed a character either good or bad, an object of the divine complacency and favour. The complacency and favour of the Creator are expressed in all the kind provisions that are made by the constitution of things for his improvement and happiness. He is by nature no more inclined or disposed to vice than to virtue, and is equally capable, in the ordinary use of his faculties, and with the common assistance afforded him, of either. He derives from his ancestors a frail and mortal nature ; is made with appetites, which fit him for the condition of being in which God has placed him ; but in order for them to answer all the purposes intended, they are so strong, as to be very liable to abuse by excess. He has passions implanted in him, which are of great importance in the conduct of life, but which are equally capable of impelling him into a wrong or a right course. He has natural affections, all of them originally good, but liable by a wrong direction to be the occasion of error and sin. He has reason and conscience to direct the conduct of life, and enable him to choose aright, which reason may yet be neglected, or perverted, and conscience misguided. The whole of these together make up what constitutes his trial and probation. They make him an accountable being, a proper subject to be treated, according as he shall make a right or wrong choice, being equally capable of either, and as free to the one as to the other.

That this, and not the scheme of innate moral depravity, is the truth, I shall endeavour now to show by arguments drawn

1. From observation and experience, and
2. From the Scriptures.

It is my purpose, previous to entering on this discussion, to observe, what the Orthodox will not hesitate to admit, that judging beforehand, the scheme of total moral depravity, or of any original bias to evil rather than good, is something different from what we should expect, and involves great difficulty in reconciling it with the moral perfections of God. This, as I have before observed, is implied (p. 29) by Dr. Woods himself. I admit, with him, that this is not a sufficient reason for rejecting it in opposition to the evidence of fact, and of scripture, and for the reason which he gives, viz. that we are finite, and cannot so comprehend the purposes and conduct of an infinite being, as to be certain, that what *seems* to us inconsistent with his moral character, is so in reality. But *it is* a good reason for yielding our assent with caution, not till we have examined with care, and not without very satisfactory evidence. It is a reason for suspending our assent, and reexamining, so as to be entirely satisfied as to the fact. I have another remark also to make. The doctrine, it is confessed, is repulsive. The mind naturally revolts at it. It *seems* at first, to all men, universally, to be inconsistent with the divine perfection. But the first impression is made upon us by the nature which God has given us; and I think we should be slow to believe that a nature, thus given to all, is intended to mislead and actually does mislead all, on so important a question. It is certainly an extraordinary fact, if a fact it is, that God should first give to man a corrupt nature, wholly averse to good and inclined to evil, and at the same time endow him with a moral discernment and feelings, which lead him instinctively to deny that God can so have made him, because inconsistent with justice and goodness; that is, that he has given him a natural sense of right and wrong, which lead him to arraign the conduct of the Being who made him.

I proceed now to the inquiry, what observation and experience teach us, as to the fact of human depravity. And here we must not forget, that the question is, not whether there is a great deal of wickedness in the world, but what is the source of that wickedness; not whether mankind are very corrupt, but how they become so; whether it is a character born with them, or acquired; whether it is what God made them, or what they have made themselves. All that is said of the prevalence of wickedness in the world may be true, and yet none of it the effect of an original taint, which men brought into the world with them; none of it making a part of their original nature. I may acquiesce in the mournful and humbling representations given of the violence of human passions, the brutal excesses that follow the unrestrained indulgence of the appetites; the intemperance and self-indulgence of individuals; the wrongs, violation of the rights, and neglect of the duties of domestic life; the injustice, and fraud, and violence, prevalent in every form in all the transactions of social life; the pride, and selfishness, and regardlessness of the rights and feelings of others, appearing in a thousand forms; the wars which desolate the earth, the abuses of government, and the oppression and tyranny, that are exercised by some over the rest of their fellow-beings. All these representations may be true, and no more than a just account of what actually takes place, and yet the whole be fairly accounted for, without any original and natural bias to sin. All may be but the effect of neglect to restrain appetites, in themselves useful and good, to control and give a proper direction to passions designed to be useful and capable of the very best effects, and in general a failure to exercise properly, in temptations and trials, the powers of direction and resistance, which were in themselves sufficient.

But, although this reply may be made, were the representation usually given of the human character, and of the prevalence of wickedness, correct in its fullest extent; I am satisfied that I am not called upon by truth to make that concession. I insist, that the account usually given of human wickedness is exaggerated. It is a partial account, and such as gives a very wrong impression. Men are not the mere brutes and fiends, which it would make them. There is much of good as well as of evil in the human character, and in the conduct of man. Indeed I hesitate not to say, that as much as there is of wickedness and vice, there is far more of virtue and goodness; as much as there is of ill-will, unkindness, injustice, and inhumanity, there is incomparably more of kindness, good disposition, pity, and charity. I insist, that if we take a fair and full view, we shall find that wickedness, far from being the prevailing part of the human character, makes but an inconsiderable part of it. That in by far the largest part of human beings, the just, and kind, and benevolent dispositions prevail beyond measure over the opposite; and that even in the worst men good feelings and principles are predominant, and they probably perform in the course of their lives many more good than bad actions; as the greatest liar does, by the constitution of his nature, doubtless speak many truths to every lie he utters. One great source of misapprehension is, that virtues and good qualities are silent, secret, noiseless; vices are bold, public, noisy, seen by all, felt by all, noted by all.

But whether this be so or not, the ground for rejecting the doctrine of innate original moral depravity will not be materially affected. It is not supported by observation and experience, as we have a right to demand of a doctrine so apparently inconsistent with the moral attributes of the Deity.

What I assert upon this point, and think to be very obvious and capable of being made out to entire satisfaction is, that observation and experience are altogether favourable to the view I have stated of the human character and condition, and that without revelation there is nothing that would lead a reflecting man to the thought of an innate moral depravity.

It is easy to bring together into one picture, and place in a strong light, with exaggerated features, all the bad passions in their uncontrolled and unqualified state, all the atrocious crimes that have been committed, all the bad dispositions that have been indulged; but the picture, though it contain nothing, but what is found in men, will be far, very far, from being a just picture of human nature. Let all that is virtuous and kind, and amiable, and good, be brought into the picture, and presented in their full proportions, and the former will be found to constitute a far less part of it, than we were ready to imagine.

Our most correct ideas of human nature will be drawn from the characteristics of infancy, and the earliest indications of disposition, tendency, and character in the infant mind; and if the nature of man be corrupt, inclined to evil, and evil only, it will appear there with its unequivocal marks. But do we find it there, and is it the common, untaught sentiment of mankind, that it exists there? Far from it. Innocence, and simplicity, and purity are the characteristics of early life. Truth is natural; falsehood is artificial. Veracity, kindness, good-will flow from the natural feelings. Duplicity, and all the cold, and selfish, and calculating manners of society are the fruit of education, and intercourse with the world. We have marks enough of a feeble, helpless nature, calling for sympathy, assistance, support, kindness; but we see no proofs of depravity, of malignity, of inclination to evil in preference to good. How early does the infant discover affection, attachment, gratitude to those from whom it receives kindness! How universally is it an object of interest to those about it! Would it be so, if it manifested such tokens, as the Orthodox doctrine of depravity supposes, of an inclination, disposition, and tendency, wholly directed to evil, and if it appeared to possess nothing good, and no tendency to good?

Instead of this, must it not naturally be the object of aversion and disgust, and especially so to pious and virtuous persons, who can only love and approve those, whom God loves and approves; and who therefore can see in little children, only objects of the divine displeasure and wrath, beings wholly averse to God and all that is good, and who deserve, not sympathy and affection, but all punishments of this world and the world to come?

It is often said, that children are naturally inclined to falsehood and deception, and that they early lie and deceive, rather than speak the truth. But this charge needs proof; and I apprehend it will be found, that evidence is abundantly against it, and in favour of the natural veracity of children. It will rarely be found, that children disregard the truth, till by example, or bad education, or peculiar circumstances of temptation, they have learned to overcome and counteract the tendency of nature. That they are so proverbially simple, unsuspicious, and easily imposed upon, arises from their judging others by themselves. It is because they themselves are conscious of no thought of deceiving, that they never suspect others. Great differences of character in this, as in other respects, appear at an early age; but what I have stated, I am persuaded is the general character, until the disposition and tendency of nature has been changed by education, example, and circumstances.

It is alleged also, that children are naturally cruel, and in proof of it, the pleasure they seem to take in torturing insects and small animals is sometimes mentioned. But the pleasure, which the convulsions and throes of a tortured insect or animal give to a child, arises from another source than cruelty, or the desire of giving pain. It is wholly to be attributed to the love of excitement, and the pleasure it takes in rapid and violent motion; and is wholly unconnected with the idea of suffering in the creature, with whose convulsions it is delighted. The same pleasure would be derived from the power of producing the same convulsive motions, and the same appearance in any inanimate substance. In proof of this, let a clear idea of the suffering of the insect be communicated to the child, and it will no longer take pleasure in its convulsions. A sentiment of compassion will be raised. It will be as eager to rescue it from its suffering, as before it was to inflict that suffering. This I am persuaded will usually, if not always, be the case. But if it were from native cruelty, the *love* of inflicting pain, or from any depravity of nature; instead of ceasing from it the moment it was made acquainted with the suffering of the animal, that knowledge would be a new motive to proceed; as it would give it the satisfaction of knowing, that its malignant purpose was effected, its cruel design accomplished. The same account is to be given of what is often called a mischievous disposition in children. It is not the love of mischief, but an exuberant love of activity. The mischief or inconvenience which they occasion to others is no part of the motive, but simply the love of action and strong excitement; and it may be accompanied with the kindest feelings, the most sincere desire of giving pleasure to others, and as sincere an unwillingness to give pain or to cause uneasiness or displeasure.

Indeed I know not a single mark of early depravity, common to children in general, which may not, as these are, be fairly traced to causes, which imply no degree of depravity, and no fault of character, or of disposition. Individuals there may be, who give very early tokens' of great perversity of mind, and corruption of heart. But these are exceptions from the general character of human nature, and, as such, have no place in the present argument ; and if they had any, would be decisive, not in favour of the Orthodox doctrine, but against it; as the *exception*, in its nature, proves the *opposite rule*. If great depravity is the exception, exemption from depravity must be the rule.

No man, I am persuaded, was ever led by personal observation and experience to the thought of an original depravity of human nature, according to which, by the bias of nature, all, without exception, who come into the world, are from their birth inclined wholly to evil, and averse to good.

And as little, I am persuaded, would any one be led to such an opinion by the general current of scripture. I am led to think so by a general view of the commands, precepts, exhortations, promises, and threatenings of religion, and by the whole history of the divine dispensations to men ; and also by attending to a great number of particulars, each of which, separately, seems to me to imply, that mankind come into the world innocent and pure, the objects of the complacency of the Creator, and no more inclined, by the nature God has given them, to sin, than to virtue ; no more disposed to hate and disobey, than to love and obey their Maker. I shall instance only in one, but that alone, in my opinion, is decisive of the question. I refer to the manner in which little children are, on two occasions, spoken of by our Saviour, and on one by the Apostle Paul. (Matt. xix. 14.) " Suffer little children to come unto me—for of such is the kingdom of heaven." These appear to have been infants, or at least very small children, for he took them into his arms and blessed them. There is no intimation of any thing peculiar in them; no evidence that they were a few selected from among many ; nothing to suggest that they were different from other children; but rather, that they were like other children. There is not the slightest intimation that these particular children had become the subjects of any great moral change. But if they were depraved, destitute of holiness, averse from all good, inclined to all evil, enemies of God, subjects of his wrath, justly liable to all punishments, could our Saviour declare respecting them, "of such is the kingdom of God?" And could he, on another occasion, say, (Matt. xviii. 3,) " Unless ye be converted, and become as little children, ye cannot enter into the kingdom of God ?" And again, (Mark x. 14. Luke xviii. 16,) " Whosoever shall not receive the kingdom of God as a little child, he shall not enter therein ?"

Could the Apostle Paul recommend to the Corinthians (1 Cor. xiv. 20,) "Be not children in understanding, but in malice be ye children, but in understanding be men;" that is, in understanding, in the power of distinguishing right and wrong, and perceiving the truth, show yourselves to be men; but in your dispositions, in your moral characters, manifest the gentleness, and mildness, and purity of children? I know not how those passages are to be explained, so as to consist with the doctrine of innate depravity, rendering those who are the subjects of it enemies to God &c. until renewed by the special influence of the spirit of God. I have never seen them satisfactorily explained upon that supposition, nor do I believe that they admit of such explanation. They most clearly imply, until turned from their obvious meaning, that young children are objects of the Saviour's complacency and affection; that their innocency, gentleness, and good disposition, are the proper objects of imitation; that they are, what men are to become by conversion or regeneration.

But there are, as I have said, a few texts, from which the doctrine I am considering is inferred, and these have been brought forward, and placed in all the strength of which they are capable, by those who believe and defend the doctrine, and particularly by the able advocate it has found in the author of the pamphlet before me.

It is not pretended, I believe, by any of the defenders of the native, hereditary depravity of the human race, that the doctrine is, any where in scripture, expressly asserted. It is not a matter of direct assertion, but of inference. It is considered as implied in several passages. Now I admit that a doctrine, no where expressly taught, may yet be so clearly, and constantly implied, may so enter into the whole texture of the sacred writings, and appear in every part, as to be as reasonable an object of our faith, as those doctrines, which are the most distinctly and formally enunciated. But examples of this kind are usually (I will not affirm always, but usually) such as are presented, not a few times only, and then in a doubtful form, but such as appear constantly, and enter as it were into the very substance of the whole. Such, for instance, is the being of God, no where asserted, but every where implied. Such is the moral freedom of man, upon which rests his accountability as a moral being; and such, in my apprehension, is the doctrine, that men become sinners, guilty before God, and objects of his displeasure only by their personal acts, and not by the nature with which they came into being.

The first text adduced, as implying innate total depravity, is Gen. vi. 5. A few remarks will show how little it is to the purpose, and how far from supporting what is made to rest upon it. For, in the first place, it relates not to mankind universally, but to the degenerate race of men of that age, so remarkably and universally corrupt, beyond all that had gone before, or have followed since, as to call for the most signal tokens of the vengeance of heaven. In the second place, were it said of all men in every age, instead of being confined, as it is, to the inhabitants of the earth at that particular time, it would still be nothing to the purpose, for which it is brought. There is no assertion of native derived depravity, none of a corrupt nature, no intimation of hereditary guilt, no reference to innate aversion to good and inclination to evil. It is the mere assertion of a state of great corruption and wickedness, which no one denies ; and not only of external actions, such as " the world being full of violence," but of purposes and dispositions of the heart, implying deep-rooted and radical wickedness, expressed by " the imaginations of the heart." But this is all perfectly consistent with their coming into being, innocent and pure. It is not what they are by nature, but by habit; not what they were as they came from the hands of the Creator, but what they have become in the use or rather abuse of his gifts, and of the condition in which he placed them.

It is said that the language here is universal, as also when it is used again in the viii. chapter ; and that its application to *man universally* in all ages and nations, is confirmed by the passages quoted by Paul, in the iii. chapter of Romans from Psalms xiv. liii. v. cxl. x. xxxvi. and Isaiah lix. where he describes Jews and Gentiles of that age, in passages borrowed from the Old Testament, and applies them as descriptive of the character of mankind without exception. But in each case the argument wholly fails of proving what it is brought to prove ; because it depends for its force on an interpretation of language, which cannot be adopted without leading to consequences, which the advocates of universal original depravity would be as slow to admit, as its opposers.

It goes on the supposition that the sacred writers used words, as no other writers ever did use them, with perfect philosophical exactness, instead of the popular sense; and that their writings were to be interpreted by rules, to which no other writings will bear to be subjected.

Universal expressions, like those in the texts in question, are so far from being always used in their strict literal sense, that they are *usually relative*, to be understood and interpreted in relation to the subject and occasion. Thus when it is said, (1 Tim. ii. 4,) " God will have all men to be saved and come to the knowledge of the truth," it relates to the question, whether any class or nation of men are excluded from the favour and good will of God, and therefore ought to be excluded from a share in the benevolent regards and prayers of Christians; so that *all men* means, not every individual, but all ranks, descriptions, and conditions of men. In the unlimited sense of the words it is not true. It is not true that God wills every individual to come to the knowledge of the truth, i. e. of the Gospel; for thousands are precluded from the possibility of it by the circumstances of their being. Nor is it true, that he wills all men to be finally saved; but only all of every rank, and every nation, who are penitent, obedient, and faithful. He wills none to be excluded from having the truth proposed, and salvation offered to them. And that *all* who receive and obey it, shall actually obtain the salvation offered. So also (Tit. ii. 11) when it is said, "the grace of God bringing salvation hath appeared to *all* men," the meaning cannot be, *every individual,* for it never has been published to *all* in that sense. But, as in the other case, to men of every nation, age, rank, condition, and in the same sense in which Paul (Col. i. 23) spoke of the Gospel as "preached to every creature under heaven."

It is in a similar, popular, qualified sense, a sense never leading men into mistakes upon other subjects and common occasions, that Moses, speaking of the general wickedness and corruption of manners, which were the occasion of the flood, uses language, which in its strictly literal import might be understood to mean, that there was no virtue remaining on the earth; though he immediately tells us, that Noah was an exception to the prevailing wickedness, that "he found favour in the eyes of the Lord, (ch. vi. 8, 9) being a just man, perfect in his generations, and one who walked with God."

The same remark occurs with equal force in respect to the passage so much relied on in the xiv. Psalm. Not only is there no intimation as to the origin and source of the evil, no intimation of an inbred, innate, hereditary depravity, but only of great and general corruption of manners; but though a verbal universality is expressed, the very Psalm itself takes care to teach us with what qualifications it is to be understood. For while it asserts, in the strong language of emotion and eastern hyperbole, "that all were gone aside, all together become filthy, none that did good, *no, not one,*" the writer seems wholly unconscious of a design to have his language understood according to its literal import; for he immediately goes on with expressions absolutely incompatible with such a meaning. He goes on to speak of a " people of God, a generation of the righteous, whose refuge was God." The same is the case with each of the other Psalms, quoted by Paul in his Epistle to the Romans.

But it is of little comparative importance, whether the authors of the Psalms, or the Apostle in quoting them, meant to be understood as expressing a general truth in popular language, or as expressing themselves with literal philosophical exactness. Understand them in the most unlimited, unqualified sense, of which their words are capable, they express only what no one will deny, that all men are sinners. The question will still be open, as before, how this universality of sin and great corruption of manners are to be accounted for. Whether, as the advocates of Orthodoxy contend, men come into the world with a corrupt nature, prone only to wickedness, and utterly incapable of any good thought or action, till renewed by an influence of the holy spirit, which they can do nothing to procure; or as Unitarians believe, this corrupt nature is not what they received from God, but what they have made for themselves. That they were not made sinners, but became so by yielding to temptations, which it was in their power to resist, by obeying the impulse of the passions, and the calls of appetite, in opposition to the direction of reason and the notices of conscience; by subjecting themselves to the dominion of the inferior part of their nature, instead of putting themselves under the guidance of their superior faculties.

Questions may be asked upon this statement, which cannot be answered, because we have not faculties which enable us in any cases to trace things up to the first cause and spring of action. But no difficulty so great and insurmountable meets us, as, on the opposite theory, is the moral difficulty in which it involves the character of the Author of our being. When we have traced back the wickedness of men, as it actually exists, to the voluntary neglect, and perversion, and abuse of the nature God has given them, we can go no farther.

It is asserted, (pp. 38, 39) "that when we read in the Bible the highest descriptions of human wickedness in the old world, in Sodom, in Canaan, in Jerusalem; or of the wickedness of individuals, as Pharaoh, Saul, Jeroboam, and Judas; it is perfectly just and natural for us to reflect, *such is human nature, such is man;* and Orthodox writers reason in an unexceptionable manner, when they undertake to show, what *human nature* is, from the description which is given of the wickedness of man in the Old Testament."

The writer, I think, must perceive that he has expressed himself rashly or carelessly, when he considers clearly the force and bearing of what he has said in the above paragraph. Are we to consider those places, which, singled out and distinguished from all others, are expressly declared to have been destroyed for their enormous and incorrigible wickedness, as fair representatives of the usual state and character of the human race? People, who were ordered to be wholly extirpated for the very purpose of stopping the contagion of their vices, preventing the spread of the infection, and serving as a warning to other nations to prevent their becoming like them? Are Pharaoh, Jeroboam, and Judas, fair examples and representatives of human nature? Men, singled out in a history of two thousand years, as instances of uncommon wickedness, visited with as uncommon tokens of retributory justice? Let it be asked, why the cruelty and obstinacy of Pharaoh, rather than the humanity, and piety, and meekness of Moses; why the idolatry, and unprincipled ambition, and selfishness of Jeroboam, rather than the piety, tenderness of conscience, and public spirit of Josiah; why the single wretch, who was so base and sordid as to sell and betray his Master, rather than the eleven, who were true and faithful to him, should be selected as specimens of the race to which they belong, and the great community of which they make a part?

Would you select the period of seven years' famine, as an example of the usual fertility of Egypt? The desolating pestilence in the days of David, as a fair specimen of the salubrity of the climate of Israel?

Would you go to a lazar-house or hospital, rather than to the fields, the wharves, and the factories, to know what is the usual state of human health and activity? Is an ideot or a madman a just specimen of the human intellect? Or are we to find in our prisons, and at the gallows, in highwaymen, pirates, and murderers, a true index to point out the general morals of the community?

It is unnecessary to multiply remarks on the next text brought to prove human depravity. (Jer. xvii. 9) "The heart is deceitful above all things, and desperately wicked." Admit that it relates to a prevailing trait in the human character; do we not well know, that in the common use of language, such general expressions are seldom to be understood as universal in their application? They are to be understood in a limited and popular sense. What is more than this, though the text were intended to express a trait of character absolutely universal, it has no more relation to the question respecting the source of human wickedness, whether it be natural or acquired, than any other descriptions of prevalent wickedness in the world. But the total irrelevancy of the text to the purpose for which it is brought, appears best by considering the subject matter, about which it is introduced. The prophet is stating the safety of trusting in God, and the insecurity of trusting in man. The reason is, that men are deceitful, and not to be depended on. Now this reason would be good, and support the prophet's conclusion, though deceit and treachery were not the universal, though they were not even the general character of men. Were there many to be found, who would deceive and betray, it would be sufficient to justify the prophet, in withdrawing men from their confidence in man, and teaching them to place it in him, who can *never* fail, and will *never* deceive. And it would sufficiently account for his adding in the next verse, "I the Lord search the heart." However deceitful men may be, and able to impose on men; there is one, who is able to detect, and will not fail to punish.

From the New Testament, the first passage selected, as implying the doctrine under consideration, is the answer of Christ to Nicodemus, (John iii. 3) " Except a man be born again, he cannot see the kingdom of God." It is contended, (pp. 42, 43) that the universal necessity of regeneration, expressed in this text, implies universal depravity. "That this necessity of a moral renovation arises from the character man possesses in consequence of his natural birth; that all must be born again, because, and only because, all without exception are, by nature, or in consequence of their natural birth, in such a state of moral impurity, as disqualifies them for the enjoyments of heaven, unless they are renewed by the holy spirit."

A single consideration convinces me, that the inference is without foundation, and that the universal necessity of regeneration may consist with original innocency, and exemption from any prevailing tendency, as we are born into the world, to vice rather than virtue. By their natural birth men only become human, reasonable, accountable beings. "What is born of the flesh is flesh." They receive by their natural birth only the human nature. They receive no moral character, but only the faculties and powers, in the exercise of which a moral character is to be formed. The formation of this character introduces them into a new state of being, and by whatever means, and at whatever time it takes place, it may be called, by no very remote or unusual figure, a new birth; and those, who have thus acquired a moral character, and received the principles of a spiritual life, in addition to the natural human life, may be said to be born again. Now if this was what Jesus meant in what he said to Nicodemus, it will no more imply original sin, than original holiness. It will only imply the absence or want of that, which was necessary to becoming a subject of the kingdom of God. The terms *new birth, born again, born of the spirit, renewed, become a new man,* are applied with as much propriety to those, who receive the influences of the Gospel, and acquire the character, which it is intended to form, on the supposition of original innocence and purity, as upon that of native depravity and original sinfulness. In each case alike, it expresses a great moral change, and implies the formation of a new character, not possessed before. On the supposition, therefore, that this passage refers, as is generally supposed by interpreters, to that great moral change, which the religion of the Gospel is to produce on those who embrace it, in order to their being fit members of the kingdom of heaven on earth and in glory; it will be seen to be nothing to the purpose of those, who attempt to build upon it the doctrine of a moral depravity, with which all men are born into the world. It will only imply, that they do not possess by birth that character of personal holiness and positive virtue, which is necessary to their being Christians, fit subjects of the present and future kingdom of God.

The passage, (Rom. v. 12) "Wherefore, as by one man sin entered into the world, and death by sin, and so death passed upon all men, for that all have sinned," is of another kind, and to be shown to have no relation to the subject by other considerations. The whole force of this passage, (if it have any, as relates to this subject,) lies in the last clause, "For that all have sinned." Now if this clause be understood in a sense, which shall prove any thing to the purpose, it will prove the genuine old Calvinistic doctrine, the imputation of Adam's sin. It leads back to the notion of a federal head, of Adam's acting not only on his own responsibility, but for all his posterity; acting in their stead, so that his action was theirs, and they "sinned *in him* and fell *with him* in his first transgression." They are all sinners by the sin of him, their representative, federal head. The myriads who die in earliest infancy, before it is possible for them to perform any act, or to have any volition, either sinful or virtuous, yet die because they are sinners. They are sinners then by the sin of another, by the imputation of sin to them; and this is the true doctrine of Calvinism; and this, it seems to me, is also the doctrine of Dr. Woods, notwithstanding his explicit rejection of it, as stated in words. For besides that he acquiesces in the qualified statement of Stapfer, (p. 45) (which, after all, must mean the doctrine of imputation in its full extent, if it have any intelligible meaning; since God's giving Adam a *posterity* like himself, if it mean any thing to the purpose, must mean *sinners* like himself;) besides this, he asserts, that the Apostle's reasoning goes on the ground, that (p. 46) "Adam's transgression had, in the plan of the divine administration, such a relation to his posterity, that in consequence of it, they were *constituted sinners,* and subjected to death and all other sufferings, as *penal evils.*" Now if the posterity of Adam being *constituted sinners,* and subjected to all sufferings, as *penal evils,* that is, as punishments, in consequence of his transgression, mean any thing to the purpose for which it is introduced, and yet short of the common Calvinistic notion of imputation, I am unable to perceive what it is, and it needs explanation, and a more definite statement, than I have seen.

But I am persuaded the passage has no such meaning. It is a single phrase taken away from its connexion, and what is more, out of the middle of an argument. Did it therefore, as it does not, express distinctly our original native depravity, it would give very little satisfaction alone; for there is no sentiment so absurd, that it may not be supported by single sentences, thus detached from the connexion in which they are used. But I have observed that in its most obvious sense it expresses no such native corruption. Understood literally, the only assertion it contains with certainty is that of a fact, which none will deny, the universality of sin, that *all* have sinned. Now the nature of the universality intended to be asserted, in this, as in every case, is to be learned from the circumstances of the case. All who are *capable of sinning*, all *as soon as* they are capable of it, all as soon as they are *moral agents*. Such limitations of the sense of universal expressions in other cases are constantly occurring. Were all the inhabitants of a country required to take an oath of allegiance to the government; the requisition would be considered as complied with, though no infants and small children had taken the oath, and all would be considered as included under its obligation. But there is another consideration, which ought to prevent this text from being considered of any weight on the subject. The whole passage in which it stands is one of the most intricate and difficult in the New Testament. The phrase,* on which so much is made to depend,

---

* 'Εφ' ᾧ, in our translation, "*for that,*" has been rendered by the several phrases, *because, inasmuch as, as far as, in whom, unto which, after whom, on account of whom.* When meanings so various are assigned to this text by Schleusner, Elsner, Taylor, Doddridge, Whitby, and Macknight, I am justified in attributing to it a degree of obscurity and uncertainty, which should prevent it from being alleged with much confidence in proof of any doctrine, which it may be supposed to express.

admits equally well of several different translations, each of which will give it a different meaning; and its connexion with the passage in which it stands is not such, as to help us, to any degree of certainty, in determining by which version its true sense is expressed. Dr. Woods himself, " allows it to be in some respects very obscure." He will doubtless admit then, that the support derived to a doctrine, depending on any particular translation of this text, or any particular meaning assigned to it, will be of very little value ; of none indeed any farther, than it receives support itself from other plainer passages.

Ephesians ii. 3. " And were by nature children of wrath, even as others." The connexion and circumstances of the case show the meaning of this verse, and that it furnishes no proof of inbred moral corruption, but only of corrupt and wicked habits. It refers to the former state of Jews as well as heathen, before their conversion to Christianity. In that state, they were all alike, children of wrath, deserving of wrath, not as they came into the world, not as they came from their Maker's hand, but as they became by the habits, and customs, and practices of that state, into which they were born ; which was a state of nature, as compared with the state of grace, into which they were introduced by Christianity. What they were before they became Christians, they were by nature ; what they became afterward, was by the grace of God, which appeared bringing salvation. The state of nature was that, into which they came by their birth; as distinguished from the state of grace into which they came, when they embraced Christianity. When they received Christianity, they were born again, born of water by their baptism, born of the spirit by receiving the spirit of Christianity, by being renewed in the temper of their mind. Then they were no longer children of wrath, when the new birth was completed, and their religion had produced all its moral effects.

According to this view of the subject, the state of nature has no reference to what a man brings into the world with him, but it stands opposed to a state of grace. It is that state in which all are, Jews as well Gentiles, before they become Christians. This language of the Apostle, like much of that in the Epistles, referring to the same subject, relates to men, as bodies of men, not as individuals. It compares them together as bodies, not as individuals. It speaks of them *generally*, as in their heathen and Jewish state, and then in their Christian state. In the former " dead in sin," in the latter " quickened, and raised up," and (v. 5, 6.) " made to sit together in heavenly places."

The former, (12, 13.) " Strangers, aliens, without God, without hope, afar off;" the latter, " made nigh by the blood of Christ."

The former, (19.) " Strangers and foreigners;" the latter, " fellow-citizens with the saints, and of the household of God."

The former, (3, 1.) " children of wrath, having their conversation in the lusts of the flesh, dead in trespasses and sins;" the latter, (4, 5, 10.) " by the rich mercy of God, quickened, saved by grace, created by Christ Jesus unto good works."

The whole of this refers to the same thing; not to the personal condition of individuals as such, but to that of the whole body of Christians, as quickened and raised from the moral and spiritual death of their original Jewish and heathen state; as delivered from the state of wrath, in which they had lived from their birth; and by the rich mercy of God and the faith of the Gospel, made to sit together in heavenly places, that is, to enjoy all the privileges and hopes of Christians.

It has no reference therefore to the state in which persons are born into the world in all ages. Those now born into the world in Christian lands, are not in the same sense that these Ephesians were, *children of wrath by nature,* but as these same Ephesians were after their conversion to Christianity, *saved by the grace of God, quickened, raised from the dead, made nigh by the blood of Christ, fellow-citizens with the saints, of the household of God.*

All this language was applied to the Ephesians universally after their conversion, and all of it is as applicable universally now to those, who are Christians by birth; as distinguished from those, who are heathen by birth.

The phrase we are considering then must be seen to be wholly inapplicable to the purpose for which it is alleged.

We are called upon by the advocates for the doctrine of depravity to show, that it is inconsistent with the moral perfection of God; that it is not taught in the scriptures; and that all the wickedness in the world may be accounted for without admitting the doctrine.

With respect to the first, I might satisfy myself with saying, that it belongs to those, who maintain the doctrine, to prove its consistency with the moral perfection of God. But I have no wish to avail myself of the right, which every one has, who is called upon to prove a negative, of throwing back the burden of proof. It is one of the cases in which the negative is susceptible of satisfactory proof.

When we charge the common doctrine of depravity with being inconsistent with the moral character of God, it is, as taken in connexion with the rest of the system, of which it makes a part. It is the whole system together that we maintain is incapable of being defended in consistency with the moral attributes of the Author of our being. Whatever the nature of man be, it is such, as he received at the hand of his Maker. Whatever tendency and proneness to evil there may be in him, as he is born into the world, it is no greater than his Maker gave him. We assert then that no guilt, no fault can be attributed to him by his Maker for such proneness. If God be a just being, he cannot be displeased with him for being what he made him. If he be a good being, he cannot punish him for it. To subject him to *penal evils* for a propensity to sin, born with him in consequence of his descent from a sinful ancestor, is not the less cruel and unjust for his being *voluntary* in following that propensity, unless he had also the natural of communicated power to resist it. If he have that power, then he becomes guilty and deserving of punishment, so soon as in the indulgence of the propensity he actually becomes a sinner, but no sooner. Till then, even on the supposition above, no guilt is incurred. The propensity itself is no sin and implies no guilt. And afterward the justice of his subjection to penal evils depends on his power of being and acting otherwise than he does. Had he no power to be, to feel, and to act otherwise than he does, he could not be guilty and deserving of punishment for continuing in his present state. But according to the scheme, which assumes to be that of Orthodoxy, those who are the subjects of this innate moral depravity, inclination to evil, and wholly " wrong state of the moral affections and actions," (p. 31) are utterly incapable of doing any thing toward producing in themselves a moral change, or which shall be a reason with God for granting to them that grace, which is necessary to their regeneration and sanctification. It is only the irresistible influence of the spirit of God, which can renew and change their nature. Now we assert, that until this grace has been imparted and resisted, there can be no blame-worthiness. Beings so situated may be the objects of pity to the Author of their being, and his pity may be manifested in bringing suffering upon them in the way of dicipline, for the purpose of promoting their renovation, and bringing them to a state of holiness : but it cannot be inflicted by a just being as punishment. Now, if I rightly understand the scheme of Calvinism, divine punishments are not, according to that scheme, disciplinary, but vindictive. God punishes his offending creatures, not to reform them, but to vindicate his authority. The sufferings of the wicked have no tendency to reform, but rather to harden and confirm them in their opposition to God and their duty.

Now however consistent with justice may be the infliction of vindictive punishment, where it is in the power of the subject of it to be different from what he is, and to act otherwise than he does; it is contended that it cannot be so, where the guilt to be punished is inbred, a part of man's original nature, such as he came from the Creator's hands ; where, in fact, the sinner is as his Maker sent him into the world, not as he has made himself by his own act, by the abuse, or neglect, or perversion of his power, and his faculties and affections.

That the doctrine is not contained in the scriptures I have endeavoured to show, by showing the insufficiency of the several texts from the Old and New Testament, on which Dr. Woods relies for its support; and that they admit of a satisfactory interpretation, which gives no countenance to it. I know very well, that these are not the only texts which are supposed to relate to the subject ; but I do not know that any others are thought to have more weight, or to present greater difficulties. I have limited myself to these, solely from a wish not to extend the discussion beyond what was rendered necessary, by the course pursued by Dr. Woods; and presuming that the texts, which he has selected, were those on which he would place his chief reliance.

When the extent and prevalence of wickedness in the world are urged as indicating an original inherent corruption, and we are called upon to account for it in a satisfactory manner, without admitting the Orthodox doctrine of depravity; I shall think it sufficient to refer you to the account which I have given of our moral constitution, and the state of trial in which we are placed. Being, by the whole of our nature and condition, equally capable of virtue and of vice, of a right and of a wrong course; it is no more difficult to account for the actual existence of the highest, than of the lowest degree of either. But I have also another consideration to suggest. It will not, I suppose, be pretended, that our first parents were, previous to their fall, subjects of the same moral depravity, which is attributed to their descendants. It will be admitted that they were created innocent and pure, "in the image of God in righteousness and holiness;" yet they became sinners. Now it belongs to him, who urges the wickedness of mankind as a proof of innate original depravity, to account for the sin of our first parents, who are admitted to have been created, not only in a state of innocence, but of positive holiness.

I have one only remark more, which I wish to make in conclusion upon this subject. The doctrine, which I have been considering in this letter, Dr. Woods styles, (p. 31) his "humbling conclusion." In this he intimates, what is often more distinctly expressed by Orthodox writers, that the doctrine is of a more humbling nature, more expressive of self abasement, and of a sense of human demerit and unworthiness, than that which declares our nature to be originally pure, innocent, free from enmity to God, and from an inclination only to evil. But with how little justice this is claimed, I am persuaded you will be convinced, by a moment's reflection. Can that be thought a more humbling doctrine, which traces all our wicked actions up to an original constitution, given us at first by our Maker, and a depravity of nature which he gave us when he gave us being; than that which attributes all our sins to our own neglect, and abuse, and perversion of the gifts of God? We have certainly no cause to feel ourselves humbled under a sense of any thing that we are by nature. We have occasion to be ashamed only of what we have become by practice. For the nature God has given us no sentiment but that of gratitude is due. Humility and self-condemnation should spring only from the consciousness of a course of life not answering to the powers, and faculties, and privileges of our nature. What God has made us, we should think of with unmingled satisfaction; what we have made ourselves, we cannot think of with too deep regret, and sorrow, and shame.

LETTER IV.

In the system of Orthodoxy defended by Dr. Woods, the doctrine of Election stands in immediate and close connexion with that of the total depravity of human nature, and is brought forward by him the next in order. He seems to enter upon the discussion of this subject with the impression, that he has strong prepossessions to encounter, and that these prepossessions are not without foundation. "I acknowledge," he says, (p. 52) "that orthodox writers and preachers of high repute, but deficient in judgment, have, in some instances, exhibited the doctrine in a manner, which has given too much occasion for these prepossessions; and too much occasion for this author (Mr. Channing) to think, that the doctrine is inconsistent with the moral perfection of God." Again, (p. 63) "Orthodox writers have not unfrequently made use of expressions, which, at first view, may seem to furnish occasion for some of the heavy charges brought against us by our opposers. But for the rash, unqualified expressions of men, who have become hot and violent by controversy, we are not to be held responsible. We here enter our solemn protest against the language, which has sometimes been employed, and the conceptions which have sometimes been entertained on this subject by men, who have been denominated Calvinists." Again, (p. 79) "I am willing to concede, that *those views* of the doctrine of Election, against which Whitby and many other respectable writers direct their principal arguments, are *justly liable to objection.*" From these passages one might be led to suppose, that those, whose opinions Dr. Woods professes to represent, maintain the doctrine of Election in some qualified sense, and not as it is to be found in the popular writers, and confessions. And in this he would be confirmed by the statement at the close of the discussion. (p. 81) " You now see what we mean by the doctrine of Election, and in what manner we believe it. *As the result of his own unsearchable wisdom and grace, and for reasons which relate to the great ends of his administration, God eternally purposed to save a great number of our race, and purposed to save them precisely in the manner in which he actually does save them.*" From this form of the doctrine, I presume no Unitarian would dissent; and were there nothing in the Letters of Dr. Woods to show that the Orthodox faith is something more than is here expressed, one would have supposed he might have been spared the labour of any formal defence of it against objection, and all that solicitude which he seems to have felt " in disclosing to his readers with the utmost frankness his inmost thoughts upon the subject." (p. 82.)

If this is a complete statement of the doctrine of Election, as it is understood by the Orthodox, and if Dr. Woods and those whom he represents, and for whom he professes to speak, do not maintain the opinions against which the Sermon of Mr. Channing is directed; there seems to have been no good reason, why he should feel himself concerned at all in the charge. *Calvinists* only, who *do* maintain them, can fairly consider their opinions as attacked, and themselves called upon to defend them.

But Dr. Woods has no where informed us, who those " Orthodox writers of high repute" are, who have exposed the doctrine to objection by their injudicious exhibitions of it; nor has he told us in what respects they have given a false representation of it. It is to be regretted that he did not think it necessary to do this, as he must perceive how much it is calculated to perplex, and how much it may mislead, his readers. For, as a simple statement drawn from the several parts of his letters will show, it cannot have been his design to express his dissent from the *doctrine* of Election as expressed in the strongest language of orthodox writers; but only to guard against *the impression,* which he supposes the strong and naked statement of it may be likely to make.

The following is the statement of this doctrine by the Westminster Divines, as it stands in their Confession of Faith, and more briefly in the Assembly's Catechism.

" God did from all eternity freely and unchangeably ordain whatsoever comes to pass."

" By the decree of God some men and angels are predestinated unto everlasting life, and others fore-ordained to everlasting death."

"These angels and men, thus predestinated and fore-ordained, are particularly and unchangeably designed, and their number so certain and definite, that it cannot be either increased or diminished."

"Those of mankind that are predestinated unto life, God, before the foundation of the world was laid, according to his eternal and immutable purpose, and the secret counsel and good pleasure of his will, hath chosen in Christ unto everlasting glory, out of his mere free grace and love, without any foresight of faith or good works, or perseverance in either of them, or any other thing, in the creature, as conditions or causes, moving him thereunto."

"As God hath appointed the elect unto glory, so hath he, by the eternal and most free purpose of his will, fore-ordained all the means thereunto. Wherefore, they who are elected, being fallen in Adam, are redeemed by Christ, are effectually called unto faith in Christ, &c. Neither are any other redeemed by Christ, effectually called, &c. but the elect only."

"The rest of mankind God was pleased, according to the unsearchable counsel of his own will, whereby he extendeth or withholdeth mercy, as he pleaseth, to pass by, and to ordain them to dishonour and wrath for their sin."

I will now place before you, in the best manner I am able, such a view of Dr. Woods' opinions upon the subject, as is to be found in scattered passages through his VIIth and VIIIth letters.

"The Father has given to Christ a part of the human race, and those, who have thus been given to Christ, are the persons, who shall have eternal life;"

(p. 54) and this, he goes on to prove at large, "denotes *all who shall finally be saved.*" (p. 55.)

"In every case, a person's being given to Christ *secures* his coming to Christ; and, when Christ speaks of those, who were given him of the Father, he includes the whole number that shall be saved." (p. 56.)

"God has a *purpose, choice, will,* and *good pleasure,* respecting those who are saved; a *purpose* or *choice,* which was in the mind of God before they existed; a purpose, which does not rest upon any personal merit in those, who are its objects; of grace, excluding *all works of righteousness* from having any concern in this subject." (p. 57.)

"Nothing is effected by the efforts of man, but every thing depends on the mercy of God." (p. 59.)

"The sovereign purpose of God relates to man's eternal interests, to their religious character and salvation."....."I could, as I think, make it appear, that the doctrine of God's sovereign Election is the only doctrine, which accounts satisfactorily for *the actual difference, which exists between true believers, and the rest of the world.*" (pp. 61, 62.)

"We hold it as a fact, universally, that impenitent, unrenewed sinners do no good work, which God regards as a condition of their being renewed, or on account of which he has promised them regeneration: that, in all cases, he calls and renews them according to his own purpose and grace." (pp. 67, 68.)

"We believe that those, who are chosen of God to salvation, are not chosen because they were, in themselves, more worthy of this blessing than others, that God looked upon their moral feelings and conduct with the same disapprobation, and had the same view of their ill-desert, and that he chose them, as we may say, *for reasons of state;* for general reasons in his government, which he has not revealed."...." The purpose and administration of God are, in this respect, different from what our wisdom would dictate, or our affections choose; they cannot be accounted for by any principles known to us, but result from the infinite perfection of God, and are conformed to reasons, which he has concealed in his own mind." (p. 74)

If you will compare these passages with those before quoted from the Westminster Confession, you will find that they differ from each other only in the degree of clearness and explicitness, with which the same doctrine is expressed.

I shall now endeavour to show, that the " method of designating the heirs of salvation," which this doctrine implies, can neither be reconciled with our natural notions of the moral character of God, derived from the use of the faculties he has given us, and our observation of his conduct in the government of the world ; nor with what he has made known to us of his character, and purposes, and government in the Christian revelation.

How repugnant this doctrine is to our natural reason, Dr. Woods himself seems to be fully sensible. " If it were put to my natural reason," he says, (p. 54) " to judge by its own light respecting what is called the doctrine of Election; my judgment might agree with the judgment of those, who reject the doctrine. If the question were, what difficulties attend the doctrine, I might perhaps bring forward as many as others."

Now, as God is the Author of our being, and as that portion of reason, which we have, was given us by him for our guide, it is certainly very remarkable, and what we should not expect, that instead of indicating to us truly his character, and dispositions, and purposes; so far as it gives us any information, it should universally mislead us respecting them. Following the light of our reason and the natural impulse of our feelings, we find it impossible to imagine, that the Author of our being, the common Parent of all, can regard and treat his offspring in the manner, which the doctrine in question attributes to him. That, without any foreseen difference of character and desert in men, before he had brought them into being, he should regard some with complacency and love, and the rest with disapprobation, and hatred, and wrath; and without any reference to the future use or abuse of their nature, should appoint some to everlasting happiness, and the rest to everlasting misery; and that this appointment, entirely arbitrary, for which no reason is to be assigned, but his sovereign will, should be the cause, and not the consequence, of the holiness of the one, and of the defect of holiness of the other. A man, who should do what this doctrine attributes to God, I will not say toward his own offspring, but toward any beings that were dependent on him, and whose destiny was at his disposal, would be regarded as a monster of malevolence, and cruelty, and caprice. It is incredible that the Author of our being should thus have formed us with an understanding and moral feelings to lead us without fail to condemn the measures and the principles of the government of him, who so made us.

Will it be said that this repugnance which we feel to the doctrine in question is one of the proofs of the corruption of our nature? Yet whatever that nature may be, it is such as he gave us. And however imperfect our reason, it is what he gave to be our guide. It is the only immediate guide he has given us ; and it is that, which must be the ultimate judge of the evidence, and of the nature and value, of any notices which he may give of his will and purposes, by his providence or his word. Can it have been the design of the Apostle to put down our reason, our moral feelings, and natural conscience, as seems to be intimated in the pamphlet, "*by the appalling rebuke,* Who art thou that repliest against God?" But who is the man, that in the truest sense is chargeable with replying against God? Is it not he, who would set aside, as false and dangerous, the guide he has given to all for the direction of life? Is it not he, who refuses to listen to the voice, by which he speaks to all? Who calls in question the notices he gives of himself and of the principles of his government, in the only universal revelation that he has made of himself? He, it seems to me, *replies against God,* who rejects or undervalues the notices, which he has in any way given us, of himself or of the principles of his government. Not less he, who refuses to follow reason and natural conscience, than he, who will not submit to the demands of a written revelation. Not less he, who turns his back upon the works of God, than he, who closes his eyes against his written word.

But my objection to the orthodox doctrine of Election is grounded not solely on its being irreconcileable with our reason and moral feelings; I find it not more easy to reconcile it with the instructions of the holy scriptures. I look to the general scope of the sacred writings, as regards the disposition of the Author of nature toward his creatures, and the principles of his government; and I find nothing to support this doctrine, but much with which it seems to be wholly incompatible. I ask how this sovereign appointment of the everlasting condition of men, "excluding all works of righteousness, as having any concern in it," and with reference to which " nothing is effected by the efforts of men," can be shown to consist with all that we find in the scriptures so clearly implying, that something is depending on the exertions men will make, and the part they will act ; for, according to this doctrine, what they are to be and how they are to act is determined beforehand, without any reference to such exertions ; with all that implies the influence of motives, since it is no such influence of motive, but " God's sovereign election, that is to account for the actual difference between true believers, and the rest of the world;" with all that implies guilt, ill desert, blame-worthiness in the unholy, disobedient, and impenitent; for how can men be guilty of being what they were made to be? how are they deserving of blame for remaining in that moral state, in which it was determined by the sovereign appointment of God, that they should remain? With all those promises, threatenings, warnings, admonitions, exhortations, and entreaties; which imply in those, to whom they are addressed, a power of being influenced; with all that implies, that men are capable of duty and obligation, and are the proper subjects of praise and blame, and of reward and punishment?

This charge of inconsistency with the general scope of the scriptures, and the doctrine every where taught or implied in the sacred writings, has never been removed; nor can it be, I am persuaded, but by violating the plainest principles in the interpretation of language.

There is another view, in which this doctrine is at variance with what the scriptures every where present to us. I mean the righteous and benevolent character of the Author of our being. It represents him to us as a cruel and unjust being, exacting endless punishment for sins committed in following the nature he had given, and acting in pursuance of his decree. It represents him, as arbitrary and partial in his distributions; making a distinction the most momentous that can be imagined in his treatment of those, between whom there was no difference of character or of desert as the ground of the distinction; from his mere sovereign will and good pleasure, ordaining *these* to eternal blessedness and glory, and appointing *those* to endless and hopeless misery. That it is the *righteous* only, who will thus be raised to glory, and the *wicked* only, who will be the subjects of condemnation, will make no difference in the case; since, according to the doctrine we are considering, it is not merely an absolute appointment to salvation on the one hand, and to condemnation on the other; but also to the different dispositions, character, and course of life, which are to have these opposite results. Those, and those only, who are ordained to eternal life, are also ordained to be effectually called, to be regenerated by irresistible grace, and thus to be brought, not by any thing they do, or can do themselves, but solely by the immediate power of God, out of that state of sin, in which they are by nature, to that holiness, which is to qualify them for salvation. The rest of mankind, " passed by, and ordained to dishonour and wrath for their sins," have that effectual and irresistible grace withheld from them, which was necessary to their regeneration, and without which it was impossible for them to attain to holiness and salvation.

To say, that those who are appointed to salvation, are chosen from among mankind "*for reasons of state,*" (p. 74) is to say nothing that is intelligible. But to say, that they are chosen (ib.) " for reasons, which God has not revealed;—reasons, which he has concealed in his own mind; such as cannot be accounted for by any principle known to us," is something more.

It is a position, I think, unsupported by proof, and confuted distinctly by what we constantly meet with in the New Testament. In the appointment to privileges, means, and external condition, God has indeed given no account of his motives; nor assigned his reasons for the infinite variety that appears. He has exercised an absolute sovereignty, of which no account is given, and the reasons of which we are not competent to understand. But it is clearly otherwise as to the final condition of men. So far is that from being determined *by reasons of state, which he has not revealed ;* that the reasons, upon which the final salvation or condemnation of every man is to take place, are distinctly assigned by our Saviour and his Apostles; not once only, but as often as they have occasion to speak of the final distinctions that are to be made between men. Those distinctions we are again and again told, are to be wholly according to the difference of moral character. It is that *these* are righteous, and *those* wicked ; *these* have done well, and *those* have done ill; *these* have been faithful, and *those* unfaithful. So far are the reasons of the final distinction to be made between those who are saved, and those who perish, from being concealed in the divine mind, that nothing is more distinctly made known. The New Testament is full of it.

Nor is it with any better reason said, that, " in this respect, the purpose and administration of God are different from what our wisdom would dictate, or our affections choose." They are precisely what the wisdom and the affections of every man in their uncorrupted, unperverted state, would approve and concur in. And they are accounted for by principles well known to us; principles of eternal and immutable justice. Not reasons which he has concealed in his own mind, but such as he has made us perfectly capable of understanding; and such as he has clearly revealed to us in his word.

But though the general tenor of scripture seems so foreign from the doctrine we are considering, and not easily reconciled with it; there are particular texts in which it is thought to be expressly taught, or so clearly implied, that their force cannot be evaded.

The first text alleged by Professor Woods, in the pamphlet before me, is (John xvii. 2) " That he should give eternal life to as many as thou hast given him," and, (John vi. 37, 39) " All that the Father giveth me shall come to me, and him that cometh to me, I will in no wise cast out. And this is the Father's will, who sent me, that of all which he hath given me, I should lose nothing, but should raise it up at the last day."

With respect to the first of these, it cannot have been our Saviour's intention to declare, that a certain definite number of mankind were appointed by the Father to receive the benefit of his mediation and sacrifice, and obtain salvation, exclusive of all others; and without any thing in them, as the ground of this preference and choice, for the reasons that follow.

In the discourse with his disciples, (ch. xv.) which stands in immediate connexion with the prayer, of which this text is a part, he addresses the same persons, of whom he here speaks as " given him of the Father," in language implying, that they might " abide in him, and bring forth much fruit," or failing to abide in him, might be " taken away, cast forth, cast into the fire and burned." As those who, though chosen and ordained, might or might not keep the commands, and abide in the love of him, who had thus chosen and ordained them. But according to the doctrine in question, there could be no such contingency in the case. All who are thus given, chosen, ordained, and those only, are to bring forth fruit, to keep his commands, to abide in his love, to have eternal life.

In this same discourse, again, (ch. xvi. 27) we meet with the following sentence. " For the Father himself loveth you *because ye have loved me*, and have believed that I came out from God." Here the love of God is represented, not as the cause, but the consequence, of the faith and love of the disciples, and the plain and obvious meaning of the texts in question, in their connexion with this is, that they were given to Christ, not by an arbitrary selection of them from the mass of Jews, without any thing in their character and disposition leading to the choice; but, because they were seen to be fit subjects for the kingdom of God, ready to receive the faith of the Gospel when offered to them, having already something of the Christian disposition and character, already manifesting an obedient temper, as expressed (ch. xvii. 6), they were already children of God, and were given to Christ, and came to him, because they were God's in a sense, in which the rest of the world were not; and were then chosen, and ordained to partake in the final benefits of the Gospel, because of their faith and fidelity. This interpretation renders the whole discourse and the following prayer consistent throughout in the several parts, and consistent with the moral character of God, and the moral state of man, as a free and accountable being. With the other interpretation, I do not perceive how the texts that have been mentioned can be fairly reconciled. If by *those given to Christ*, we are to understand, as Dr. Woods asserts, (p. 54) " a certain part of the human race, who are to have eternal life, and those, denoting *all*, to whom Christ will actually give eternal life," and as his argument requires, and as he elsewhere states with sufficient distinctness, this choice and appointment to Christian faith, obedience, and eternal life, is wholly independent of any thing in them as the ground of this distinction from the rest of the world; it is impossible to see with what propriety it could be said, that " God loved them, because of their faith and love to Christ," for his distinguishing love was, by that supposition, the cause of their faith, &c.; or how any intimations could be given, that something was yet depending upon themselves; that it yet depended on themselves, whether they should abide in Christ, keep his commandments, continue in his love, and share in the great salvation; for the appointment to all this was absolute, and without any condition on their part, as the ground of it. Besides, I observe that other language of our Saviour in the discourses recorded by this same Evangelist, is equally favourable to the supposition, "that coming to Christ, believing on him, and having eternal life," are events, not flowing from a sovereign unconditional appointment, but the result of a faithful use of means, in the exercise of a right disposition; and that the difference of character thus appearing between them, and others who neglect to come, who refuse to believe and obey, and fail of eternal life, is the ground and not the consequence of their being chosen, given to Christ, and ordained to eternal life. Thus, (John iii. 19) the ground of men's condemnation is, not an irrespective decree of God, "but their hating the light, loving the darkness, because their deeds are evil." It is their being in character and disposition opposite to those, who escape the condemnation, because they do the truth, and willingly come to the light.

Thus it is, that the reason assigned, and as is clearly implied, the *criminal reason* why the unbelieving Jews rejected the Gospel (John v. 40) was, not that they were ordained to this condemnation without any thing in them, by which they were distinguished from those, who accepted the invitation; but because they wilfully rejected the Gospel, and refused the eternal life it offered. "Ye *will* not come unto me, that ye might have life." Again, the same great moral ground of distinction appears in the declaration, (John vii. 17) "If any man *will do his will*, he shall know of the doctrine, whether it be of God." Those, who are given to Christ, chosen, ordained, who are to know of his doctrine, to believe in him, and thus to obtain eternal life, are those, who are well disposed to it, who have an obedient temper, who are *willing to do his will.*

The observations which have been applied to this text are equally applicable to the other text under consideration. (John vi. 27) " All that the Father giveth me shall come to me;" that is, those only are given to him of the Father, those only are to receive the final blessings of the Gospel, who come to Christ. It was so when the Gospel was first promulgated. The humble, the pious, the teachable received the Gospel; all those who were of God. The proud, the irreligious rejected it; those who were not of God, but of the world. It has been so in every subsequent age.

And none of those who thus come, bringing with them the spirit of the Gospel, abiding in it, and bringing forth the fruits of righteousness, none of these will he cast off. Of all those, thus given to him, thus coming to him, thus abiding in him, thus bringing forth fruit, it is the Father's will that he should lose nothing.

From this expression in the text, however, as well as the other, an unwarrantable inference is probably drawn; that of the absolute certainty of the final salvation of all those persons, concerning whom it is spoken. But this form of words was evidently intended to express, not the particular decree, but the general purpose of heaven; not the specific effect, which is without fail to be produced, but the object and design of the divine dispensation; to be understood with similar limitations with those, which we apply to the expression, (1 Tim. ii. 4) "who will have all men to be saved." Not that every human being will be actually saved, in the sense in which *saved* is here used, but that the salvation of all was the object and design; that the offer of it was made to all, an offer which yet might be rejected. Again, (Col. i. 23) "the gospel, which was preached to every creature which is under heaven." Here the literal meaning of the sentence is not the true meaning. The Gospel had not been preached to every living creature. But the direction of the Saviour to his disciples was to preach it to every creature, that is, to *all men*. It was intended in general for all. None were excepted in the commission; none were passed by in the execution. As far as the design of the commission had been accomplished, it had been done agreeably to the direction of the Saviour. To these instances many others might be added to show, that expressions of *universal* import are often, as in the text in question, to be interpreted only in a *general sense;* and that they are frequently used to express, not an absolute decree, but a purpose or design depending on contingences, and which *may in fact* be either universal or only general. And that the example we are considering is clearly of this kind, and that it does not warrant the use, that has been made of it, we have the farther positive proof in this circumstance; that notwithstanding this unqualified expression, *one* of the persons given to Christ had been lost. "Those that thou gavest me I have kept, and none of them is lost, but the son of perdition." The son of perdition, it is here clearly implied, had been given to Christ in the sense of the passage, and yet had been lost. The declaration then, "It is the Father's will that he should lose nothing," is manifestly designed to express, not a specific personal decree, but the general purpose and design.

The next passage quoted by Dr. Woods to prove an absolute personal election to salvation is Ephesians i. 3—11. "Blessed be the God and Father," &c. To all the observations made by Dr. Woods on this passage, I give my entire concurrence; yet have no hesitation in asserting, what I hope satisfactorily to prove, that it has no relation to the doctrine, which he has brought it to support.

It refers not to individuals as such, but to the Christian community. Not to final salvation, but to Christian privileges. In the first place, the Epistle is addressed to the whole Christian community at Ephesus, without any intimation, that any expressions in it are applicable to some and not to others. The terms, *saints* and *faithful in Christ Jesus,* (ver. 1) are applied alike to all, and are evidently to be understood as terms which designate the whole company of believers, and external professors, without any reference to the personal character of any, as individuals. It is again in the name of the whole Christian community, Jews and Gentiles, that the Apostle speaks, when he says, that " God hath blessed us with all spiritual blessings, chosen us in *him* [that is, Christ] before the foundation of the world, predestinated us to the adoption of children, predestinated us according to the purpose of him, who worketh all things after the counsel of his own will." (ver. 3, 4, 5, 11) That this choice or predestination was not that of individuals to eternal life, but of all, who received the Christian faith, to the profession and privileges of the Gospel, (besides its being thus generally addressed, and in the name of Christians at large and universally) appears still further from other expressions, addressed in the same manner. It is for these same persons, saints, faithful, chosen, predestinated, that the Apostle thought it needful very devoutly and earnestly to pray to God, " that they might be strengthened with might by his spirit in the inner man, that Christ might dwell in their hearts by faith, that they might be rooted and grounded in love;" very suitable to be addressed to professed believers as a promiscuous body: but such as we should hardly expect, if the persons designated were by the very designation understood to consist only of persons certainly chosen to eternal life, and were already certainly grounded in love, were already strengthened in the inner man, had already Christ dwelling in their hearts by love.

Further, these same persons, he thinks it proper to exhort, (ch. iv. 1) "to walk worthy of the vocation with which they were called," " to walk henceforth, not as other Gentiles walk," (ver. 17) " but to put off, concerning the former conversation, the old man, which is corrupt according to the deceitful lusts, and to be renewed in the spirit of their mind, and to put on the new man, which after God is created in righteousness and true holiness," and " not to grieve the holy spirit of God." (ver. 22, 23, 24, 30.) Implying, that they are liable to retain still their heathen character, notwithstanding their Christian profession; that they *may* still pursue the former conversation, which, by their profession, they have renounced ; that they are in danger of failing to put off the old man, and to be, as their Christian profession requires, " renewed in righteousness and true holiness;" that they finally may, instead of following the guidance of the spirit of God, grieve it. Very suitable, therefore, to be addressed to the promiscuous body of professing Christians ; very suitable if by *saints, chosen, predestinated,* this only were meant; but certainly not so, if by these terms were designated persons chosen from eternity to final salvation, and already saints and faithful in the highest and literal sense of the words. *Such,* as distinguished from the rest of the world, are not the proper subjects of exhortation to walk worthy of their Christian vocation; for the very terms applied to them imply that they cannot fail to do so ; being certainly predestinated to life, they are as certainly predestinated to that character and state, to which life is promised. They cannot be exhorted to be renewed and to put on the new man ;—for by the supposition against which I am contending, their renewal is already certain. It is what they have no power, either to prevent, or to bring about, or even to accelerate. Their renewal has indeed already taken place; for they are addressed, not only as chosen and predestinated, but as saints and Christians, which, according to the scheme under consideration, they were not, till they were renewed. And with what propriety can such be exhorted " not to grieve the holy spirit of God ?"

The next, and only other passage, to which Dr. Woods has referred for the direct proof of the doctrine of sovereign personal election to eternal life, is that contained in Romans ix. 11—24. A similar method of investigation to that, which was applied to the passage in Ephesians, will convince you, I think, that this is as little to the purpose as the other; and that it has no relation to an election to eternal life, but only to the privileges of the Gospel.

This will appear to you in the first place by an attention to the general scope and design of the Epistle, the subject of which was suggested by the great controversy of that age, respecting the extension of Christianity to the Gentiles, and their admission to its privileges and hopes, without being subjected to the observance of the Mosaic ritual. The Apostle combats the exclusive spirit of his Jewish brethren, by showing them, that those distinctions, on which they so valued themselves, as the chosen people of God, were done away; that Gentiles were admitted to the same rights, and to the opportunity of securing the final favour of Heaven on the same terms with them.

The Jews, as descendants of Abraham, disciples of Moses, children of the covenant and of the promises, enjoyed a high distinction and valuable privileges.

But these privileges were no security of their final acceptance with God. They were disciplinary and conditional. The knowledge of the law would be of no avail to those, who did not faithfully observe it. The sign of the covenant would not save those, who should violate it. The oracles of God, which were committed to them, would but enhance the guilt and the condemnation of those, who, with all their superior light and motives, lived no better than ignorant heathen.

On the other hand, the Gentiles, without the light of the written law, and without the sign of the covenant, the external mark of being the people of God; if, guided by the light they had, (Rom. ii. 26, 27, 29) they fulfilled the law by a virtuous life, thus showing practically " the work of the law written in the heart," (ver. 15) would secure that acceptance of God, of Him, " with whom is no respect of persons," (ver. 11) and " who will render to every man according to his deeds," (ver. 6) which the Jew must lose, who being " a Jew outwardly" only, (ver. 28) and relying on the letter and circumcision, was emboldened to neglect its moral design, and to live as a heathen. The final condition of every individual, whether Jew or Gentile, was to depend on individual personal character. (ver. 5—10) "Indignation and wrath to every soul of man that doth evil: glory, honour, and peace to every man that worketh good, to the Jew and also to the Gentile."

Now with this general scope and design of the first

part of the Epistle, that interpretation of the ix. ch. which refers " the purpose of God according to election," (ver. 11 et seq.) to an unconditional election of individuals to eternal life, seems to be wholly irreconcileable: whereas that, which refers it to an appointment, free and unconditional, to the participation of privileges, not only comports well with the general design of the Epistle, but makes the latter part of it a continuation of the former, and a completion of the design, that prevails in the whole preceding part.

This appears again not less clearly, when we come to a separate examination of the passage itself.

The first instance mentioned of the accomplishment of " the purpose of God according to election," is that of the appointment of Isaac, and pretermission of Ishmael and the other children of Abraham. But what purpose of God was accomplished by this? Not the salvation of Isaac, but the fulfilment of the promise to Abraham in the whole series of dispensations for promoting the knowledge of God and true religion in the world; and especially in raising up one from among his descendants, in whom " all the families of the earth were to be blessed."

The next instance, is the choice of Jacob in preference to Esau, a choice which preceded their birth, and could therefore have no respect to their good or ill desert. And this, the whole reasoning of the Apostle assures us, is applied, not to Jacob personally, but to the race descending from him; and not to them in their personal character, but solely to their designation, as a people, to a certain part in accomplishing the great purposes of heaven. In this appointment, the same free, sovereign, uncontrouled will was exercised, which is seen in the appointment of all the other circumstances, which make up the state of trial of every human being. It is "the power of the potter over the clay, of the same lump to make one vessel to honour, and another to dishonour." Upon this interpretation there is room for the appeal, (ver. 20) " shall the thing formed say to him that formed it, why hast thou made me thus?" Upon that interpretation, which supposes a reference to the final lot of individuals as determined by a decree that has no respect to different desert, the appeal could not be sustained.

In each of these cases we perceive a peculiar propriety in the expressions, which the Apostle applies by way of reflection, (ver. 16) "So then it is not of him that willeth, nor of him that runneth, but of God that sheweth mercy." It was the wish of Abraham, that the blessing might be given to his eldest son Ishmael. It was the desire of Isaac, that it should descend with his eldest son Esau. But the will of neither of them was permitted to prevail; nor yet the prompt obedience of Esau, by which he hoped to secure it to himself.

I am ready to admit, with Dr. Woods, that this reflection of the Apostle implies a general principle; but it is a principle to be applied to similar cases only, not those that are dissimilar. Now similar cases are those and those only, which relate to privileges, opportunities, blessings, which are disciplinary in their design, temporal in their duration, and make a part of human probation. That which relates directly to final salvation is dissimilar, and the same principle is not to be applied.

The case of Pharaoh is as little to the purpose as either of the others. For when it is said, (ver. 17) "For this same purpose I have raised thee up, that I might shew my power in thee, and that my name might be declared throughout all the earth;" whether by the phrase, *raised thee up*, be meant, as some suppose, *his recovery* from the effects of the preceding plague, which had been inflicted *on his person* and his people ; or as others understand it, his being exalted to high power, and placed in a situation to act so important a part ; in either case, there will be no reference to his final personal destiny. For how did God actually show his power in him, and make him the instrument of his glory? It was by giving him the opportunity to act out his character, by allowing full scope for displaying the incorrigible obstinacy of his disposition, and by then inflicting upon him exemplary punishment, for the instruction and warning of mankind ; thus making him the instrument of promoting some of the best purposes of heaven, in the free and voluntary exercise of his power.

I should have passed by what is said (p. 72) on the doctrine of Reprobation, as expressing no other sentiment than what all Unitarians, as I believe, hold on the subject, but that I think it calculated (unintentionally I am persuaded as respects the writer) to mislead the reader, as to the opinions of the Orthodox on that point. Dr. Woods has in fact given us, not as he professes to do, the *doctrine* of the Orthodox, as to the decree of Reprobation; but only his *opinion of the character of the doctrine.* He says, " it is the determination of God to punish disobedient subjects *for* their sins, and according to their deserts." Now this, I observe, is not a statement of the orthodox doctrine, but his opinion of the character of that doctrine. What it belongs to him to state and defend is, not an opinion upon the subject, which he holds in common with all Christians, but that, by which the system he defends is distinguished from others. That opinion I will now state in the language of one of the most approved symbols of Calvinistic faith; and it is such as follows very clearly from his own statement of the counterpart of the doctrine. "The rest of mankind," i. e. all but the elect, " God was pleased, according to the unsearchable counsel of his own will, whereby he extendeth or withholdeth mercy as he pleaseth, for the glory of his sovereign power over his creatures, to pass by, and to ordain them to dishonour and wrath for their sin, to the praise of his *glorious* justice." Again, " Others, not elected, though they may be called by the ministers of the word, and may have some common operations of the spirit, yet they never truly come to Christ, and therefore cannot be saved; much less can men, not professing the Christian religion, be saved in any other way whatsoever, be they never so diligent to frame their lives according to the light of nature, and the law of that religion, which they do profess: and to assert and maintain that they may, is very pernicious, and to be detested." *(Westminster Confession.)*

I am very willing to believe that the doctrine, as thus stated in the orthodox confessions, does not make a part of Dr. Woods' faith; though I am unable to perceive with what consistency he can reject it, while he retains the other parts of the system that are connected with it.

If the doctrines of original hereditary depravity, absolute personal election, effectual calling, and special irresistible grace be true; that of reprobation, as stated above, follows of course, and must be true also. Whether it be that Dr. Woods, with a fair and inquiring mind, actually shrinks from this doctrine, because he finds it cannot be defended consistently with the moral character of God: or only thinks it desirable to keep out of view a feature of Calvinism, which shocks our moral feelings more than any other; in either case, I deem it an auspicious circumstance, a favourable omen. Men will not long continue to hold an opinion, after it has got to cause a painful struggle with their moral feelings, such as to dispose them to endeavour to keep it out of sight. They will not suffer themselves to be long encumbered with that, which they are unable to defend or unwilling to avow. Besides this, it cannot fail to open the eyes of men to the difficulties of the other parts of the system, which are intimately connected with this, which necessarily flow from it, and are in fact no better supported by Scripture nor by reason than this.

LETTER V.

Following the arrangement adopted by Dr. Woods, the next subject to which I am to call your attention is that of the Atonement. It is a doctrine on which great stress is laid by orthodox writers generally. The author of the Letters addressed to Unitarians says, " If there is any one doctrine of Revelation which the Orthodox distinguish in point of importance from all others, it is the doctrine of Atonement." It must accordingly be thought, that the importance of having clear conceptions and just views on the subject will bear some proportion to the importance of the subject itself. After such an introduction, therefore, to a letter devoted expressly to the discussion of that subject, it was certainly reasonable to expect a distinct statement of the orthodox explanation of the texts of scripture, in which it is supposed to be taught, and a defence of the interpretation by which those texts are understood to express the meaning that is assigned to them. More especially was this to be expected of one, who complains that the opinions of the Orthodox are misrepresented, and who, in their name, disclaims the opinions, which are attributed to them. But in this expectation I am disappointed. There is much complaint of misrepresentation, but I find no distinct statement in what the alleged misrepresentation consists, nor. what are the precise opinions maintained by the Orthodox on this subject. I am able to collect but a very imperfect and indistinct idea, what the scheme, which claims to be Orthodox on this subject, is. It is asserted, that the language used by orthodox writers on this subject, like that used by the sacred writers, is highly figurative, (p. 86, &c.) that it is not to be understood literally, that it does not mean, what it seems to express. It would have greatly assisted us, and possibly put a period to all controversy on the subject, had the writer seen fit to explain the figures, and give the true interpretation of the metaphors, which it is complained have been so misunderstood, and have thus laid the foundation for misrepresentation.

The first charge of misrepresentation is, that the author of the Sermon makes it a part of the orthodox system, " that God took upon him human nature, that he might pay to his own justice the debt of punishment incurred by men, and might enable himself to exercise mercy"—" that he might appease his own anger toward men, or make an infinite satisfaction to his own justice." The unfairness alleged in this representation is, that it does not recognize the distinction of persons in the Deity, which is maintained by the Orthodox, and it is implied, that if no such distinction do exist, the representation would not be liable to objection, for no objection is made to it on any other ground. It was incumbent then on Dr. Woods, not merely to assert this distinction as an article of the orthodox faith, but to explain *what* it is, and to show its foundation in the language of scripture. The former he has declined, as not being within the scope of our limited minds, (p. 84) the latter, as not falling within his purpose (p. 85) in the discussion of the subject. But until both are done, I can see no ground for complaining of the absurdity charged upon the doctrine. It is a legitimate and necessary consequence of the orthodox faith, that Jesus Christ, whom the Father sent into the world, is the same being with the Father who sent him; that Christ, who interposed and made an atonement for sinners, is the same being with that God, who, it is alleged, (p. 65) "would never have saved them without such an interposition." It was the same God, the same being, who sent, and was sent, who made the atonement, and whose anger was appeased by the atonement, who made satisfaction to offended justice, and whose justice was satisfied. It is not enough to assert, (p. 64) that " the Father and the Son are *two* as *really* as Moses and Aaron, though not in the same sense, nor in any sense inconsistent with their being one." It belongs to him, who asserts this, to state intelligibly, what is the nature and import of the distinction here intended; to explain in what sense *two*, and in what sense *one*. No man knows better than Dr. Woods, that until he has done this, he has done nothing to the purpose. He uses words without meaning, and merely casts a mist, where he is bound to shed light.

The next imputation on the orthodox faith, which Dr. Woods endeavours to remove is, that it conveys to common minds the idea, that " Christ's death has an influence in making God placable, or merciful, in quenching his wrath, and awakening his kindness towards men." Now to vindicate the system, and those who support it, from this charge, it was necessary to show, that the language in which the doctrine is expressed and enforced by the Orthodox, is not calculated to produce this impression. But has this been done? By no means. The contrary is frankly admitted. It is conceded that the literal sense of the orthodox writings amounts to this. It is *asserted* indeed, that the doctrine of the Orthodox is the very reverse of this, "that the mercy of God, not the interposition of Christ, was the origin and moving cause of the work of redemption;" (p. 68) " that the mercy or placability of God could neither be produced nor increased by the atonement of Christ." These are noble, correct, scriptural views. We are delighted to find on this point an opinion so highly important, in exact coincidence with that of Unitarians, and one to which they attach a very high degree of importance. We are glad too to find a strong sensibility expressed to the honour of the divine character, and horror at the thought of an opinion, so derogatory to it, as that which is attributed to the influence of the language they use on the subject. But why then does he go on to defend the use of that language, instead of correcting it? Since it is admitted not to be the language of scripture, and that understood literally it does convey the ideas objected to; that it does make the impression at which so much horror is expressed, does express a doctrine acknowledged to be false and unfounded;

why is it not given up? Especially as it would, on this point, put an end to all controversy. And why complain that the opinions of the Orthodox are misrepresented, when it is acknowledged that the opinions attributed to them are the literal and obvious meaning of the language they employ?

It is to little purpose to say, that the figurative language used on this subject, though not the same, resembles that employed by the sacred writers in reference to the same subject. Dr. Woods admits that the language of the sacred writers is highly figurative. He admits too that such boldness of metaphor is peculiar to the Eastern, and particularly to the Hebrew idiom; (p. 88) and that it is not so consentaneous to our language. (p. 99) Why, then, will orthodox writers use it without explanation, when it serves to mislead readers and hearers who are not aware of this character of the Eastern languages; and lead them into so great an error? And if orthodox writers, instead of explaining the metaphors, so that their true meaning may be understood, "for the purpose of strong impression," use them as if they were to be understood literally; and not only so, but further sanction that interpretation by the use of other similar language of the same literal import; especially if they charge Unitarians with denying or explaining away the doctrine for the very reason, that they explain the language in question as figurative; can he be surprized that the Orthodox should be supposed to hold the opinions, which the language literally expresses?

Could it be imagined by a plain, honest man, under these circumstances, that while this strong, impressive language is constantly used and insisted on, something very different is all the time meant from that which strikes the ear? And, let me ask, does it enter into the minds of common hearers of such language, that, correctly interpreted, it expresses no ideas, which would be "objected to by Unitarians?" (p. 92) It is to be hoped that in future the opinions of Unitarians on this part of the subject will be viewed with less aversion, when we are told from so high authority, that "the language used by orthodox writers is to be understood as highly figurative; that, taken literally, it would impute a character to God, which would excite universal horror; but understood according to the legitimate principles of interpreting metaphors, it teaches the simple truth, that the death of Christ was the means of procuring pardon, or the medium, through which salvation is granted." (p. 93) Dr. Woods is right in supposing, " that no objection will lie in the minds of Unitarians," against the doctrine thus expressed. It is the very manner of expressing the influence of the Atonement, which has been adopted by unitarian writers.

Dr. Woods proceeds to the notice of several other modes of expression, the use of which by the Orthodox he supposes to have been misunderstood, in a similar manner, and from the same cause, the misinterpretation of figurative language. When it is said that Christ bought us, redeemed us by his blood; when he is said to have paid our debt, to have satisfied divine justice, to have redeemed us from the curse of the law, being made a curse for us, and that our sin was imputed to him; when these and other figurative forms of expression are employed to set forth the design and influence of Christ's death, we are told " they are to be interpreted as metaphorical language, according to the nature of the metaphors used, and that against the literal sense, there are many objections." (p. 95) So far, there will be no controversy on the part of Unitarians, and it gives us no small satisfaction, that we have here a ground upon which we can stand together. And we are not without hope, that agreeing in this principle on which to proceed, we shall gradually approach nearer together in the result, till there shall no difference remain worth contending about.

But when Dr. Woods proceeds to explain the figures, he seems to have fallen into the same error " of mixing a degree of the literal sense with the metaphorical," which he afterwards mentions, and to which he traces some important mistakes, into which other writers have been led. To perceive this you have only to compare together the passage, (p. 94) in which he professes to explain what is meant by our being bought, redeemed, our debt paid, and divine justice satisfied; with that (p. 96), in which " the notion, that if Christ has made a perfect atonement and satisfied divine justice, those for whom he has done this are no longer under the same obligations to obey the law, and punishing them for their sins would no longer be just, is attributed to something of a literal sense being applied to the figurative language of Scripture and of orthodox writers. And it is admitted, that "if Christ paid our debt, or the price of our redemption literally, as a friend discharges an insolvent debtor, or purchases the freedom of a slave by the payment of money; it would certainly be an unrighteous thing for us to be held to pay our own debt, or to suffer the evils of servitude." For in the passage referred to, this is the very representation that is made. "As the debtor is freed from imprisonment by the friend who steps forward and pays his debt, so are sinners freed from punishment by the Saviour who shed his blood for them." The payment is as literal in the one case as in the other; and I see not how the consequence, consistently with what is admitted above, is to be avoided. The same may be said with respect to the other terms. The consequence is not to be evaded, if our redemption by Christ means, as is there stated, "his delivering us from the punishment of the law by suffering an evil, which, so far as the ends of divine government are concerned, was equivalent to the execution of the curse of the law upon transgressors." (p. 94) The ends of the divine government are answered, the demands of the law are fulfilled. It has no farther demands. When Christ has done and suffered that which answers the ends of justice in the divine government, the necessity of punishment, so far as those ends are concerned, is superseded. The sinner then is free; exempt alike from obligation, and from danger of punishment. The debt is paid; justice is satisfied; the ends of government are answered by the voluntary substitute. These consequences certainly follow from the manner which Dr. Woods has adopted of explaining the figurative language of the sacred writers.

But the language in question certainly does admit of a fair and unstrained interpretation, which leads to no such consequences. We are declared to have "redemption, the forgiveness of sins, by the blood of Christ." It will help us to the true interpretation of this language to attend to the use of the word redemption by the sacred writers in other analogous cases. Literally to redeem is to relieve from forfeiture, or captivity, or slavery, or to rescue from punishment by the payment of a price, and the price thus paid is the ransom. When, by a price paid by some friend, a captive is restored to liberty, or the punishment of a criminal is remitted, whose life was forfeited to the law; in each of these cases there is a redemption in the original meaning and literal sense of the word. In the same manner also, if "Christ delivers us from punishment by suffering an evil, which was equivalent, so far as the ends of the divine government are concerned, to the execution of the curse of the law upon transgressors," (p. 94) that is a literal redemption, and that and the other correspondent terms, such as *bought* and *ransomed*, are applied, and are to be understood, not in a metaphorical but a literal sense. And here I cannot but observe, that the error complained of, that of mixing a literal with the metaphorical sense of such phrases, consists, not as intimated, (p. 95) " in the manner of reasoning upon them," but in the interpretation of the language itself.

Now it is not difficult in this case to trace the passage of the term in question from its original literal meaning to its metaphorical use. For as the deliverance from captivity or punishment was the principal thing, and the price paid as a ransom only a secondary consideration in making up the complex idea of redemption, it is easy to see how the term came to be used to denote the principal thing alone, where this accessory circumstance was wanting; and thus any kind of deliverance, by a very common change in the use of language, was called a redemption. Examples occur in the sacred writings as well as in our constant use. The deliverance of the Israelites from Egyptian bondage is called a redemption, and God is said on this account to be their redeemer, to have redeemed them from the house of bondage, and out of the hand of Pharaoh the king of Egypt.

But how was this redemption effected? Was a ransom paid as the price of their deliverance, as an equivalent for their services, as a consideration, for which their oppressors were to let them go? Let the sacred historians and prophets answer this question. (Exod. vi. 6) " I will redeem you with a stretched out arm, and with great judgments." (Deut. ix. 26) " Destroy not thy people, which thou hast redeemed through thy greatness, which thou hast brought forth out of Egypt with a mighty hand." (Neh. i. 10) "Now these are thy servants and thy people, whom thou hast redeemed by thy great power and thy strong hand." The nation of Israel then was redeemed, not by a ransom paid to their former oppressors, as the price of their emancipation, but by the mighty power and strong hand of Jehovah, stretched forth in those signs and wonders in Egypt, in the Red Sea, and in the wilderness, by which the Egyptian monarch was compelled to suffer their departure, by which they were protected and avenged, when pursued by their oppressors, and were conducted in safety to the promised land.

The term is applied also in a similar manner to the deliverance of that nation from the Babylonian captivity. (Micah iv. 10) "Thou shalt go even to Babylon; there shalt thou be delivered; there the Lord shall redeem thee from the hand of thine enemies." It is applied in many instances also to the deliverance of individuals from danger, captivity, slavery, or any great calamity; and the propriety of the term is sufficiently maintained, where something important is done, though nothing is literally paid, to procure the deliverance.

These examples of the use of this term may lead us to some just notions of its meaning, as applied to express the benefit we receive, when it is said we have redemption by the blood of Christ. It is not, that his death was a price literally paid, either to God, to satisfy the demands of vindictive justice, or to the enemy of God and man, as the purchase of our release from his power. He was our redeemer in the same sense, in which God was the redeemer of the children of Israel ; and he redeemed us by his blood, as they were redeemed by the mighty power, and the strong arm of the God of Israel. As God was the redeemer of Israel by the miracles of Egypt, so Christ was our redeemer by those miracles which proved him to be a messenger and teacher from God; by those instructions and that example, which were to remove our ignorance, and deliver us from the slavery of sin, and bondage of corruption ; by those high motives to repentance and holiness, which are found in the revelation of a future life and righteous retribution ; and especially by the confirmation his doctrine and promises received, and the persuasive efficacy given to his example, by his sufferings, his voluntary death, and his resurrection. He was our redeemer by doing and suffering all, that was necessary to effect our deliverance from the power of sin, to bring us to repentance and holiness, and thus make us the fit objects of forgiveness and the favour of heaven.

This view of the subject will enable us to correct an error, into which we are liable to be led by language, which we frequently meet with ; as when it is said in the Letters to Unitarians, that "when Christ is said to pay our debt, it is simply signified, that by means of his sufferings, he delivers us from punishment." (p. 94) Christ delivers us from punishment not *directly* by his sufferings. It is not that his sufferings are in any sense a substitute for ours. It is not that satisfaction is made by his sufferings to divine justice, so that the sinner escapes, because " there is no further need of punishment." It is not that our sin was so *imputed to Christ,* that he " suffered, in some sense, as he would have suffered if our sin had been really imputed to him," and that we are directly in consequence of this vicarious suffering exempted from the punishment. But his sufferings are the means of delivering us from punishment, only as they are instrumental in delivering us from the dominion of sin. They are the grounds of our forgiveness, only as they are the means of bringing us to repentance, only as they operate to bring us to that state of holiness, and conformity to the will of God, which has the promise of forgiveness, and qualifies us for it.

There is another term also used by the sacred writers to express the efficacy of Christ's death, which admits of a satisfactory explanation somewhat similar to that which has been given of *redemption,* and is to be understood as having passed to a similar metaphorical sense. The whole of *that,* by which the benefits of redemption are procured for us, whether it be the active obedience, or the sufferings and death of Christ, or both together, is spoken of as *a sacrifice.* (Heb. ix. 26) " He appeared to put away sin by the *sacrifice* of himself." The meaning of this is rendered perfectly intelligible, and is freed from the insuperable difficulties that attend any explanation, in which is contained " a mixture of the literal with the metaphorical sense," by attending to a change from a literal to a metaphorical sense of the term *sacrifice*, similar to that, which has been noticed in the terms *redeem* and *redemption*.

A *sacrifice*, in its primitive meaning, is an offering made to God, as an acknowledgment of dependence, as an expression of gratitude, or for the expiation of sin. It is thus applied to the various offerings appointed in the Jewish ritual. But as the effect to be produced is the principal thing, and it is of little comparative importance in what manner it is produced, and by what circumstance or act it is brought about; any other act, by which a similar effect is produced, though no proper sacrifice be offered, is familiarly called by the sacred writers *a sacrifice*. We find the term thus applied to prayer and thanksgiving. (Psalms cxli. 2) "Let my prayer be set before thee as incense, and the lifting up of my hands as the evening sacrifice." (Psalms cxvi. 17) "I will offer to thee the sacrifice of thanksgiving." (Heb. xiii. 15) "By him let us offer the sacrifice of praise, that is, the fruit of our lips." It is applied to a holy life. (Rom. xii. 1) "that ye present your bodies a living sacrifice, holy, acceptable to God." It is finally applied to an act of kindness and relief. (Phil. iv. 18) "I have received the things, which ye sent, a sacrifice acceptable, well pleasing to God." It is by a use of the term similar to what we find in these examples, that sacrifice is applied to whatever was done by Jesus Christ for our benefit, especially to the labours and mortifications of his life, and the sufferings that attended his death; and that he is said to have "put away sin by the sacrifice of himself."

It may further help us to correct notions on this subject, to be reminded of what a change the word Atonement itself has undergone. This term is now more used than any other to express the popular doctrine of an expiation for sin procured by the death of Christ, a satisfaction made to divine justice, the Deity thus rendered propitious, his anger appeased, his mercy conciliated, and forgiveness obtained for those, for whom this atonement was made.

But it is evident, I think, that this was not the original meaning of the word. It occurs but once only in the New Testament, (Rom. v. 11) "By whom we have now received the atonement." And in that case it is translated from a word, καταλλαγη, which in every other instance is rendered *reconciliation*. The same is undoubtedly the meaning of the word also in this place. And we have reason to think, that it was understood to be its meaning by the translators, and that they meant to use the word *atonement* in that sense only. This is rendered probable by the formation of the word itself. It is a compound word, and in some early English writers the composition of the word is indicated, and thus its meaning pointed out in the manner of writing it, *at-one-ment, at-one*. Atonement then expressed the condition of being at one, in a state of agreement, reconciliation; and to atone was to produce reconciliation, to bring parties to agreement, so that they shall be at-one.

Dr. Johnson has mentioned two instances of this use of the word in a writer of the next age preceding that, in which our translation of the Bible was made.

"He and Aufidus can no more atone,
Than violentest contrariety."—*Shakspeare's Coriolanus.*

That is, can no more agree, be reconciled, be at one. Again,

"He seeks to make atonement
Between the Duke of Gloster and your brothers."

That is, to produce a reconciliation between them, to bring them to agreement.

Now, when we thus consider the change of meaning, which this word has undergone, from expressing simply the state of agreement, the fact of a reconciliation, to express that, by which the agreement is produced, the reconciliation is effected; we find in the use of the word itself no support of the doctrine it is usually understood to express. The term has evidently a different meaning as used by St. Paul, and probably as understood by his translator, from what it has in modern books of controversial theology.

According to the explanations which have now been given, of the language of the New Testament on this subject, it will be seen, that those Unitarians who reject the popular doctrine of the Atonement, yet attribute an important efficacy to the sufferings and death, as well as the instructions and example of Jesus Christ, in procuring pardon and salvation. But this efficacy consists, not in their appeasing the anger of God, and disposing him to be merciful, but in their moral influence on men, in bringing them to repentance, holiness, and an obedient life, and thus rendering them fit subjects of forgiveness and the divine favour. The sufferings and death of Christ are thus represented as being not in our stead, but for our benefit; and intended to render the forgiveness of sin consistent with "the honours of the divine law, the character of the lawgiver, and the interests of his moral kingdom," (p. 102)—not by satisfying justice, but by subduing the spirit of rebellion, restoring the authority and power of the law, and making men obedient subjects.

And these explanations meet in a satisfactory manner the true meaning of the two texts, which Dr. Woods has introduced for the purpose of illustrating (p. 101) the " bearing which the death of Christ has on the moral government of God, and *how* it secures mercy to penitent sinners." According to this view of the subject, " Christ was made a curse for us," not in our stead and as our substitute, but for our benefit. And his being made a curse for us redeemed us from the curse of the law, from the punishment due to us as transgressors of the law, by its influence in bringing us back to repentance and subjection to the law. And when this was done, the sinner reconciled to God, brought to repentance, subjection to the law, and a life of holiness, the purposes of God's moral government are answered, its authority is supported, his law is vindicated, " God is justified, is seen to be just, is perceived to have a regard to justice, in justifying him, who believes in Jesus." It is seen that in extending pardon to the penitent believer, he has not yielded up the authority of his law, nor subjected his government to contempt.

The question which Dr. Woods here asks himself, (p. 102) " what hindrance there is in the way of God's showing the same favour to transgressors as to the obedient," is incorrectly stated, so as to give a deceptive view. The question is not, whether God can consistently with his character of moral governor, and the honour and safety of his government, show favour to *transgressors*, but whether he can extend forgiveness to the *penitent*, to those who have ceased to be transgressors, and have returned to their allegiance. The answer to this question would be very different from what the other requires. None of the consequences, which it is readily admitted must follow on *that* supposition, would have any place on *this*. God's readiness to show favour to those who repent and return to virtue, does not show, " that the authority of the law is set aside, and that no distinction is made between virtue and vice." Nothing indeed can show in a stronger light than this, God's love of virtue, and desire to encourage it by encouraging the first return to it. No other expedient which the wisdom of God could devise, certainly not that which consists in an atonement by the substitution, either literal or figurative, of the sufferings of an innocent person in the place of the guilty, will show better than the necessity of repentance and holiness and their efficacy in order to forgiveness and the divine favour, " that God does and forever will make a distinction between holiness and sin."

I have next to make some remarks on the defence of the orthodox faith against the objection, that it " lowers the value of Christ's sacrifice and robs his death of interest ;" because consisting, according to this scheme, of a divine and human nature united together, the human nature only could suffer and die. So that, instead of the infinite atonement made by the sufferings and death of an infinite being, it is in fact only the sufferings and death of a man. The defence is made on the common ground, of the "human and divine nature in Christ constituting but one person, so that all his actions and sufferings belong to him *as* one person." As this is the only defence that is, and the only one that can be set up, let us examine a little its value and force. It is admitted, that if the premises are true, the conclusion does follow; if Jesus Christ is both perfect God and perfect man in one individual person, the defence is complete.

But in the first place I remark, that the possibility of two distinct intelligent natures making but one person, has never been shown to the smallest degree of satisfaction ; especially of two natures so distinct and distant as the divine and human, a finite and an infinite mind. No Trinitarian can deny, that in Jesus Christ are two perfectly distinct minds, two perfectly distinct, intelligent natures, as distinct as any two intelligent beings can be. But two distinct minds, two distinct intelligent beings, with each its separate consciousness, knowledge, capacity, will, and action, cannot be other than two distinct persons. But all these the trinitarian doctrine attributes to Jesus Christ. Separate consciousness, for the divine nature by the supposition was not conscious of any of that suffering, by which the atonement was made. Separate knowledge, for it is alleged, that the divine person knew that, of which the human person was ignorant. Separate capacity, for the human nature of Christ could increase in wisdom and knowledge, while the divine nature, being omniscient, was incapable of increase. Separate will; for the human person most earnestly prayed for that to take place, which it could certainly be no wish of the omniscient mind should take place. Separate action, for while the human nature of Christ was limited to the labours only of a man, and confined to a narrow space, the divine nature was extending its influence to all beings and events, and producing its effects over worlds and systems throughout the universe. It is impossible for any reasoning to show more clearly, than this simple statement, the absolute incredibility of this. But this is not all. The identity of person is not only shown to be impossible, upon the trinitarian hypothesis. The only ground upon which some of the strongest objections to the trinitarian doctrine, that part of it, which consists in the supreme Deity of Jesus Christ, can be evaded is, by the assumption of two distinct persons in Jesus Christ. By assuming that he spake, and acted, and suffered, and was spoken of in two different characters. And this assumption has been made, as far as I have seen, universally by trinitarian writers, not in words indeed, but in fact. " *Here* it is asserted, no argument lies against his divinity, for he is speaking not as God, but as man. Of *this* indeed he was ignorant as man, but he knew it as God, and *this* he might truly say he was unable to do as man, though as God he could do all things." This, I observe, is the answer on which Trinitarians have rested, and it is the only one they have offered to all those texts, and they are very numerous, in which inferiority to the Father, limited knowledge, and limited power are expressed or implied. And this goes on the supposition of two distinct persons, and is utterly absurd on any other supposition. It is indeed a palpable contradiction to say, that the same person knows and does not know the same thing at the same time, can do and cannot do the same thing at the same time. And this contradiction, and worse than trifling, is attributed to the Saviour in some of his most solemn declarations, by the supposition in question. With these brief hints I am willing to leave the reader to make up his judgment, " how far the views of the Orthodox in this case are capable of being defended in a satisfactory manner."

I would gladly have passed unnoticed what I find on the last page of the Letter respecting the Atonement, as it is unpleasant to be obliged to express the censure, to which I think a charge of so serious a kind, as is there brought against those, who reject the doctrine of the Atonement, is entitled to. This subject, it seems, is one, which it is dangerous to discuss, and on which it is not safe even to inquire. For certainly, if the rejection of the doctrine is in itself " a plain indication of the disposition of the heart, and a proof of a temper of mind, which is in total contrariety to the humble spirit of Christian faith," it is not a subject on which it is safe to trust ourselves in speculating. The only safety is in believing without inquiry, receiving implicitly without examining. For if we allow ourselves to inquire, the result *may* be, that we shall reject, and rejection will indicate " a disposition of heart, inconsistent with the humble spirit of Christian faith."

But this, I am persuaded, cannot have been the intention of the author of the Letters. The expressions must have been used in haste, without well considering their import and bearing. It cannot have been his design, to deter those whom he addresses from examining the evidences of a doctrine, respecting which Christians have been so little agreed, and which has been so variously understood and explained, by those who receive it.

A doctrine which we cannot deny, without incurring the charge of wanting the humble spirit of Christian faith, and about which it is therefore unsafe to allow ourselves to inquire, we have certainly a right to demand to find either distinctly and intelligibly expressed in the scriptures, or clearly stated and explained in the writings of those, who propose them as essential parts of the Christian doctrine. But where, I ask, are we to look for a clear and distinct statement of the orthodox doctrine of Atonement? The genuine doctrine of Calvinism is indeed stated by the early writers of that school in a manner sufficiently clear and intelligible. But every feature of that is denied as a misrepresentation of the orthodox faith. We are told that the language of the orthodox, like that of the scriptures, is metaphorical, not to be understood literally; and I in vain seek for such an explanation of the metaphors, as to enable me to understand what is the distinct doctrine, which is intended to be maintained. A fleeting and shadowy image is presented to the view, which eludes every attempt to fix its shape, and dimensions, and features. And can it be, that my inability to receive a doctrine, expressed in words, of which I am only told what they do *not mean*, and not what they do, is to be regarded as " an indication of a disposition of heart and temper of mind, which is in total contrariety to the humble spirit of Christian faith?"

There are some other sentiments in this paragraph also, which must not be passed without notice. It is asserted, " that God, having sent his Son to be a propitiation, has told us, that we must rely upon his atoning blood, as the *sole ground of forgiveness.*" I would ask where God has told us, that " the atoning blood of Christ is the *sole* ground of forgiveness."

I find the prophet Isaiah, without any reference to any kind of atonement, referring the forgiveness of sin solely to the mercy of God, by which he is ready to accept reformation and a return to virtue. (Is. lv. 7)

" Let the wicked forsake his way, and the unrighteous man his thoughts, and let him return unto the Lord, and he will have mercy upon him, and to our God, for he will abundantly pardon." I find David, in the depth of his sorrow and distress in the consciousness of deep and aggravated guilt, by which he had incurred severe tokens of the divine displeasure; in pouring forth his humble supplications for pardon, placing his hope, in no sacrifice, or atonement, but solely in the mercy of God, and the evidence he should give of true repentance. (Psalm xli. 1, 16, 17) "Have mercy upon me, O God, according to thy loving kindness, according to the multitude of thy tender mercies, blot out my transgressions."...." Thou desirest not sacrifice, else would I give it. The sacrifices of God are a broken spirit; a broken and contrite heart, O God, thou wilt not despise." I find John the baptist announcing the approach of the kingdom of heaven, with the call to repentance, and intimating nothing else as requisite, preparatory to being the fit subjects of it, but that men should " repent," and " bring forth fruits meet for repentance." (Matt. iii. 2, 8) I find Jesus Christ himself declaring, (Matt. vi. 14) " If ye forgive men their trespasses, your heavenly Father will also forgive you." And I find it the object of one of his most beautiful and touching parables (Luke xv.) to teach his followers, not that God demands with unrelenting severity full satisfaction " in the atoning blood and perfect righteousness" of another, as the foundation of hope, and ground of forgiveness; but proclaiming the essential mercy and placability of our heavenly Father, and his readiness, not only to receive and restore his penitent children, but to meet with joy the first workings of ingenuous sorrow and a sense of guilt, and the first symptoms of a disposition and wish to return to duty. "When he was yet a great way off, the Father had compassion on him, and ran to meet him." To this compassion and reconciliation he was solely moved, as far as we are informed, by the return of the penitent to a sense of his guilt and his duty; "Father, I have sinned against heaven and in thy sight, and am no more worthy to be called thy son."...."This, my son, was dead, and is alive again, he was lost and is found." I find it was the prayers and alms of Cornelius that "came up into remembrance with God," and that "in every nation he that feareth God, and worketh righteousness, is declared to be accepted with him." (Acts x. 4, 35)

These declarations, and numerous others of the same import, must surely have been out of the mind of the writer, when he asserted, in the words I have before quoted, "that God has told us, that we must rely on the atoning blood of his son, as the *sole* ground of forgiveness."

I must take leave also to correct some other expressions, standing in close connexion with this. It is implied in a manner not to be misunderstood, in the paragraph in question, that Unitarians, or those who reject the doctrine of the atonement, "hope for heaven on the footing of their own virtue or good works," (p. 105) that they "think themselves entitled to future happiness on their own account, and rest their hopes of heaven on their own goodness." But is there no alternative between "relying on the atoning blood of the son of God, as the *sole* ground of forgiveness," and relying on our own merit, as the *sole* ground of acceptance? Unitarians, as far as I know, and as far as I can learn from their writings, are equally distant from each of these extremes. Their dependence is wholly on the mercy of God, for they believe that all men, on account of their actual sin, stand in need of mercy, and are wholly incapable of meriting salvation, and claiming it as a matter of right; *that* mercy, they believe, is promised to all who repent: yet that the salvation of the best of men is of grace, and not of debt, what they cannot demand as a right, yet may claim on the ground of the divine promise. A promise, too, not in consideration of satisfaction having been made by the vicarious suffering of a substitute, but originating in free sovereign mercy, and contemplating the change of character implied in repentance, as alone a sufficient reason for this exercise of it.

But though Unitarians, in rejecting the orthodox doctrine of atonement, do not maintain the opinion attributed to them of the worth and sufficiency of human merit; yet they will certainly not acquiesce in the opinion, so strongly expressed by the author of the Letters, of the entire worthlessness of all the works of righteousness and good dispositions of men. They think such expressions equally inconsistent with truth, and of pernicious tendency. For if human virtue be thought of no value, and of no estimation in the sight of God, the motive for its practice is weakened, if not destroyed. We shall feel little interest in seeking high attainments in that, which is of so little consideration, or is so offensive, that it must not be named in the presence of God. But let me ask, where we are to find the inhibition so confidently asserted. Where " has God taught us, (p. 105) that no works of righteousness which we have done, and no accomplishments or dispositions which we possess, must ever be named in his presence?" I find instances innumerable, in which the reverse of this is expressed in a very clear and unequivocal manner. It is expressed by Paul, when he said, (Rom. ii. 6, 10) " God will render to every man according to his deeds," and has prepared "glory, and honour, and peace, for every man that worketh good." And as he thus believed that the good deeds of good men were regarded with approbation and complacency by their Maker; so he was certainly not aware that it was either criminal or improper to *name them in his presence*, when he so exultingly appealed to the course of his past life, and expressed his so strong assurance of the future rewards of virtue; (2 Tim. iv. 7) " I have fought a good fight, I have finished my course, I have kept the faith; henceforth there is laid up for me a crown of righteousness, which the Lord, the righteous Judge, shall give me at that day."

Such a thought must have been far from the mind of our Saviour, when he directed his disciples to plead their good deeds in their supplications to God for his mercy; (Matt. vi. 12) "Forgive us our debts, as we forgive our debtors," with the express assurance, that this plea will not be disregarded, "for if ye forgive men their trespasses, your heavenly Father will also forgive you." Such a thought seems wholly inconsistent with the declaration, "That the son of man will come in the glory of his Father, and will then reward every man according to his works;" (Matt. xvi. 27) for such a declaration implies, that the works of men are of some account in the mind of Him, who will be their judge, are to be brought into solemn account, and to furnish the grounds of the decisions of the great day.

I would request you also to compare with the assertion under consideration, "that God has taught us that no works of righteousness which we have done, and no accomplishments or dispositions, which we possess, must ever be named in his presence;" the parable of the talents in the xxv. chap. of Matthew, and the representation of the final judgment in a more direct form, which immediately follows it. To whom and upon what ground, in the former case, was the eulogy pronounced, and the reward assigned; "Well done, good and faithful servant, thou hast been faithful over a few things, I will make thee ruler over many things?" And in the latter, to whom was addressed the welcome, "Come, ye blessed of my Father, inherit the kingdom prepared for you from the foundation of the world?" It was in each case the faithful, the humane, and the obedient; and in each case it was the good deeds they had done, " the good dispositions they had manifested, the fidelity with which they had used the talents entrusted to them, the kindness with which they had conducted in the relations in which they were placed, that recommended them to the approbation of the judge, and procured for them the rewards he had to distribute. No allusion is made to a " perfect righteousness, which God has provided for them" to supersede their own personal righteousness, or to render it valueless. Indeed nothing can be more clear, than that if it be of no value, of no account, and not to be named in the presence of God, it is not worth our pursuit, and those are the truly wise, who place their whole dependence on the worthiness of Him, who was righteous for them, and trouble not themselves about the attainment of personal righteousness, which being of no account, can be of no use.

I know that this consequence will be rejected with abhorrence by every serious believer in the doctrine; but I know, too, that it does not follow with the less certainty from it.

LETTER VI.

The subject to which I would next call your attention is that of *divine influence;* the discussion of which occupies the Xth letter of Dr. Woods. Upon this subject we must keep carefully in mind the distinction between the general doctrine, and that which is peculiar to Calvinism. It is with the latter only that we are concerned as a subject of controversy. To the indistinctness and obscurity, which arises from confounding them together, we owe much of the difficulty, in which this subject is usually involved.

As to the general doctrine of divine influence, I observe, there is no controversy. It is implied in the government of providence, in the acknowledgment of dependence on God, and in every prayer. We may suppose it to be direct and immediate, or only such as reaches us through the instrumentality of those means, by which common effects are usually produced, and thus not distinguishable from the common course of nature. None, I suppose, will deny the possibility of a direct access to the human mind by him, who gave being and all its powers to that mind; and the reality of it will always be a fact, depending like every other fact upon evidence; to be received or rejected, as the evidence is perceived to be satisfactory or not.

It will not, I presume, be pretended, that the direct influence of the spirit of God upon the mind is of such a nature, that men can be conscious of it at the time, so as to distinguish it with certainty from the natural operations of the mind under the influence of external circumstances, and the variety of motives, which are presented to it. There can then be no evidence of it in any particular instance. Our proof of the doctrine must be drawn, not from experience or observation, but solely from those texts of scripture, which are supposed to assert it; and those are to be subjected to just rules of interpretation, in order to ascertain, whether that, and that only, can have been the meaning of the spirit that dictated them.

But without any immediate and direct influence upon the mind, the most important effects may be produced, and changes brought about within us, by a variety of instruments and means, in a manner analogous to that, in which all the great purposes of God are accomplished in the natural and moral world. God is to be acknowledged, his hand is to be seen, the operations of his spirit appear in all the events that take place. Yet not a direct and immediate agency is to be perceived. Instruments and means are employed, but the hand that employs them is unseen. Not seldom a long and circuitous train of them, the connexions and combinations of which it is not in our power to trace, conceals from our view the spirit that guides, and the power that effects the whole.

Nor is it only great events, and the accomplishment of great purposes, that we are to trace to the agency of the spirit of God. It extends not less to the common provisions and constant occurrences of life; to the food by which our life is supported, and every provision by which it is made comfortable. These are the gift of God; not directly, not independently of our exertions, nor without the exertions of others, but by employing them both. God is also the preserver of our lives, and is to be so acknowledged in all the common, as well as the uncommon exigences of our being. Not, however, by immediate acts of power, and a direct agency, is this done, but by the instrumentality of an infinite variety and complicated system of means. Of these means, our own exertions, and the assistance of others, constitute an essential, and a principal part. If they are neglected or withheld, the protecting care of heaven is withheld. We perish. A miracle is not wrought to save him, who takes no care to save himself.

It is in a similar manner, by instruments and means, not by a direct action upon the mind, that the spirit of God produces its great effects in bringing men to repentance, holiness, and virtue. Among these, the most important are the instructions of the holy scriptures. "The word of God (1 Pet. i. 23) is the incorruptible seed, by which men are born again." Whatever good influences are produced by it, are influences of the spirit of God. The same may be said of christian institutions, religious assemblies, public worship. The usual course of providence, but especially deviations from it in remarkable events and uncommon phenomena, are means for accomplishing the same purposes. The same also is to be said of the priesthood, religious rites, and prophetic office under the former dispensation, and the christian ministry, and the whole system of written and oral instruction under the present. And those who are thus employed in "converting sinners from the error of their ways, and turning many to righteousness," are represented as "ambassadors of Christ." They are his agents, act in his stead, and whatever effects are produced, they are the proper fruits of the spirit, and may be considered as the work of that spirit, which projected the great scheme, and which provides for and directs its execution.

Now, were there nothing more direct and immediate, than those influences, which have now been mentioned, there would be enough to answer to most of the language of the Bible on the subject; enough to give a fair and important meaning to all the texts alluded to by Dr. Woods. (p. 107) Those are the instruments and means by which God is constantly "working in men both to will and to do; creating in them a new heart and a new spirit; opening their eyes, drawing, turning, renewing, strengthening them, helping their infirmities."

All that is said to show, that a divine influence upon the mind *may* be consistent with human liberty and proper activity, is to no purpose; for neither the reality of a divine influence, nor its consistency with human liberty and activity is denied. That is not the question in dispute between Unitarians and Calvinists. The question is, whether the doctrine of divine influence, in the peculiar sense in which it is held by Calvinists, is consistent with human liberty and activity. Nor is it whether they affirm it to be so, but whether it can be shown to be so in reality.

It is in vain that Dr. Woods has blended together and confounded the general doctrine of divine influence, which is held by Christians in common, with the peculiar doctrine of Calvinism respecting special irresistible grace. In vain has he softened down the offensive features of the system, and explained away, or endeavoured to give an unexceptionable meaning to the terms *irresistible, overpowering, invincible,* used by the Orthodox in relation to the subject. The import of these terms is to be found in the known and avowed doctrines of Calvinism, as they are stated by the most approved writers, and in the Confessions of Faith deliberately drawn up by Councils, and received by churches, which profess to make the Calvinistic faith their standard.

Now according to these, " All those, whom God hath predestinated to life, *and those only,* he is pleased in his appointed time, effectually to call by his word and spirit, out of that state of sin and death in which they are by nature, to grace and salvation by Jesus Christ."—" This effectual call is of God's free and special grace alone; not from any thing at all foreseen in man, who is altogether passive therein, until, being quickened and renewed by the holy spirit, he is thereby enabled to answer this call."—" Elect infants, dying in infancy, are regenerated and saved by Christ, so also are all other elect persons, who are incapable of being outwardly called by the ministry of the word."—"Others not elected, although they may be called by the ministry of the word, and may have some common operations of the spirit, yet they never truly come to Christ, and therefore cannot be saved. Much less can men, not professing the Christian religion, be saved in any other way whatever, be they never so diligent to frame their lives according to the light of nature, and the law of that religion they do profess." *(Westminster Confession.)*

In the above extracts from an instrument of high authority, we have a clear and distinct statement of the orthodox doctrine respecting that influence of the spirit, by which regeneration is effected; and by which alone men can be brought out of that state of sin and death in which they are by nature, and brought into a state of salvation. It is an influence confined to the elect; granted exclusively to those, who are predestinated to eternal life; granted to them also in a perfectly arbitrary manner; not being on account of any thing foreseen in them, still less on account of any thing already in them; since, until it takes place, they are, according to this scheme, in a state of sin and death, wholly inclined to evil, and indisposed to all good. In those, upon whom this influence is exerted, its effects take place without any agency or cooperation of theirs, for they are wholly passive in it. It is the irresistible and unaided work of the spirit of God, which man can do nothing either to assist or to prevent. In all those, who are the subject of it, it is effectual, and their regeneration and final salvation are sure. Those to whom this influence is denied, or from whom it is withheld, are not elected; and they can never be regenerated, and consequently their salvation is impossible.

It will be objected, perhaps, that the Orthodox, though they receive in general and substantially the doctrines contained in the Westminster Confession of Faith and Catechism, yet they are not satisfied with them in all respects, and do not subscribe to all their language.

To this objection they have an undoubted right, and Dr. Woods, as their representative, has a right to be judged upon a fair construction of the language, which is used in the Creed of the Theological Institution with which he is connected; and that which he has himself used, as far as he has proceeded in giving a statement and explanation of the doctrine.

But, little I think will be gained by this toward relieving the doctrine, which he means to maintain, from the charges which are brought against the orthodox system on this point.

In the following extracts from the Creed of the Theological Institution at Andover, I think you will find every important idea expressed or implied, that is to be found in the passages before given from the Westminster Confession. "By nature every man is personally depraved, destitute of holiness, unlike and opposed to God, and previously to the renewing agency of the divine spirit, all his moral actions are adverse to the character and glory of God ; being morally incapable of recovering the image of his Creator, which was lost in Adam, every man is justly exposed to eternal damnation ; so that except a man be born again, he cannot see the kingdom of God ;....God, of his mere good pleasure, from all eternity elected some to everlasting life....no means whatever can change the heart of a sinner, and make it holy....regeneration and sanctification are effects of the creating and renewing agency of the holy spirit."

A cursory reading of Dr. Woods' Letter on this subject might lead to an impression of something short of the doctrine expressed in these extracts ; but the following sentence, taken in the connexion in which it is used, and in connexion with the other doctrines defended in his Letters, will be found, I think, to express or imply all that is contained in the fuller, and more naked and undisguised statement of the Westminster Divines. He is speaking of the meaning of the words *irresistible, overpowering*, as used by orthodox writers, in reference to the divine influence upon the minds of men, when he says, (p. 116) " What the nature of the disorder is, God knows, and is perfectly able to apply a suitable and efficacious remedy. Now, when this almighty Physician kindly undertakes the cure of our souls, the obstinacy of the disorder yields ; its resistance is taken away ; that is to say, the heart is effectually cleansed from its pollution ; love of sin, enmity to God, pride, ingratitude, and selfish, earthly desires are subdued, and man is induced to love God, and obey his commands." He had before explained the orthodox faith in general by saying, (p. 108) "We believe, that all virtue or holiness in man is to be ascribed to the influence of the divine spirit, and that without the effectual agency of the spirit, man would have no holy affections, and perform no acts of holy obedience."

Now what is the disorder, to which the efficacious remedy is to be applied; and for which, as we shall see, there is no other cure? If we look back to the Vth and VIth letters of Dr. Woods, we shall find it described. It is a state of entire moral corruption, in which every man is born into the world, and in which every man continues until he is renewed by the holy spirit. It is, that men are by nature, that is, as they came first from the hand of the Creator, destitute of holiness; not only so, but subjects of an innate moral depravity, from the first inclined to evil, and while unrenewed, their affections and actions wholly wrong. This is the disease, as to its nature and extent.

Passing to the next letters, VIIth and VIIIth, we are told to whom, and on what ground, a cure is applied. Those, who are to be delivered from this moral bondage, this original state of depravity, to be regenerated, renewed, and saved, are selected from the mass of mankind by a sovereign act of the divine will, without any thing in them, as the reason why they were chosen, rather than the others, who are passed by, left to remain in sin, and to perish forever.

Being thus elected, thus predestinated to eternal life, they become the subjects of the efficacious, renovating influence, under consideration. And when this "almighty Physician undertakes the cure, the disorder yields." He cannot be defeated. He cannot be resisted. The fact then is, that all, whom God undertakes to renew, all to whom he applies that effectual influence, which is to subdue the obstinacy of the disorder, are in fact renewed. The love of sin and enmity to God are subdued, and they are brought to the love of God and obedience. And this effect is produced, because he who knows the disorder has known how to apply a remedy; and has applied one, which must produce a cure.

It follows, then, that this remedy has been applied to *no others*. Those who are not renewed have none of this influence employed upon them; for if they had, they also would have been renewed; since this influence is efficacious, cannot be resisted, cannot be defeated. Their failure then is for the want of that, which is granted to the others, and without which it was impossible for them to be renewed and saved. "All virtue, all holiness in man is to be ascribed to this efficacious influence; without it man would have no holy affections, and would perform no acts of holy obedience." (p. 108) Those, then, who have holiness and virtue, have it solely in consequence of their having this influence, which makes them, and cannot fail to make them holy; and those who have none, but remain unholy, sinful, enemies to God, are destitute of it solely because they have not that influence, which, if they had, could not fail to produce the same effect in them, which it has produced in others. This is but a fair and full, unexaggerated development of the doctrine, according to Dr. Woods' own statement of it. And whether it be not in every point the same as that which is more clearly stated in the Westminster Confession, every one can judge.

From the doctrine thus stated, Unitarians, I believe, generally dissent, and maintain a very different opinion on the subject. They dissent, because they think it inconsistent with all the representations we have in the scriptures of the moral character of God, and with the condition of man, as a free and accountable being; —inconsistent with all those texts, which complain of the sins of men; because, by the supposition, they act only according to the nature given them, and could not act otherwise without assistance and influence, which are not given to them;—inconsistent with all the commands of the Gospel to believe, repent, be renewed, and to love God with the whole heart; since they have no ability to do any part of this, till almighty power is exerted to make them willing; and it is equally impossible for them not to do it, when this power is exerted;—inconsistent with the sincerity of all exhortations, encouragements, and promises to the exertions of men, since it supposes them incapable of willing to perform either of these acts; that it is not of themselves to will any thing good, but they depend for it on an influence, over which they have no control, and which they can do nothing to procure.

Taking this doctrine of an efficacious influence, without which there can be no holy affection, and no act of holy obedience, in connexion with the whole scheme of doctrine, of which it makes an essential part; we are unable to reconcile it with the paternal character of God, or a righteous government, or to perceive how it can consist with a moral accountability. We are unable to see how the character of God can be vindicated, in creating beings with a nature totally depraved, inclined only to evil, demanding of them holiness, which they are utterly unable to exercise, without an irresistible influence in renewing their hearts, and giving them right dispositions and desires; which influence he grants to some, and denies to others, without any difference in them as the ground or reason of the distinction; and punishing those for not exercising this holiness, to whom he had never granted the assistance, without which it was never possible to them. And we are equally unable to see how those could be accountable for their actions, and the subjects of reasonable blame for their unholy and wicked lives, who were brought into being with hearts totally corrupt, inclined to evil, and evil only, and from whom that efficacious renovating influence has been withheld, without which it was never possible for them to be renewed, to " have any holy affections, or to perform any acts of holy obedience." The sinner seems upon this scheme to have a perfect apology to offer for his continuing in sin; a complete and satisfactory excuse for every defect and for every crime, however numerous, and however great.

It may be useful to give you a distinct statement of the several points, in which our views upon this subject are at variance with those, which we find advocated by Dr. Woods. In the first place, a different account of the moral nature of man, and his character and disposition, as he comes from the hand of the Creator, leads to a different opinion correspondent to it, of what is necessary, in order to his becoming holy, and a fit subject of the approbation and favour of the Author of his being. Not seeing in him a nature wholly corrupt, inclined only to evil, and an enemy of God, we perceive no necessity for an almighty, irresistible influence to be employed for the purpose of producing an entire change of nature, opposite inclinations, dispositions, and course of action from those, to which he was directed by his natural constitution. Believing him to possess faculties and affections, equally capable of a right and a wrong direction, neither morally good nor bad by nature, but equally capable of becoming either, we see a moral discipline under which he is placed, adapted to such a nature, such capacities, and such dispositions. The influence and agency of the spirit of God is to be acknowledged in the whole of that discipline which is intended to improve, exalt, and perfect our nature, or to correct any wrong tendencies it may have acquired, and restore it to a right direction, and its previous purity.

In this light are to be viewed all the means and the motives of religion, the institutions of society, the course of providence, events calculated to lead to reflection, to produce seriousness, to give us just views of our nature, condition, duty, prospects, and hopes; what we are, and what we ought to be, or are designed to be. Whatever is adapted to subdue the power of sin, to control the bad passions, and to bring us to the love of holiness, and the practice of every virtue. In all this the agency of God is to be acknowledged, as the purposes of God are to be perceived. Not a direct and immediate agency, but such as we see exercised in every thing else through the universe; God bringing about his ends by a variety of means, and employing in them the subordinate agency and instrumentality of his creatures.

It is by such means, that the spirit of God produces its great moral effects, operates on the minds and hearts of men, reconciles them to God, works in them to will and to do his good pleasure. These influences are distributed to men in very unequal measure, and with infinite variety, as to kind and degree. The impartiality of the common parent is manifested, not in employing the same means with all, and exerting upon all the same influence, but by rendering to all according to the manner in which they act under the influence that is employed upon them, whatever that may be, as to kind and degree; not in giving to all the same number of talents, and of the same value, for use; but rendering to all according to the use they make of their talents, whether few or many. And here they find room for the particular and perhaps direct and immediate influence of the spirit upon those, who have made a good use of common privileges, upon the principle, that "to him that *hath*, more shall be given." More shall be given to him, who has made a good use of that which he has, whether much or little.

Accordingly, Unitarians generally do not reject the notion of a direct and immediate influence of the spirit of God on the human mind. They believe that there may be circumstances of great trial, strong temptation and peculiar difficulty, that call for extraordinary assistance, and that those who have manifested a disposition to make a good use of the ordinary means afforded, will have further aid suited to their exigences, and sufficient by a proper use to answer to their necessities. They suppose also that any extraordinary assistance will be granted only to those, who ask it; that it will be granted to previous good disposition, and a sense of need and dependance. That God will give the holy spirit to them who ask, to them who have already right feelings, are sensible of their weakness and wants, and ask the mercy of God to supply them.

LETTER VII.

I now follow Dr. Woods in calling your attention to a few remarks on *the influence and moral tendency* of the Unitarian compared with the Trinitarian and Calvinistic scheme; premising however the caution, that we must not confound, in our examination, as is too apt to be done, the moral tendency with the effects actually produced; and that even when this error is not committed, too much weight is not to be given to any argument drawn from such a comparison on either side. The reason is, that mankind are less influenced in their conduct by their speculative opinions, and the character of their faith, than we are ready to imagine. Were we purely intellectual beings, governed wholly by reason, there would be no such uncertainty or fallacy in our deductions. We could calculate with certainty how men would act, by knowing what they believed; and on the other hand, what was the character of their faith, by their course of life. But men have also passions and affections, on the one hand; and these not only serve to corrupt and pervert the understanding, but where they fail to do this, they yet are able to overpower the will, so as to lead them to act in opposition to reason and faith;—and on the other hand they have conscience and a moral sense, which, however the understanding may have been blinded, or misled, or perverted, will sometimes preserve them in a right course of conduct, in defiance of an absurd or a corrupting faith. Still there is a general influence of right views and a pure faith, which is not inconsiderable, nor uncertain.

But when we come to speak of the practical influence of different forms of christian faith, we are to take into our consideration, that there are certain great principles, and those the most fundamental, and influential upon the conduct of life, which the several sects of Christians hold in common. So that great as the difference is between the Unitarian and the Trinitarian faith; on account of the fundamental principles held in common, the difference of their practical tendency is less, probably, than ardent and zealous partizans on either side are ready to imagine. Still, however, it is believed that the difference in several respects cannot be very small.

I am ready to accede to the statement implied in what is said by Dr. Woods, pp. 135—141; that the practical influence of a scheme of faith will bear some proportion to the exhibition it gives, " of a being of infinite perfection as the object of worship; a moral government marked with holiness and righteousness throughout; and the manner in which mercy is exercised toward offenders under this government."

These are the great points, upon which the Unitarian and Calvinistic doctrine are at variance, and with this difference in view, Dr. Woods endeavours to show the favourable influence of the latter above the former in several respects.

In the first place, with respect to *love to God*.

Now it will be sufficient to remark on this point, that the practical influence of a doctrine will depend, not on the words in which it is expressed, but on the images, which are presented to the mind. However we may speak in words of the perfect justice, benevolence, and mercy of God; our feelings and affections will wholly follow the images, in which he is presented to us in the dispositions towards his creatures, and the actions respecting them, which are attributed to him. If those are such, as in any other being would be thought arbitrary, or unjust, or cruel; it will be in vain for us to speak of them in words, that express all the kindness and benignity of the paternal character. The question then will be, not what are the epithets which the two systems apply to God, for they both apply the same; but what are the actions they attribute to him, what the images, under which they present him, what the principles and measures of his government? In these respects enough has before been said to show how the comparison will stand.

Love to Christ, and the value at which we estimate the benefits we receive through him, will depend on our view of the nature and value of those benefits, and not at all on the rank he holds in the scale of being. Unitarian views indeed ascribing to him only what he claimed himself, derived excellences, and a subordinate agency, will not allow us to give him the supremacy of affection, any more than the glory, which was due to God only. It teaches us to love him, to be grateful to him, and trust in him, as him who was appointed by the Father to execute his purposes of benevolence; and who voluntarily did and suffered all that was necessary to procure for us the forgiveness of sin, reconciliation with God, and eternal life. These are benefits, with which nothing that is done by any other finite being can bear any comparison; they are such as entitle him to affection, and gratitude, and trust; such as we owe, and can owe to no other being, but to "his Father and our Father, his God and our God."

Unitarians are unable indeed to express these sentiments in the language applied by Dr. Woods, p. 145. Such expressions of confidence and trust they can apply to God only. They have but one object of supreme trust and dependence. Were they to make Jesus Christ that object, they would fear to incur the rebuke, which the prophet received from the angel before whom he fell down to worship, " See thou do it not, I am thy fellow-servant, worship God." I am ready therefore to answer to the questions, with which Dr. Woods closes the paragraph which relates to faith in Christ, (p. 145) " Does the Unitarian system teach any thing like this? Does such a faith spring from the principles which it inculcates?" to say no! Most of what is there said, Unitarians would apply to God, but not to Christ. We find nothing in the Bible to justify us in transferring our supreme confidence and trust from God to Christ. It is accordingly the power and wisdom and goodness of *God*, which inspire us with humble and joyful hope; and which put our hearts at rest respecting the important concerns of the creation. It is to *his* care, that we cheerfully and entirely commit our interests, temporal and eternal. It is in *him* that we trust for all that is necessary to purify our hearts, to guide and protect us during our pilgrimage, to comfort us in affliction, and to give us peace and triumph in the prospect of death. In these great interests and concerns, we cannot consent, and we do not find ourselves taught, to leave our heavenly Father wholly out of the account.

The tendency of any scheme of doctrine to produce *the dread of sin, and a watchful care to obey the divine precepts,* will depend essentially on the view it presents of the rewards and punishments prepared for men in another life, the heaven it provides, and the hell it reveals. Now it is not a little remarkable, that Dr. Woods should claim an advantage, in point of moral influence, to the orthodox faith, on the ground that " it contemplates a state of higher perfection and purer and more elevated enjoyment, than the Unitarian describes." (p. 146) And " that the contemplation of a future reward, *to be obtained by virtuous efforts,* must evidently tend to excite those efforts, very much in proportion to the greatness and excellency of that reward."

For, besides that the claim of higher perfection and greater purity is without any foundation to justify it; upon what ground can he speak of a future reward to be obtained " *by virtuous efforts ?*" The reader has not forgotten, that the sinner has no encouragement to virtuous efforts: " That no works of righteousness, and no accomplishments or disposition, must ever be named in the presence of God.....That the only righteousness, which is to be the foundation of hope to men is a perfect righteousness which God has provided..... That we must rely on the atoning blood of Christ as the sole ground of forgiveness."

Unitarians may be allowed to speak of the motives to virtuous efforts arising from the future rewards to be obtained by them; but with what propriety can the *Calvinist* do this, who believes, that the future condition of men is determined from eternity by an irreversible decree; that by nature they are totally depraved and inclined only to evil; that they remain so till brought out of that state by regeneration, and that regeneration is effected only by the special irresistible influence of the spirit of God, granted only to the elect, and to them, not on account of any disposition or efforts of theirs, which have any tendency to produce or to procure it?

And as to the influence of the different views of future punishment;—it might at first be thought, that the advantage were on the side of those of Calvinism; but there are two considerations that convince me to the contrary. For, in the first place the punishments as well as the rewards provided by that scheme, are administered on the principles of a sovereign, unconditional election; the desert of punishment, and consequently the punishment itself, not being subject to any human efforts, but following necessarily the divine decree. Bad men may be expected to avail themselves of the plea of a moral inability, which, to all practical purposes. is in fact the same as a natural inability, or physical coercion. They may be expected to go on quietly in the course of vice in the persuasion, that if they are not predestinated to holiness and eternal life, no efforts of theirs can avail thêm ; and if they are, God will, in his own time, draw them to him, by his effectual, irresistible grace ; that nothing, which they can do, till thus regenerated, will have any tendency to bring about this effect, or prepare them for it ; on the contrary, that they are as likely, I believe they are sometimes told more likely, to be thus arrested by sovereign grace in the full career of wickedness, than when using endeavours to recover themselves out of the hands of satan by their own strength. This reasoning, and I cannot see that it does not proceed fairly on the acknowledged principles of Calvinism, must check instead of encouraging the efforts of wicked men to disentangle themselves from the snare of the devil.

In the second place, we are to look for the efficacy of punishment and its moral influence in preventing sin or reclaiming men from it, not to the degree of its severity and duration only, but to its certainty, and the evidence brought home distinctly to the minds of men of its certainty. Now if you endeavour to enhance the fear of punishment, by representations of its severity or of its duration far disproportioned to what can be the apprehension of the demerit, to which it is to be applied ; if you carry it beyond the bounds of probability, that the threat will be executed ; if it be such, that to a reflecting mind, it is impossible it should be executed by a just, and good, and merciful being, the Parent of the creation; you weaken its effects as a motive, you lose in probability, and the firmness of faith, more than you gain in the force of fear. You excite a vague and indistinct terror and dread; but so mingled with incredulity, arising from a natural and unconquerable sense of the essential kindness and benignity of the Author of nature, as to impair, if not destroy its practical effects.

The surest and highest, the purest and most permanent influence will be that, which arises from such views of the future punishment awaiting the wicked, as are consistent with the character of a Sovereign of the world, who has nothing vindictive in his nature, who adjusts punishment to the degree of demerit, who inflicts it solely for the purpose of promoting holiness, and accomplishing the purposes of his moral government, and only to the degree which these purposes require, and so long as they require it.

From these considerations, I am persuaded that the moral influence of the views of future reward and punishment, maintained generally by Unitarians, is far more certain, and powerful, and salutary, and purifying, than that which is the result of the Orthodox views on this subject. And I am persuaded of this by another consideration still. It is this—The virtue that is produced by cheerful views, and by the contemplation of kindness, benevolence, and mercy in God, is of a more pure, generous, and elevated kind, than that which arises from cold, austere, and gloomy views, and the contemplation of severe, unrelenting, vindictive justice, and the execution of eternal wrath.

Unitarians believe that the representations in scripture of the future punishment of the impenitent wicked are, for the purpose of impression, highly figurative; but they believe that the figures, like all others used by the sacred writers, are intended to mean something, something of vast moment; that in degree and duration it will be such, as is calculated to produce the highest practical influence. In either respect we can have clear and distinct conceptions only to a certain degree. All beyond that, therefore, can add nothing to the effect.

Dr. Woods proceeds to a comparison of the different influences of the systems in question, as respects *reverence for the word of God*. To show that Unitarians have little reverence for the scriptures, and treat the sacred writings with little respect, he asserts, (p. 148.) That, " the grand maxim of the Polish Socinians was, that *reason is our ultimate rule and standard*, and that whatever in religion is not conformed to this, is to be rejected. This maxim, as they understood it, gave them perfect liberty to alter or set aside the obvious sense of the bible, whenever it did not agree with the deductions of reason. Unitarians, in general, have, with more or less decision, adopted the same maxim." The impression intended here to be made on the reader must be, That " Unitarians, generally think themselves at perfect liberty to alter or set aside the obvious sense of the bible, whenever it does not agree with the deductions of reason." Dr. Woods has not seen fit to refer us to his authority for the assertion, as respects the Polish Socinians. This it was his duty to do, in laying against them a charge of so serious a nature, that the reader might be able to judge of its justice. What authority he may be able to produce, I know not. But I presume it must have been derived from a passage, which I shall subjoin, which is found in the Racovian Catechism, which contains a summary of the Socinian doctrines, as drawn up by the celebrated Polish Divines. But if this passage be the only authority to which he will appeal, the charge is made with less care, than were to have been expected of one, so frequent and loud, as he is, in his complaints of the misrepresentations and unfairness of adversaries. The passage is this—

"By what means may the more obscure passages of scripture be understood?

"By carefully ascertaining in the first instance, the scope, and other circumstances, of those passages, in the way which ought to be pursued in the interpretation of the language of all other written compositions. Secondly, by an attentive comparison of them with similar phrases and sentences of less ambiguous meaning. Thirdly, by submitting our interpretation of the more obscure passages to the test of doctrines, which are most clearly inculcated in the scriptures, as to certain first principles; and admitting nothing that disagrees with these. And lastly, by rejecting every interpretation, which is repugnant to right reason, or involves a contradiction."

The reader is now requested to compare this with the assertion of Dr. Woods, and to judge of the fairness of the representation. The principles of interpretation, as here stated, are such, as no Divine of any school will at the present day call in question. They are such as Dr. Woods himself, I will venture to affirm, continually applies in practice. The difference between him and the Polish Divines is only as to the cases, to which the principle is to be applied, and not as to the principle itself. A thousand instances may be brought, in which Dr. Woods will apply the principle without hesitation. No one will reject with more decision than Dr. Woods the obvious meaning of all those passages, numerous and frequent as they are, in which bodily organs and human passions are ascribed to God. He will exercise his reason in the interpretation of all those passages, which will teach him to set aside as inadmissible, the plain, obvious, and literal meaning of the words that are used.

Luke xiv. 26. Our Saviour says, "If any man hate not his father, and mother, and wife, and children, and brethren, and sisters, yea, and his own life also, he cannot be my disciple." Dr. Woods, I trust, will be slow to insist on the plain and obvious sense of this text, as the true meaning of it. He will doubtless make reason his guide, in its interpretation; and applying his knowledge of oriental idioms, will set aside, as utterly inadmissible, the literal and obvious meaning of the words; not suspecting that he is thus exposing himself to the harsh censure from some less enlightened and liberal interpreter of scripture, of taking the liberty to alter or "set aside the obvious sense of the Bible."

Matt. xxvi. 26, 28. Our Saviour says, "This is my body,—this is my blood;" and John vi. 53. "Verily, verily I say unto you, except ye eat the flesh of the son of man and drink his blood, ye have no life in you." Dr. Woods, I suppose, will be as much shocked as any Polish Divine of the whole Socinian school, or any English or German Unitarian, at the idea of adopting the obvious sense of these expressions, as the real meaning of him who uttered them. Nor will he much regard the honest Catholic, who, pressing him with the literal meaning of the words, charges him with perverting the scriptures; and destroying their authority by thus subjecting them to reason in their interpretation. But why thus shocked, and why not adhere to the literal sense with the Catholic, unless the principle be admitted, that reason is to be employed in the interpretation of scripture? Unless calling to its aid all the resources of learning, experience, and common sense, it may authorize us to set aside the obvious sense by supplying us with proof, that, in any given case, the obvious sense cannot be the true sense? This is quite a different thing from such an arbitrary alteration of the word of God, or setting aside its true meaning, as is implied in what Dr. Woods has laid to the charge of the Polish Socinians and modern Unitarians.

But who, let me ask, is the man that manifests the truest reverence for the word of God? Is it he who indolently and carelessly takes the meaning that first presents itself, however absurd, or contradictory, or even impossible that may be; or he who, when the meaning that first presents itself is attended with difficulty or doubt, sets himself with patient and laborious study to ascertain, whether it be the meaning intended by the writer; a meaning, which if it be the word of God, will certainly contain neither an impossibility, a contradiction, nor an absurdity? Is it he, who without suffering his reason to judge in the case, accepts the meaning, which has been assigned to it in an age of ignorance and superstition, and which ecclesiastical authority has sanctioned, enforced, and perpetuated; or he, who using his own reason, instead of trusting that of another, applies all the helps that time, and industry, and learning have furnished, to the discovery of its true meaning?

We not only avow the principle, that reason is to be our guide in the interpretation of Scripture, but we declare that we know not a higher act of disrespect and irreverence to the word of God, than he is guilty of, who, rejecting the free use of reason in its interpretation, exposes it to contempt by attributing to it communications, which could not have been made by the same God, who is the author of our reason. We profess none of that loyalty of faith which consists in implicit subjection to the creed of a master; which is expressed by degrading and undervaluing our reason or refusing its use, and thus becoming prepared to receive absurdities, contradictions, and impossibilities for divine instructions. We think it to be doing no honour to our sacred books to be ready to believe both sides of a direct contradiction, because we think that we find them there. We are satisfied, from the very circumstance that it is a contradiction, or an absurdity, that we must have misunderstood what we there read. We suspend our faith, and apply ourselves with all the aids that reason, learning, industry supply to ascertain the source of our error, and to discover the truth. We believe that Unitarians, by doing this, have done much toward relieving our religion from articles of faith, and the scriptures from opinions attributed to them, which they never taught, which have been a reproach to our religion, and the occasion of its being rejected by many; who would gladly have received all that it has taught, had it been presented to them unmixed with the absurdities and impossibilities, with which they have seen it associated in popular creeds.

In order to estimate the relative tendency of the two systems, as respects *benevolent action*, whether in relation to the common interests of life, or that highest kind of it, which is directed to *the spread of the gospel, and the salvation of men;* we have only to compare together the views which have been given of the leading doctrines of the two systems; particularly as they relate to the character and dispositions of the Author of nature, his moral government, and the moral nature of man, and his condition, as a state of trial and probation for an endless being.—To this comparison I confidently invite you, in the assurance that no further illustration is necessary; and that you cannot fail to be convinced, that no opinions on these subjects can be better calculated, than those which we maintain, to purify and exalt our best affections, and to strengthen the motive to every kind of benevolent exertion.

I am persuaded too, that upon a fair comparison, Unitarians will not be found in fact to be behind other Christians in their benevolent exertions. Neither in Europe nor America are they liable to any peculiar reproach for the want of activity and engagedness in promoting humane and benevolent designs. In accomplishing all the great purposes of christian charity, as relates both to this and another life, it is believed they have taken their full share of interest, and have contributed their full share of exertion with their persons and their property.

In proportion to their numbers, no denomination of Christians has furnished more distinguished examples of ardent and disinterested zeal, personal sacrifices, and active exertion in the cause of truth, for the advancement of pure religion, and to promote humane and benevolent objects. None have contributed more largely to some of the most valuable institutions, by which the present period is distinguished. They have taken an active and leading part in promoting the great ends of the Bible Society, and the Peace Society.

In each of these they have united together with Christians of all other denominations. Their exertions and their contributions to the purposes of christian charity have been less the subject of public notice, than equal and similar exertions of others, for reasons which are obvious. They have not been exclusive. They have not been made separately. They have usually been thrown into a common stock. They have had no desire to be distinguished from other Christians,—have been willing to act with them, and wherever the object proposed, and the means for attaining it were such, as they could approve, to unite with others in promoting it. They have done, what every one, who regards the great interests of religion more than personal reputation, or the advancement of a party, ought to do. They have exercised their judgment in selecting the objects to which they should lend their aid; not always choosing those, which would excite the admiration of the world, or contribute most to give consideration or power to a sect, or serve to distinguish them from others. They have accordingly been less engaged than some other denominations of Christians, in projecting and supporting foreign missions, which though the most splendid and imposing, they have thought to be one of the least useful of the achievements of christian charity. For this apparent backwardness and lukewarmness, with which they are sometimes reproached, reasons may be assigned, which are not inconsistent with their taking as deep an interest in the cause of Christianity, and the salvation of their fellow-men, as others; and being ready to contribute as much and as cheerfully to extend the knowledge, the influences, and the blessings of our holy faith to all lands and to every people.

The imaginary cases, which Dr. Woods has allowed himself to state, (pp. 154, 155) are wholly gratuitous. He would have spared himself and the reader, had he reflected for a moment, that a Unitarian might invert the picture he has drawn, and it would be entitled to the same consideration as that, which he has presented; that is, to none at all. Were it even in his power, instead of a mere supposition, to produce an example, he must perceive, that it would prove nothing to the purpose, for which it was alleged; since that would not be inconsistent with an opposite example at the same time. Were it a fact, *instead of a mere imagination*, that an individual Unitarian by becoming orthodox had become more zealous and engaged, both in personal religion and in benevolent exertions; and that an individual Calvinist, on the other hand, had lost much of his piety and zeal in becoming a Unitarian; it would not prove that others might not experience an equally salutary change of character in passing from the orthodox to the unitarian faith,—or one equally unfavourable by passing from the unitarian to the orthodox. I may have as good reason for believing that the one event would take place, as Dr. Woods has for the probability of the other. And our opinions are each alike of no value.

I have observed that satisfactory reasons could be assigned, why Unitarians are not seen, as distinguished from others in those "remarkable movements," which in Dr. Woods' opinion " present the only prospect we have of the salvation of the world." (p. 153.) Some have had the opinion, in common with intelligent and pious Christians of other denominations, that little hope was to be entertained, of any important benefit from missionary exertions in heathen countries. So little success has attended all endeavours in modern times to extend the bounds of Christendom by missions for the conversion of barbarous pagan nations, that some have been ready to think, that no hope was to be entertained from human exertion, until it should be accompanied, as it was in the apostolic age, with some visible supernatural aid; until those, who are sent forth to carry the Gospel to the heathen, should have the power given them to propose its doctrines with the same authority, and accompanied with the same miraculous evidence, as it was when presented by its primitive teachers. Nor has this opinion been confined to Unitarians.

Others again, who have had more confidence in the efficacy of human exertions, and who believe that Christianity will finally triumph universally through the instrumentality of ordinary means; have yet not been satisfied with the means they have seen employed. They have believed that direct endeavours for the conversion of the heathen to Christianity have been premature; and have been wasted by being ill-timed and misapplied. They have thought that no permanent or extensive good was to be expected, except where the arts and some of the habits of civilized life, and some of the human literature of Christendom have been first carried, to prepare the way for its reception. They have thought that those, to whom the Gospel is sent, must be prepared to understand it and to feel its value by some previous education; and some have been disgusted, no doubt unjustly, by thinking that they saw, in the *remarkable movements* alluded to above, too much of ostentation and worldly motive; too much that seemed like a call upon an admiring world, " *Come and see my zeal for the Lord.*"

By some it has been thought, that to bring men from the grossness and absurdities of paganism to pure Christianity, the progress must be gradual. The transition is too great, and would give too violent a shock, to take place at once. They must pass to it through several intermediate steps. Light must be thrown in gradually, as they are able to bear it. Christianity is more likely to be received, if it be first introduced in forms mingled with considerable degrees of superstition; with pomp, and form, and ceremony, and even with corruptions of doctrine, which bring it nearer to the faith to which they have been accustomed. Polytheists, for example, it has been supposed, may be more easily reconciled to Christianity, and more ready to embrace it in that form, which leaves them a threefold God, or three Gods (for they will be able to understand none of those nice distinctions, which exercise the wits of learned theologians and acute metaphysical divines on this subject,) than that, which reduces the object of human worship to a perfect unity.

With such views and such impressions, they have seen their duty, so far as respects exertions in the Christian cause, lying in a different course; not in sending Unitarian missionaries into barbarous nations, but in studies, and labours at home to purify the Christian doctrine, and restore it to its primitive state. They have believed, if the Unitarian doctrine is to be sent any where abroad, it is to the Jews, and the followers of Mahomet, among whom all attempts to introduce Christianity have been defeated by the corruptions, with which it has been accompanied; and where better success may be reasonably expected, when it shall appear stripped of those appendages, which constitute their objection to it.

Other reasons also are to be assigned for that appearance of apathy, want of interest and want of exertion, with which Unitarians are sometimes charged. As has been said before, they have never been forward to distinguish themselves as a sect from the rest of their fellow Christians. They have never united their exertions together for the purpose of establishing a separate interest. They have felt no separate interest. They have been willing to remain, as long as they were allowed to remain, mingled together with their fellow Christians, undistinguished from the general mass, throwing in their contributions both of money and of personal exertion with theirs. They have thus contributed to swell the amount of charities and exertions, for which they have had no share of the credit.

To this course of conduct they have been induced in part by the love of peace, a desire to escape odium, and to avoid disturbing the public tranquillity and order. But neither the purity of their motives, nor the peaceful and silent course they have pursued, was sufficient to shield them from reproach. This very quiet and silence were brought against them, as an evidence of lukewarmness, and heartlessness, and indifference to the cause of religion; and their alleged inactivity was attributed to an opinion, that Christianity was of little value, and that men might do well without it.

They have accordingly found, that the reasons for their former course no longer continued; and they have changed that course. They have been convinced, that the state of things called upon them to use those exertions in the maintenance, defence, explanation and propagation of their opinions, from which only a regard for peace had hitherto restrained them; since the same peaceful and silent course could no longer shield them from reproach, nor prevent the mischiefs that they wished to avert. And now what is the consequence of this change of measures? They are reproached with that very activity and zeal, with those very exertions, which but a short time since, it was their reproach not to make.

These exertions are accompanied with the happiest effects. They have awakened a spirit of inquiry, which will go on and increase. They appear not yet, and it may be long before it will be proper that they should appear, in some of those particular things, in which they are reproached with being deficient. They have much to do at home, before it will be in their power advantageously to the Christian cause to extend their exertions abroad. They have to awaken a livelier interest in the cause of Christianity and the progress of rational and just views of its doctrines in their own body; to excite a deeper tone of religious feeling in that part of the Christian community, to which they have access, whether from the press or the pulpit; to engage the wealthy to cooperate with them, by bringing home to their feelings, the great good they have it in their power to do, and to their consciences the solemn responsibility connected with every talent, and every opportunity and power of doing good. They have to excite literary men to give more of their studies and labours, and more of their zeal to the promotion of so great and desirable a purpose. They have to induce enlightened and liberal men, who by their professions or public stations have an opportunity of exciting a salutary influence in the community, to a more open and manly avowal of their opinions, and to unite with them in all fair, and moderate, and temperate measures, with the Christian spirit, yet with ardour and lively interest, to promote and extend them.

It is not doubted that throughout our country, a very large proportion of these men, who for their talents, and learning, and virtues have the most influence in the community, and have it in their power to do the most toward giving a right direction to the public feeling or public sentiment, are dissatisfied with the Calvinistic and Trinitarian form, in which they have had religion presented to them; and if they have been led by circumstances to free inquiry on the subject, are Unitarians. But various causes prevent them from making a public avowal of their opinions. Among these, not the least is, usually, an unwillingness to encounter opposition and obloquy, and the loss of confidence, and of the power of being useful. It is among the encouraging prospects of the present time, that the reasons for reserve are ceasing to operate with all the force they have done in times past, and that the reluctance to an undisguised avowal of Unitarian sentiments is in a great degree overcome.

It is asked, by what motives Unitarians are influenced in their endeavours to disseminate their peculiar opinions. The answer is easy, and I think such as to justify at least all the zeal and earnestness they have yet discovered in the defence or the publication of their views of Christianity. They are earnest and active then, because they have a firm faith in the truth and the importance of their opinions, and that it is their duty to bear their testimony to the truth, and to leave no proper means untried, to cause it to be attended to, and understood, and respected. And they are fully persuaded, that the course they are pursuing in this respect, is in fact attended with very salutary effects. One, to which they attach no small importance, is the well known fact, that wherever the Unitarian doctrine prevails, and the rational views with which it is accompanied, a very important portion of society, the most elevated, intelligent and enlightened, become serious and practical Christians, who, in catholic countries, or where Calvinism prevails, are oftener unbelievers, and sceptics, and treat Christianity with neglect at least, if not with disrespect.

The reason of this is obvious. Men of cultivated minds and enlarged views are often so engaged in the business, and engrossed by the interests and cares of the world, as to depend for their views of Christianity wholly on what they hear from the pulpit, and what they find in the popular creeds and catechisms, which, they take for granted, exhibit fairly to them the Christian doctrine. Finding the system as it thus presented to them, such as their understanding and moral feelings will not admit of their receiving, they reject Christianity without further examination; not thinking themselves bound to inquire into the evidence of a system of faith, which carries in itself, in their view, intrinsic marks of incredibility. When to persons of this character and in such circumstances unitarian views of the christian doctrine are afterward presented, their attention is arrested by their reasonableness, and their consistency with what the light of nature teaches of the character and government of God. They are induced to examine the claims of a religion to their faith, which is presented to them in a form, so agreeable to the reason God has given them, and to the natural notions that arise from what they see of his character and dispositions in the government of the world; and the effect of examination is a firm conviction, that the new views in which Christianity has been presented to them, are the result of a fair and just inteppretation of the scriptures in which it is contained; and that the religion itself is as well supported by evidence, as it is worthy of the faith, and approbation, and affection of a wise and enlightened mind.

The time has been, within the memory of men now living, when in that class of society now alluded to, the most elevated, enlightened, and influential, in giving the tone to the public sentiment, and the direction to the manners and practice of society, infidelity and contempt for religion were far more prevalent, in this vicinity, than they are at the present day; and at that time the religion which issued from the pulpit, and which was the only faith that reached them, was Trinitarian and Calvinistic. I hazard nothing in asserting, that in proportion as those views of religion, which are generally adopted by Unitarians, have become prevalent, infidelity and contempt of religion have become less and less frequent; and our most enlightened men, with scarcely any exception, are among its most efficient friends and serious and practical professors.

I have now said all that I meant to say upon the doctrine of Christianity, as held by Unitarians, its comparison with the Trinitarian and Calvinistic faith, and its tendency and moral influence. I have endeavoured to express myself with the most perfect freedom and plainness; yet with the decorum and respect due to the solemn and interesting subjects which have come before me, to the author of the book which I have had so much occasion to notice, and to those fellow christians, who may dissent from the opinions and views which I have expressed.

For the declaration made with emphasis by Dr. Woods at the close of his book, "that in his honest and serious apprehension, the Unitarian system *is indeed another Gospel,*" I was not wholly prepared; though it is one which we have before been accustomed to hear in different forms from other sources, for which we have less reason to feel respect. We are consoled, however, with the thought, that an excommunication, though pronounced *ex cathedra,* carries not with it now the terror, which it once did. Christians will venture to judge between the rival systems, and will take the liberty to decide, each one for himself, whether the gospel, as it is held by Unitarians, or as it is held by Trinitarians and Calvinists, be *the Gospel of Christ.*

For Product Safety Concerns and Information please contact our EU representative GPSR@taylorandfrancis.com
Taylor & Francis Verlag GmbH, Kaufingerstraße 24, 80331 München, Germany

www.ingramcontent.com/pod-product-compliance
Lightning Source LLC
Chambersburg PA
CBHW072132220426
43664CB00013B/2218

www.ingramcontent.com/pod-product-compliance
Lightning Source LLC
Chambersburg PA
CBHW052124230426
43671CB00009B/1106